TELEVISION AND PSYCHOANALYSIS

PSYCHOANALYSIS AND POPULAR CULTURE SERIES

Series Editors: Caroline Bainbridge and Candida Yates

Consulting Editor: Brett Kahr

TELEVISION AND PSYCHOANALYSIS
Psycho-Cultural Perspectives

Edited by

Caroline Bainbridge, Ivan Ward, and Candida Yates

Series Editors: Caroline Bainbridge and Candida Yates

Consulting Editor: Brett Kahr

KARNAC

First published in 2014 by
Karnac Books Ltd
118 Finchley Road
London NW3 5HT

British Library Cataloguing in Publication Data

A C.I.P. for this book is available from the British Library

ISBN-13: 978-1-78049-173-8

Typeset by V Publishing Solutions Pvt Ltd., Chennai, India

Printed in Great Britain

www.karnacbooks.com

CONTENTS

v

ACKNOWLEDGEMENTS

This work was supported in the UK by the Arts and Humanities Research Council (grant numbers: AH/J00541X/1 and AH/G014329/1) as part of the Media and the Inner World research network activity and we are grateful for the research leave afforded to us by this funding which has enabled the production of this volume. We are also grateful for the support of the University of East London and the University of Roehampton. Special thanks are due to Brett Kahr, Carol Seigel, Ivan Ward, and all staff at the Freud Museum for their enthusiastic collaboration with the research network which culminated in the organisation of the "Remote Control: Psychoanalysis and Television" conference at the museum in November 2010. Several of the essays included in this volume have been developed from presentations given at that conference and this book owes a debt of gratitude to all at the museum for their support and encouragement. We would also like to thank Constance Govindin, Rod Tweedy, and Oliver Rathbone at Karnac Books for their helpful and friendly advice in the production of this volume.

We would like to acknowledge the kind permission given by Palgrave Macmillan to reprint in full Caroline Bainbridge's article, "Psychotherapy on the Couch: Exploring the Fantasies of *In Treatment*".

This was originally published in *Psychoanalysis, Culture and Society*, volume 17, number 2 in July 2012 (pp. 153–168). We are also grateful to *Play School* author and archivist, Paul R. Jackson, for permission to include his photographs, which are copyright of the BBC, in Carol Leader's essay in Chapter Four of this volume.

ABOUT THE EDITORS AND CONTRIBUTORS

Caroline Bainbridge is Reader in Visual Culture at the University of Roehampton and a Director of the Media and the Inner World research network, which is funded by the UK Arts and Humanities Research Council. She is Editor of the journal, *Free Associations: Psychoanalysis and Culture, Media, Groups, Politics* and author of *The Cinema of Lars von Trier: Authenticity and Artifice* (Wallflower Press, 2007) and *A Feminine Cinematics: Luce Irigaray, Women and Film* (Palgrave Macmillan, 2008). She also co-edited *Culture and the Unconscious* (Palgrave Macmillan, 2007). Caroline has written widely on psychoanalysis, gender, film, television, and popular culture. With Candida Yates, she is a Series Editor of the "Psychoanalysis and Popular Culture" book list published by Karnac Books.

Brett Kahr is Senior Clinical Research Fellow in Psychotherapy and Mental Health at the Centre for Child Mental Health in London, and Honorary Professor in the Department of Media, Culture and Language at the University of Roehampton, attached to the Media and the Inner World network. A Registrant of the British Psychoanalytic Council and of the United Kingdom Council for Psychotherapy, he works in private practice with individuals and couples in Hampstead, north London. A Visiting Clinician at the Tavistock Centre for Couple Relationships at the Tavistock Institute of Medical Psychology, he is the past Chair of the Society of Couple Psychoanalytic Psychotherapists and of the British Society of Couple Psychotherapists and Counsellors. A Trustee of the Freud Museum, and Director of the Psychotherapy Service at the School of Life in London, he is the author of six books on a range of mental health topics, including *D. W. Winnicott: A Biographical Portrait*, which won the Gradiva Prize for Biography, as well as *Sex and the Psyche*, which became a Waterstone's Non-Fiction Bestseller.

Carol Leader is a psychoanalytic psychotherapist and a senior member of the British Psychotherapy Foundation (BPC). She is also a member, training therapist and supervisor for the Association for Group and Individual Psychotherapy (UKCP). Formerly an actor, writer, and presenter, Carol worked extensively in theatre, TV, and radio before retraining as a therapist. She was a member of the National Theatre, played leading roles in a number of TV series, and also was one of the regular presenters of BBC's *Play School* for ten years. She has the honour of being named as "Adrian Mole's" favourite presenter. She has been in full-time private practice as a psychotherapist for fifteen years, works as a consultant for business and projects in the arts, and lectures and leads seminars in a number of educational and business settings and teaches on a number of professional trainings. She supervises both supervisors and psychotherapists in training at the Westminster Pastoral Foundation and is "psychotherapist at large" for the newly launched *Free Associations*, now available as a journal on the web.

Siobhan Lennon-Patience is a third year PhD student at the University of East London. Her thesis is a critical cultural analysis of positive psychology, which reflects the interdisciplinary psychocultural approach of the AHRC Media and Inner World research network (*www.miwnet.org*). Siobhan is the Assistant Web Editor for the weblog of the international journal, *Free Associations: Psychoanalysis and Culture, Media, Groups, Politics* (*www.freeassociations.org.uk*). Her PhD entitled "A psychoanalytically informed investigation of the positive psychology movement: exploring its social, cultural and political contexts" is supervised by Dr Candida Yates at the School of Law and Social Sciences, University of East London and Prof. Susannah Radstone at the School of Arts and Digital Industries, University of East London.

Marit Røkeberg is a Doctoral Student at the University of Roehampton in London, where she does research within the field of media and emotions. The working title of her thesis is "Connection, emotional experience and the parasocial: a psycho-cultural study of Twitter interactions", and it focuses on issues of online connection and the formation of identity through social media. Røkeberg comes from a media production background, having worked as a professional video editor for ten years. She has a Bachelor's degree in video production from Webster University, USA (2000), and a Master's degree in media, culture, and identity from Roehampton (2011). Her broader research interests span a variety of topics within media, psychology, and technology, and she recently had the journal article "Reliving the crime: cinema, containment, catharsis and reparation" (2012) published in *Free Associations*.

Sue Vice is Professor of English literature at the University of Sheffield. Her most recent publications are *Jack Rosenthal* (2009), *Shoah* (2011), and *Representing Perpetrators in Holocaust Literature and Film*, co-edited with Jenni Adams (2013). She is at work on *Textual Deceptions*, a study of false memoirs and literary hoaxes in the contemporary era.

Ivan Ward is Deputy Director and Head of Learning at the Freud Museum, London and manager of the Museum's conference programme. Publications include *The Presentation of Case Material in Clinical Discourse* (Freud Museum Publications, 1997), *The Psychology of Nursery Education* (Karnac Books, 1998), *Introducing Psychoanalysis* (Icon Books, 2000), *Phobia* (Icon Books, 2001), *Castration* (Icon Books, 2003), and *Shame and Sexuality*, co-edited with Claire Pajaczkowska (Routledge, 2008). He is Series Editor of *Ideas in Psychoanalysis*, published by Icon Books and, with Julia Borossa, co-editor of *Psychoanalysis, Fascism and Fundamentalism* (Edinburgh University Press, 2009), which was published as a special edition of *Psychoanalysis and History* (Volume 11, No. 2).

Jo Whitehouse-Hart teaches media and communication studies at De Montfort University, Leicester. Her interests are in developing psychoanalytically informed methods and approaches to audience research in television and film. She is currently writing a book based on a research project on "favourite" television programmes and films.

Candida Yates is Reader in Psychosocial Studies at the University of East London and is a Director of the Media and the Inner World research network funded by the Arts and Humanities Research Council. She is the Co-editor of the journal *Free Associations: Psychoanalysis and Culture, Media, Groups, Politics*; a Consulting Editor of *Psychoanalysis, Culture and Society*; and with Caroline Bainbridge, she is a Series Editor of the "Psychoanalysis and Popular Culture" book list published by Karnac Books. She has published widely on the themes of emotion, gender, and popular culture. Her publications include *Masculine Jealousy and Contemporary Cinema* (Palgrave Macmillan, 2007), *Culture and the Unconscious* (Palgrave Macmillan, 2007), and *Emotion: New Psychosocial Perspectives* (Palgrave Macmillan, 2009).

SERIES PREFACE

The application of psychoanalytic ideas and theories has a long tradition of engaging with culture, and especially with cultural artefacts that we might regard as "classical" in some way. For Sigmund Freud, the works of William Shakespeare and Johann Wolfgang von Goethe were as instrumental as those of the great poets and philosophers of classical civilisation in helping to formulate many of the key ideas underpinning psychoanalysis as a psychological method. In the fields of the humanities and social sciences, the application of psychoanalysis as a means of illuminating the complexities of identity and subjectivity is well established. However, despite this, there is relatively little work that attempts to grapple with popular culture in its manifold forms, some of which may seem transient and ephemeral in the moment, but which, nevertheless, reveal important opportunities for insight into the human condition.

The "Psychoanalysis and Popular Culture" book series builds on the work done since 2009 by the Media and the Inner World research network, which was generously funded by the UK's Arts and Humanities Research Council. It aims to offer spaces to consider the relationship between psychoanalysis in all its forms and popular culture as a lived experience—one that is ever more emotionalised in the contemporary age.

In contrast to many scholarly applications of psychoanalysis, which often focus solely on "textual analysis", this series sets out to explore the creative tensions of thinking about cultural experience and its processes with attention to observations from both the clinical and scholarly fields of observation. What can academic studies drawing on psychoanalysis learn from the clinical perspective and how might the critical insights afforded by scholarly work cast new light on clinical experience? The series provides space for a dialogue between these different groups with a view to forging new perspectives on the values and pitfalls of a psychoanalytic approach to ideas of selfhood, society, and popular culture. In particular, the series strives to develop a psycho-cultural approach to such questions by drawing attention to the usefulness of a post-Freudian, object relations perspective for examining the importance of emotional relationships and experience.

The series is edited by Caroline Bainbridge and Candida Yates, and Brett Kahr is the Consulting Editor.

PREFACE

Caroline Bainbridge, Ivan Ward, and Candida Yates

Television is still the most common form in which images and narratives are transmitted and consumed across the world and yet, to date, there has been little psychoanalytic engagement with it as a subject matter and questions abound. How does television work at the level of the psyche and what can psychoanalysis suggest about its pleasures and irritations? How do we make use of television to help us to relate to others? How might we conceive television, together with its images, stories, and characters as objects of the internal mind? How does the medium enter the sphere of clinical practice and what are the consequences of this for psychotherapy? Drawing on an eclectic array of psychoanalytic ideas, embracing the work of Sigmund Freud, D. W. Winnicott, Melanie Klein, and others, this anthology of essays and interviews tackles these questions by providing perspectives from the clinic alongside others from the realms of academic criticism and television production. Taking up a psycho-cultural approach, it explores the importance of considering what is at stake psychologically, socially, and culturally when we engage with television in all its forms. The collection includes essays on television shows such as *In Treatment*, *Play School*, and the television plays of Jack Rosenthal. It also grapples with the issues that emerge for both producers and subjects in reality documentary programming.

Lastly, it offers new perspectives on the psycho-cultural significance of television as an object of the internal world, which has lived effects on experiences of subjectivity and therapeutic practice.

The material in this book emerges from a conference called "Remote Control: Psychoanalysis and Television". Held in 2010, it was jointly organised by the Freud Museum in London and the Media and Inner World research network (MiW), which is funded by the Arts and Humanities Research Council in the UK. The MiW network sets out to explore our relationship to notions of therapy and emotion in popular culture and the media, and also the potential of psychoanalytic ideas to help us understand our relationship to the world of objects in that media context. With this aim in mind, the network has brought together psychotherapists and analysts, media professionals and academics to discuss particular themes related to emotion, media, and the unconscious. In the spirit of the psychoanalyst, D. W. Winnicott, who gave prominence to the interactive and transitional relationships between people, culture, and its objects, the aim has been to create spaces for dialogue between these different groups, to find ways in which we can perhaps learn from each other to create new interdisciplinary ways of thinking, practising, and researching. The chapters in this book apply a range of psychoanalytic perspectives to the study of television and its reception, and, in providing space for a range of different critical and theoretical positions, we hope to create a similar spirit of dialogue in the work that follows.

An important element of the MiW project and the psycho-cultural approach it develops is to draw on the experience and practice of psychoanalytic psychotherapy clinicians, in order to create a greater awareness of the processes and experiences of the unconscious. In borrowing from the culture of psychoanalytic practice and combining it with perspectives from academic research in the fields of psychosocial, media, and cultural studies, MiW has sought to create a more nuanced interpretation of the emotional work required by both the engagement with and production of contemporary media and to reflect on the significance of this in everyday life (Bainbridge & Yates, 2012). Some of the essays in this volume demonstrate a fruitful cross-pollination in the field of television studies and set out new spaces for the development of further work on the psychological dimensions of television in all its guises. The array of positions included in this volume shows the extent to which television has now become a key object of both the lived environment and its manifestions in the inner worlds of its viewers and producers. The pertinence of a psychoanalytic approach to television seems timely, given the ever more available access to television on a range of technological platforms in twenty-first-century life. We are now able to carry television programmes on pocket-sized devices, to watch on our own terms and to intervene in the programmes themselves, whether through live interaction with reality programmes or through technologies that sustain and encourage user-generated interpretations of television such as "mash-ups". The role of television as an object of fantasy and the imagination is played out across such technologies and, in order to account for the pleasures and social significance of the medium, it is essential to make an account of its psychological importance. This book marks an effort to set the scene for such developments.

Reference

Bainbridge, C. & Yates, C. (2012). Introduction to special issue on media and the inner world: new perspectives on psychoanalysis and popular culture. *Psychoanalysis, Culture and Society, 17*(2): 113–119.

CHAPTER ONE

Psychoanalysis and television: notes towards a psycho-cultural approach

Candida Yates

There is much written within the field of media and cultural studies about the pleasure and influence of television in everyday life, including its role as a purveyor of ideology and cultural struggle (Brooker & Jermyn, 2003; Newcom, 2000; Seiter, Borchers, Kreutzner & Warth, 1992; Storey, 2006). Yet an understanding of television as an object of unconscious fantasy and emotional experience remains under-researched. This anthology sets out to develop such an understanding, by exploring the relationships between psychoanalysis and television. The aim of this chapter is to introduce the reader to some of the themes raised subsequently in the book by discussing ideas taken from the fields of psychosocial, cultural, and media studies with a view to developing a new psycho-cultural approach to the study of television as an object of psychological, social, and cultural significance. The chapter draws attention to the insights of psychoanalytic theory for an understanding of television culture past and present, and the view taken here is that the study of television needs to take account of the identifications and fantasies that take place between and within the viewers, the text, and the lived experience of the immediate environment, and also the wider context of culture and society (Yates, 2010a, p. 405). Holding in mind Freud's (1900a) concept of "psychical

1

reality", and an awareness of the unconscious processes that mediate everyday experience, this psycho-cultural perspective also challenges the conceptual duality of screen studies that pitches the processes of fantasy in opposition to the experience of "reality", away from the film or television screen. Instead, I argue that the relationship between television and the shaping of subjectivity is complex, ongoing, and mutually constituted within the viewing habits of everyday life.

The media sociologist, Roger Silverstone (1994, p. 3), argues that the psychosocial and cultural processes that underpin the relationship between television and subjectivity take place on a number of levels, and he cites three areas of particular significance. First, he points to the "cognitive significance" of television as a source of information; second, he cites its "political significance" as a source of ideology, and third, he discusses its "emotional significance" as a "disturber and comforter". As Silverstone reminds us:

> Watching television and discussing television and reading about television takes place on an hourly basis: the result of focused or unfocused, conscious or unconscious attention. Television accompanies us as we wake up, as we breakfast, as we have our tea and as we drink in bars. It comforts us when we are alone. It helps us sleep. It gives us pleasure, it bores us and sometimes it challenges us. It provides us with opportunities to be both sociable and solitary. Although of course, it was not always so, and although we have had to learn how to incorporate the medium into our lives, we now take television entirely for granted in a way similar to how we take everything for granted. (ibid., p. 3)

Silverstone's insights regarding the emotional and unconscious dynamics of our engagement with television remain important for the development of a psycho-cultural approach to the study of television, and they provide a useful point of reference from which to develop an understanding of television, psychoanalysis, and the inner world. As I discuss, while the development of a psycho-cultural approach owes much to earlier studies that applied psychoanalytic understandings to the study of film and television, the approach taken here is one that draws mainly on the psychoanalytical tradition of object relations, using its ideas to discuss the emotional significance of television as a psychological object that provides a link between internal and external worlds.

To explore these themes, the chapter begins by contextualising the development of a psycho-cultural approach to television, providing a social, cultural, and historical analysis of the relationships between television, emotion, and what is often referred to as "therapy culture" (Bainbridge & Yates, 2011). I then discuss the application of psychoanalytic theories to television and popular culture in both clinical contexts and the academic fields of psychosocial and media studies. The chapter then returns to questions of television and the inner world and the kind of therapeutic work that may take place in the new psychological spaces opened up for viewers in contemporary television cultures.

Television, emotion, and therapy culture

When discussing the relationships between television and psychoanalysis, it is useful to take account of psychosocial and cultural developments in the study of what is often referred to as "therapy" or "therapeutic" culture (Richards, 2007; Richards & Brown, 2011; Yates, 2011). As recent scholarly research in the field demonstrates, the therapeutic turn in Western popular culture and the media is characterised by a heightened preoccupation with emotional experience and of the "feelingful" self in everyday life (Bainbridge & Yates, 2011, 2012). Today, it is often argued that the idea of the "affective self" has become reified, as the truth of life is represented mainly as residing in feelings and relationships, with the consumption of highly emotive television shows exemplifying this trend (Biressi & Nunn, 2005). The therapeutic turn in television is linked to wider historical developments in twentieth century culture and society defined by Cas Wouters (2007) as "informalisation", a process which led to the "emancipation of emotions" in the 1960s and to the "emotionalisation of the public sphere" more generally (Richards, 2007). As discussed elsewhere (Yates, 2010b), the foregrounding of emotions in popular media is also linked to the history of psychoanalysis and popular culture, where from cinema to advertising, the language, practice, and imagery of psychoanalysis and its concerns are evoked. Today it is widely argued that we live in a confessional culture, in which an "ego-driven sense of self has gradually predominated" (Evans, 2009, p. 77), and where the traditional boundaries between what formerly constituted public and private life are now perceived as less distinct (Evans, 2009; Yates, 2011). This development is reflected in the exchange of practices and values between the different spheres of therapy and the media, where in television, the language of emotions and psychotherapy is extensively used and applied. The emotionalisation of television output is illustrated in an example provided by Wouters:

> During the 1990–91 Gulf War, fighter pilots, interviewed for TV in their planes before taking off, admitted to being afraid. They did this in a matter-of-fact way. This would have been almost unthinkable in the Second World War, when such behaviour would have been equated almost automatically with being fear-ridden. (2011, p. 141)

Barry Richards (2007, p. 31) has documented the rise of what he calls "therapeutic culture" through his study of television "schedules and ratings" and he sees the popularity of soap operas and reality television shows as being highly significant indicators in this respect. One can cite the growth of reality television in its different formats from the *Big Brother* UK franchise (Channel 4, 2000–2010; Channel 5, 2011–present) to talent shows such as the *The X Factor* (2004–present), in which the emotional journeys of the protagonists signal the therapeutic potential of such shows, courting the attention of viewers who identify with the personal ups and downs of their life histories. The confessional style of various documentary formats and so-called "tabloid talk shows" such as *The Jerry Springer Show* (1991–present) or *The Jeremy Kyle Show* (2005–present), or self-help family programmes such as *Supernanny* (2004–2011) or *Honey We're Killing The Kids* (2005–2007), provides examples of the expansion of the therapeutic ethos on television and elsewhere today. The influence of therapy culture is not only confined to the more populist formats associated with celebrity culture and "tabloid TV" (Biressi & Nunn, 2005). One can also see the representation of psychotherapy or group therapy in television drama, as in US shows such as *Mad Men* (2007–present), *The Sopranos* (1999–2007), and *Breaking Bad* (2008–present), and as Caroline Bainbridge discusses in this volume, the series *In Treatment* (2008–present). In the UK, the characters in the BBC1 series, *Mistresses* (2008–present), visit Relate councillors, and in the recent highly successful BBC drama series, *Sherlock* (2010–2012), even "Sherlock Holmes's" sidekick, "John Watson", sees a therapist, presumably as a means of contemporising his identity through reference to the traumas of the Afghan War. Televised political culture has also followed a therapeutic trend in its focus on the emotional vulnerabilities of politicians, providing an imagined sense of authenticity to their public performances by including the personal narratives of their family life (Yates, 2012).

The emotionalisation of broadcast news, with its focus on the so-called "war on terror" since 9/11, has also been discussed by Richards (2007), who applies the ideas of Melanie Klein and the psychoanalytic object relations tradition to its coverage in order to explore the therapeutic potential of working through psycho-cultural anxieties about contemporary geo-politics. Richards argues that therapeutic culture is not just about the *representation* of therapy, as some more reductive accounts of therapy culture would have it (see for example, Furedi, 2004), but rather it connotes the potential therapeutic *process* of engaging with media, described by John Ellis (2000) as a form of "working through". As Ellis himself acknowledges, "the arduous task" of "working through the resistances" was first explored by Freud in his essay "Remembering, Repeating and Working Through" (Freud, 1914g, p. 155). Richards develops these themes and applies the work of psychoanalyst, Melanie Klein, to argue that the media has the potential to provide containing structures through which people can work through personal and cultural anxiety, and he cites the emotionalisation of broadcast television entertainment as being significant in this respect. Richards (2007) argues that therapy culture is not just about the sentimental expression of feelings, but rather signifies a potentially more complex set of psychosocial therapeutic processes, including a new reflexivity, and the development of a greater psychological awareness. As Sue Vice reminds us in Chapter Five of this volume, the everyday "taken for granted" nature of television may belie the more hidden, emotional work that takes place when watching and engaging with its programmes. As she goes on to argue in her discussions of Jack Rosenthal's television dramas, even the most "gentle" of comedies may facilitate the working through of "disruptive and uncomfortable truths".

Both Richards's and Ellis's discussion of the emotional dynamics of television engagement challenge a tradition of audience research that presents television-watching as a mindless, passive activity. In Chapter Six, Jo Whitehouse-Hart's innovative audience research challenges this stereotypical image of the "couch potato" when she stresses the active and ongoing emotional conflicts and pleasures that are experienced when watching a favourite television programme and which may be repeated as a source of comfort on a regular basis. As I discuss later in this chapter, this raises a number of questions about the unconscious processes at work when engaging with television. It may be that, in some contexts, returning to a programme on a repeated basis can imply a creative form of emotional work associated with psychoanalytic theories of transformational objects and transitional phenomena (Bollas, 1987, 1992; Winnicott, 1974). Yet in other settings, repeated television viewing can also be explained in terms first discussed by Freud (1927e) and later by film scholars such as Laura Mulvey (1975) as "fetishism", as a repetitive desire to master the psychological traumas encountered in early childhood.

In Chapter Seven, film-maker and television producer Richard McKerrow argues that programme-making can work as a form of "docutherapy" for both programme participants and members of the audience who may identify with the "emotional journey" of the protagonists telling their story. In that same chapter, documentary participant, Jonathan Phang, also takes up this theme in his discussion about his experience of taking part in the television documentary *The Marchioness: A Survivor's Story* (2009). Like McKerrow, Phang highlights the necessity of taking into account the importance of ethical production values in relation to protagonists and sees such an approach as being key to the development of an emotionally responsible approach to film-making in the future. As Ivan Ward argues in Chapter Eight, the values required for making "good television" often mitigate against a disinterested concern for the welfare of participants or the pursuit of truth.

What we hope to sketch out in this collection of essays are the beginnings of a psycho-cultural approach to the study of television that may be applied to the processes of both the production and the consumption of television. Vice's chapter on the work of Jack Rosenthal shows us that forms of representation are also significant when exploring the psycho-cultural processes of television, as they prompt and encourage the fantasies and identifications that may be experienced in response. As other chapters in this volume illustrate, the desires for self-fulfilment and self-discovery are now a key feature of television programming. Yet the psycho-cultural and political implications of the so-called "therapeutic turn" within television and popular culture need further unpacking, and the Media and Inner World research network has been at the forefront in facilitating discussions in the emerging field of psycho-cultural studies (Bainbridge & Yates, 2011, 2012). For example, does the therapeutic turn represent a positive shift towards a more empathic, thoughtful, and tolerant culture, where new spaces can emerge to facilitate self-understanding to help us live with the uncertainties of late modernity? In psychoanalytic terms, does so-called "therapy culture" provide a good enough or containing environment that facilitates the capacity to live with emotional ambivalence and the processing of complex emotions and thoughts? Or, more negatively, does the growth of a therapy culture represent something more superficial and narcissistic? These questions impact upon contemporary understandings of television production, programming, and reception and also have implications for the shaping of subjectivities in contemporary popular culture.

The sociologist, Frank Furedi (2004), writes pessimistically about what he calls "therapy culture", as it promotes new forms of social control, in which political and social issues are often reduced and redefined as personal unhappiness. Indeed, one can argue that in a neo-liberal economy, where social and economic loss is often associated with being "a loser", psychological therapy—mainly in the guise of cognitive behavioural therapy—is now often advocated as a way to get depressed people back to work (Yates, 2011). This stance is also reproduced in reality television shows such as *Honey We're Killing the Kids* (2005–2007), where the language of therapy, "tough love", and class converge in efforts to dissuade parents from "killing" their children with high-calorie crisps and other activities culturally defined as "deviant" (Ferguson, 2010). Furedi's thesis echoes that of Nikolas Rose (1999), who argues in Foucauldian terms about the colonising tendencies of "cultures of the therapeutic" upon the self, in which television can be viewed negatively, as a form of governance and as a technology of power.

Rose's and Furedi's critiques of the therapeutic cultural turn also reflect earlier discussions in the field of psychoanalytic sociology about the vulgarisation of the psychoanalytic tradition and its "analytic ethos" through popularised representations of therapy in public life. For example, Phillip Rieff (1966) argued that Freud's ideas have been co-opted in the pursuit of a mindless therapeutic ethos underpinned by individualism and the pursuit of happiness. In 1979, Christopher Lasch linked the growth of a superficial therapeutic ethos within popular culture to the development of weak and fragile narcissistic personalities. However, the pessimism of Lasch, Furedi, and Rose has been contested by those such as Bainbridge (2011), Richards and Brown (2011), and Anthony Elliott and John Urry (2010), who make positive links between the contemporary cultural focus on feelings and emotion and the creative processes of the unconscious. These different perspectives on the nature of therapy culture and its therapeutic potential have implications for a psycho-cultural history of television and debates about subjectivity and cultural change. For example, Lasch's anxieties about the media also reflect and tap into more general concerns about the fate of the self in relation to the growth of mass consumption and the lack of psycho-cultural containment associated with that development. Ellis (2000, p. 1) reminds us that in the UK context, television first emerged as a mass leisure activity during a post-war "era of scarcity" which, for UK viewers, was dominated by the standardisation of consumption and the Reithian principles of the BBC. The psychologically containing, reassuring tones and programming of public service broadcasting was associated with the wider hegemonic social formation of the social democratic settlement, where the old structures of family, class, and gender were still perceived as being in place (Hall, 1979). Ellis defines the second television era as one of consumer "availability" in which the commodification of citizenship as a lifestyle choice was evident in a more "diffuse" mode of television programming, thereby reflecting the kind of fragmented late capitalist social formation that many of those living in the West still recognise today.

Ellis's history of television and emotion was written in 2000 and the fragmentation of the television audience discussed by him at that time has since been transformed by the developments of the digital era. Yet although the experience of austerity may be relevant once more for Western consumers, fantasies of plenty may still apply to television viewing habits in the contemporary digital era, in which it is possible to watch television programmes on an array of objects, including smart phones, tablets, and computers. Social networking and the interactive engagement with television shows and with other viewers through sites such as Facebook and Twitter have transformed the viewing experience for many, and as I discuss below, such practices associated with this new television culture have implications for the psycho-cultural imagination. Thus Ellis's argument about the "emotional economy" of television in the era of "availability", with its emphasis on the "diffuse" nature of programming and watching, is still relevant when applied to discussions about the therapeutic nature of television culture today. In a networked society, the reflexive modern subject is continually faced with a number of choices related to the processing of information (Castells,

1996) and this identity work gives rise to what Ellis (2000, p. 1) refers to as the feeling "of uncertainty that haunts the modern world". Ellis argues that television, with its distinct genres of comedy, drama, sport, and so on, provides a form of stability for viewers by taking images of disorder and reordering, reframing and narrativising them, so that each genre also carries its own emotional function. Thus, comedy addresses questions of morality, and drama may invite empathy, and so on, enabling the viewer to "work through" the various emotional dilemmas of contemporary experience. For Ellis:

> ... working through is a constant process of making and re-making meanings, and of exploring possibilities. It is an important process in an age that threatens to make us witness too much information without providing us with enough explanation. (p. 79)

As the chapters in this volume illustrate, and as I also discuss below, psychoanalysis, with all its capacity for the interrogation of the textures implicit in this kind of experience, offers a particularly enriching perspective on these themes in relation to television.

Psychoanalytic approaches to television and culture

As a clinical and theoretical project, psychoanalysis has always had close ties with the culture and society in which it operates (Bainbridge, Radstone, Rustin & Yates, 2007; Bainbridge & Yates, 2011, 2012). Yet in the past, most clinical applications of psychoanalysis to culture have tended to focus their work on what might be called "high" cultural forms, including classical novels, art, and theatre, whereas popular culture and media have tended to be ignored (Bainbridge & Yates, 2012; Yates, 2012). Psychoanalytic clinicians have often been suspicious of popular culture and its products, sometimes likening it to a form of vacuous escape lacking the necessary depth for meaningful emotional work (Britton, 2007). Yet a key focus of the Media and the Inner World research project has been to put the case for psychoanalysis in helping us to understand the anxieties and desires that are stirred up through our engagement with popular culture and the media objects of everyday life. Today, popular culture is often used as a resource in various therapeutic contexts (Fingeroth, 2004; Rubin, 2008). As Brett Kahr argues in this volume, clinicians know anecdotally and from their own experience that patients have powerful emotional relationships to television and that these patients also bring those experiences of popular culture and television to the consulting room, using them in the analytic encounter.

Yet conversely, just as past psychoanalytic practitioners have given the study of popular culture a wide birth, so too have media and cultural studies scholars often resisted psychoanalytic theory as a method to analyse the experience of television and its appeal (Morley, 1992). Indeed, despite the contemporary focus within the media on emotion and therapy, media studies scholars tend to mistrust the application of psychoanalytic ideas to the study of media forms. This mistrust stems partly from the perception that psychoanalytic theory is blind to issues of ideology, cultural difference, and history (Radstone, 2007). When academic researchers have applied psychoanalytic ideas to popular culture and the media, these applications have often been underpinned by a strong political agenda. This tradition goes back to the Frankfurt school that combined the work of Freud and Marx to analyse the costs to the psyche of consumption, to suggest that mass media and television work as pacifying communicators of dominant ideology (Adorno, 1991; Adorno & Horkheimer, 1976). Over the past twenty years, British psychosocial applications of psychoanalysis to media and popular culture have tended to draw on the British school of object relations, applying the ideas of Donald Winnicott and Melanie Klein and, as mentioned earlier, this includes the work of Richards (2007), Robert M. Young (1994), and more recently Bainbridge (2011) and Bainbridge and Yates (2010, 2012), where the media subject/viewer is perceived in less passive terms.

In the past, applications of psychoanalysis have tended to use the ideas of Freud and Lacan to inform the analysis of media texts (Kaplan, 1990; Wright, 1998), and today, the cultural analyst, Slavoj Žižek (1992; Žižek & Daley, 2004), draws on this psychoanalytic tradition to carve out a place for himself as a witty and provocative commentator on the contemporary popular cultural scene. In psychoanalytic film studies, Lacanian and post-Lacanian feminist film theories have remained influential. From a psychoanalytic perspective, the darkened womb-like the conditions of the cinema are said to play an important role in promoting dreamlike, narcissistic states of mind, where infantile identifications with parental figures return to shape our identifications with the moving images on the screen (Baudry, 1970, 1975). The relationship between the unique environment of the cinema and the intense, regressive gaze of the spectator has been explored extensively in the field of psychoanalytic screen studies.[1]

Ellis (1982) was one of the first academic researchers to argue that television invites a very different response from the viewer in the form of a distracted, inattentive "glance". The glance in this context refers to the interruptions both on-screen and in the domestic setting where, say, domestic squabbles over who controls the remote control or who is making the tea may interfere with the capacity to lose oneself in a deep and focused way when watching a programme. As Whitehouse-Hart discusses later in this volume, assumptions about the links between the distracted television gaze and the domestic family environment have been recurring themes of television studies research. Yet the notion of the distracted gaze of the television viewer as being devoid of or split off from unconscious processes can be criticised on a number of counts. For example, in contrast to watching a film in a cinema, the pleasures of identifying with the Oedipal dilemmas of characters in television dramas may actually be heightened and facilitated by the many camera positions of television (Flitterman-Lewis, 1992).

As is well documented, the idea of the monolithic "male" gaze as discussed in early screen theories (Mulvey, 1975) was later replaced by an acknowledgement of the multiple processes of identification that occur when watching a film and engaging with its content (Modleski, 1988; Mulvey, 1981). Sandy Flitterman-Lewis (1992, pp. 213, 219) argues that theories of "primary cinematic identification" cannot directly be applied to the study of television, which creates a fractured, multiple, and diffuse gaze of the television viewer, but, as with cinema audiences, identifications with protagonists on the screen may also be imbued with powerful feelings and unconscious fantasy. Indeed, as studies in the field of media ethnography suggest, the fantasies and identifications that mediate our relationships to television still exist whether through watching scheduled programmes or DVDs (Bainbridge & Yates, 2010; Yates, 2010a). In Chapter Three, Bainbridge refers to the ways in which television can now be recorded, rewound, played back, and watched in a range of media contexts; programmes can also be purchased in box sets and watched on large widescreen TVs in the living room. As Bainbridge discusses, and as I also explore below in relation to the growth of social media, the many ways in which people watch television may facilitate new opportunities for working through the dilemmas of self-experience in late modern culture.

John Caldwell (1995) also critiques the notion of the distracted glance when he says that viewers may engage with television in a focused intensity—as passionate fans of HBO dramas or the acclaimed "Scandinoir" crime dramas shown in the UK and elsewhere such as *The Killing* (2011–2012) or *The Bridge* (2011–present) confirm (Billen, 2012). The intensity of the viewing experience is discussed in this book by Bainbridge, Whitehouse-Hart, Vice, and Ward, who in different ways explore the committed gaze of television viewers and how this commitment is also mediated by what Vice refers to as the "disruptive and uncomfortable truths of psychoanalysis" and unconscious fantasy. Although Caldwell falls in line with those media studies researchers who critique the usefulness of psychoanalytic theory and research methods, he also emphasises the psychological intensity of the TV gaze that is built up over time, describing "the entranced isolation" of watching TV alone (p. 27). As Whitehouse-Hart argues, television may provide a source of comfort for the lonely, isolated viewer, and Bainbridge's discussion of the identification with the psychotherapy sessions in the television drama series, *In Treatment*, examines the transferences that may take place between the viewer and the male therapist on screen, thereby echoing the actual themes of the programme itself. The Oedipal pleasures of identifying simultaneously with the therapist on screen and also with his patients, allow for the kind of multiple identifications first discussed by Flitterman-Lewis and developed in more depth by Bainbridge in her chapter.

In the past, some television scholars have applied Freud, Lacan, and Laplanche[2] in order to discuss the Oedipal identifications and primary fantasies that occur when watching television drama series such as UK police drama series *The Sweeney* (1975–1978) (Donald, 1985), *Waking the Dead* (2000–2011) (Thornham & Purvis, 2005), the long-running US science fiction drama *Star Trek* (1966–present) (ibid.), and the early BBC series *Dr Who* (1963–1986) (Tulloch & Alvarado, 1983). Yet today, the analysis of the Oedipal dynamics of watching television and its images may not be enough to capture the experience of intertextuality in the contemporary digital age (Gray, 2006).[3] Watching television may now also involve engaging with social media such as Twitter and Facebook before, during, or after the programme. Fictional characters in drama series such as *True Blood* (2008–present) or performers on the talent show *The X Factor* in the UK, now have their own Twitter accounts, thereby mobilising new modes of identification and ways of relating to television and other viewers as objects of fantasy.[4] The temporal and spatial shifts that have accompanied these changes in television viewing also connote a new, fluid, and open-ended flirtatious sensibility that is linked to the cultural shifts of late modernity (Yates, 2010b). Such changes are linked to the mediatisation of culture in which social and digital media provide new ways to experience the pleasures of play and mastery that feed the flirtatious appetites of the late modern viewing subject. Although the analysis of Oedipal identifications and primary fantasy is very useful to explore the cycles of desire that emerge for viewers in this context, object relations theory also provides a useful paradigm to explore the distinctly playful nature of contemporary television culture.

The psycho-cultural relationship to television as an object

Silverstone (1994) applies the ideas of psychoanalyst D. W. Winnicott to explore the creative potential of television in shaping subjectivity. Whereas Freud focused on fantasies related to the father of the Oedipus complex, post-Freudians such as Winnicott used an object relations approach to emphasise the importance of the first interactive relationship between the infant and the mother, and also the significance of play in that relationship for the development of creativity and the capacity to play with objects and ideas in later life (Winnicott, 1974). Winnicott and subsequent object relations theorists have been criticised for conveying a unified and developmental, linear approach to subjectivity and culture (Lacan, 1977; Greenberg & Mitchell, 1984); yet recent revised applications of Winnicott's ideas to culture have shown that this need not be the case (see for example, Bainbridge, 2011; Bainbridge & Yates, 2010; Hills, 2002; Yates, 2010a). Indeed, Winnicott's ideas about play and transitional phenomena can be usefully mobilised to explore the liminal spaces of self-experience and object relating in late modern contexts (Bainbridge, 2011). Winnicott (1974) argued that the transitional object is the infant's first possession and stands in for the "breast" which, as a metaphor, also stands in for the "mother". It functions partly as a defence against loss and separation and it also allows the infant to test reality, experience illusion, and build up a sense of trust. As Carol Leader argues in her chapter about the beloved UK children's television programme, *Play School* (1964–1988) and its presenters, a television programme can be experienced as the facilitating good enough mother, as comforting and reliable, and the viewer can feel held by it. Silverstone applies Winnicott's theory of transitional phenomena to the engagement with television as a trusted object that can be symbolically attacked, yet survives those attacks. As psychoanalyst Christopher Bollas (1987, p. 15) argues:

> With the transitional object, the infant can play with the illusion of his own omnipotence (lessening the loss of the environment-mother with generative and phasic delusions of self-and-other creation); he can entertain the idea of the object being got rid of, yet surviving his ruthlessness; and he can find in this transitional experience the freedom of metaphor.

For Winnicott, each time the subject engages with the object, she thinks she has created it, yet the object is always already there, waiting to be found. Today, the interactive nature of contemporary television culture may set in motion the creative processes of object relating described by Winnicott, in which the viewer feels a sense of emotional continuity and a "going-on-being" (1956, p. 303), by simultaneously watching and communicating with other viewers about the programme that may or may not be viewed in "real" time. The playful, transitional spaces that can emerge in the context of late modern television culture may be activated through the practice of blogging about programmes on social media sites, enabling the viewer to experience him- or herself simultaneously as a producer (who creates the text) and also as a user (who consumes television and the internet).[5] Thus, one can rework the ideas of Winnicott in contemporary settings to examine the ways in which television cultures enable the subject to refuse the limits of the self and to embrace the fluid "as-if" spaces of late modernity.

Of course, one can apply a more classically Freudian "take" on such activities in order to emphasise the neurotic aspects of endlessly returning to television programmes and the social media commentaries that surround them. Here, one could cite André Green's (2005) critique of Winnicott's theory of play. He applies a Freudian interpretation of play as being rooted in an aggressive and repetitive wish for mastery and control. Sherry Turkle's (2011) work on "being alone together" comes to mind here, in which she writes disparagingly about the essentially lonely and illusory nature of contemporary media and internet culture. One could apply Turkle's thesis to argue that in certain contexts, the television viewer may be defending herself from feelings of inner emptiness, and fragmentation—and a loss of "going-on-being", by adopting the "manic defence" of searching for outside stimulation (Winnicott, 1935). Yet some of the chapters in this book alert us to the dangers of pathologising the pleasures of returning to a favourite programme or film, which may be used as a mean of shoring up the self. Indeed, the objects of television culture may actually enrich the experience of the self and facilitate what Winnicott (1958) defined as "the capacity to be alone". It is worth emphasising that theories about the therapeutic nature of television and the viewing experience cannot be applied outside the social, cultural, and historical context in which that practice takes place. The viewing experience is always contingent upon a number of psycho-cultural and social factors related to the life history of the viewing subject, the nature of the programme, and the viewing environment. The environment includes both the domestic viewing space and also broader influences related to the forces of politics, history, culture, and society.

Living in the mood: the 2012 Olympics as a transformational object

One way to develop the discussion so far is to turn to the television coverage of the 2012 London Olympics (BBC) and the Paralympics (Channel 4), where arguably the experience of what Christopher Bollas (1987, 1992) defines as "transformational objects" came to the fore. Bollas (1987, pp. 15–16) builds on Winnicott's ideas about transitional phenomena to argue: "[W]e have failed to take notice of the phenomenon in adult life of the wide ranging collective search for an object that is identified with the metamorphosis of the self". The experience of selfhood described by Bollas is not one that evokes a tale of origins through a nostalgic return to the mother as some critiques of object relations theory imply (Frosh & Baraitser, 2008), but rather he describes a process which is more complex and fluid. Bollas argues that just as we seek objects that may hold and contain us, providing a link between inner and outer worlds of experience, we are also continually changed by those objects, and in this respect he provides us with a highly dynamic view of "working through", which we can apply to television as an object of transformation:

> Each entry into an experience of an object is rather like being born again, as subjectivity is newly informed by the encounter, its history altered by a radically effective present that will change its structure. To be a character is to gain a history of internal objects, inner presences that are the trace of our encounters, but not intelligible or even clearly knowable. (Bollas, 1992, p. 59)

Yet alongside the creative aspects of transformation, there are also more defensive and reactive ways of relating, when objects may be used as means of warding off the risks and the anxieties associated with change, difference, and the fragmentation of late modernity. Bollas's discussion of the relationship between the "conservation" of objects and "malignant" moods is pertinent here. Bollas (1987, p. 102) likens the "special state of a mood" and the emotional work that takes place within it to that of a dream, as the mood works as an environment through which the emotional work of object relating takes place:

> Moods are complex self-states that may establish a mnemic environment in which the individual re-experiences and recreates former infant-child experiences and states of being. (1987, p. 102)

Bollas distinguishes between "generative" and "malignant" moods, and in the case of the latter, the mood is used as a way to block object relating and signifies an inability to work through the "unthought known", which is beyond representation and cannot be articulated (1987, pp. 100–101). Bollas's notion of the "living through of a mood" is one that can also be applied to cultural phenomena such as television as an object of psycho-cultural significance (ibid.). Vicky Lebeau (2001, p. 6) paraphrased Freud's famous dictum on the significance of the dream when she referred to cinema as "the royal road to the cultural unconscious", and one can extend this observation to television, which serves a similar function in its capacity to both produce and reflect a cultural "mood" that enables a form of working through to take place.

I want to argue that the interactive television coverage of the 2012 Olympics and Paralympics represented an experience of "living through of a mood", an experience that seemed to take many UK television viewers by surprise. The British cynicism that surrounded the build-up to the Olympic Games is well documented in social media and the press reports in the UK and elsewhere (Jayne, 2012; Kettle, 2012; Wilde, 2012). Much of this negativity was linked to the poor weather, the anticipated disruption of travel networks, and the high cost of putting on the Games at a time of economic recession and austerity. For many, it was as if the Olympic Games were being imposed "from above" by nameless officials, and the publicity given to the so-called VIP "Zil lanes" on the roads appeared to symbolise the impinging aspects of the Games in this respect (Lancaster, 2012). Criticism about the "dumbed-down" nature of the television coverage of the Royal Jubilee celebrations held earlier in the summer provided a further context for British cynicism about being patronised by the BBC, the government, and also the Olympic planning committee (Evans, 2012). This scepticism was also parodied by the popular BBC comedy/spoof documentary, *Twenty Twelve* (2011–2012), lending a playful, postmodern edge to the UK anti-Olympic mood of the time.

Yet as documented on social media sites and in the press, the BBC television spectacle of the opening ceremony, *Isles of Wonder* (2012), designed by film-maker Danny Boyle, appeared to instantly transform this cynicism into a mood of happiness and celebration (BBC, 2012a; Cotterell Boyce, 2012). One could, of course, deploy a crude analysis of group behaviour and "the herd instinct" to explain why this occurred (Freud, 1921c), citing a manic flight from the disappointments of the present. Had the ceremony been an uncritical nationalist propaganda *fest* celebrating British imperial history, then one could have said that the national mood of that response was characterised by a defensive mood of "conservation". Yet, I would argue that this was not the case, as instead it appeared to celebrate a particular popular narrative of British history that was nuanced and playful, acknowledging the multiplicity of voices that have shaped British identities past and present. What is particularly significant for this chapter is that the historical narrative presented on the night was one that celebrated popular culture and UK television programmes in particular, working in a generative manner to evoke particular sets of memories, thereby tapping into the cultural idioms of British audiences. As Carol Leader argues in Chapter Four, about the memories of programmes such as *Play School*, television programmes from childhood lend a particular "mnemic" poignancy and pleasure to the psycho-cultural histories of the self, and at the opening ceremony the reference to such programmes generated for many a moment of cultural reverie in which they experienced the "living through of a mood". It is important to note, of course, that the emotional experience of watching the ceremony was not a universal one, as the different cultural images and themes of narrative referred largely to UK television programmes, events, and institutions. References to aspects of UK popular culture and television such as "Angie" and "Den's" fight in the British BBC soap *EastEnders* (1985–present) (YouTube, 1988), or Michael Fish's BBC weather forecast, which missed the UK's "great storm" of 1987 (YouTube, 1987), was also resonant of a particular generation of British viewers, reflecting perhaps the life history of the director, Danny Boyle, himself. Nevertheless, this event arguably constituted a kind of transformational moment for viewers in the UK and beyond, evoking the notion of "character" with all its psycho-cultural connotations as discussed by Bollas.

Reparative aspects of television and the Olympic Games

The Olympic torch relay that led up to the opening ceremony also provides a context for the success. The torch, which was carried into the Olympic stadium on the night, also worked as a transformational object, surprising those who had criticised the Games beforehand (*The Independent*, 2012). In the lead up to the Games, large crowds of people turned out to watch and cheer its progress as it was carried through villages, towns, and cities. Associations made in the media between the torch and the infamous Berlin Games of 1936 disappeared, as the torch-bearers appeared to represent the cultural diversity of the UK, and as the torch's progress mapped the nation in a series of media moments, with images of local streets and communities not normally seen on national television because it is so London-centric (BBC, 2012b; *The Independent*, 2012).

Perhaps the pleasures of the torch relay as a ritual was rooted in a desire for connection and a sense of community in an era of change and uncertainty, However, it may also be that for the viewers who watched, tweeted, and blogged about the Olympics, the appeal of the spectacle of the opening ceremony and the torch relay was that they also worked as symbols of reparation, mirroring back to the public a capacity for healing and making good.[6] Richards's (2007) thesis about therapeutic culture resonates in this context and, as he suggests, one can apply the ideas of the psychoanalyst, Melanie Klein, to explore the emotional work that such coverage may engender for the viewer. Klein (1988) wrote at length about emotions such as love, hate, and envy that are experienced in relation to the parental objects of the imagination, and she discussed the psychological defences that arise as a consequence of those early emotional experiences. At the heart of Klein's ideas about the affective subject is the notion of "reparation", and as Richards (2007) argues, the cultural fascination with wounded figures in the public eye may be related to the kind of reparative wishes she describes.[7]

The wish for reparation was a powerful theme that recurred through-out the Olympics and the Paralympics, and this was particularly pertinent given the trauma experienced in the aftermath of the London bombings, which occurred on 7 July, 2005, the day after London was awarded the hosting of the Olympic Games. Indeed, it may be that the negativity and also the satirical humour of programmes such as *Twenty Twelve* in the lead-up to the Games was also linked to such anxieties resonating with the trauma of that particular event and the fear that history might repeat itself. The 7/7 London bombings were often referred to in the lead-up to the Olympics through television documentaries such as the BBC film *One Day In London* (2012), and Akram Kahn's dance performance at the opening ceremony was choreographed as a tribute to those who suffered the traumas of 7/7 (YouTube, 2012a). The memories of that time were also made visible through the Paralympic athlete, Martine Wright, who was a survivor of those events and whose life had been transformed as a consequence (Hudson, 2012). Sebastian Coe's closing speech at the Paralympic Games also used the therapeutic language of "working through" when he referred to the 7/7 bombings, citing his meeting with the doctor who was present at the bombings and who later volunteered as an Olympic helper as a way of coming to terms with the trauma of that experience: "His name was "Andrew" and he told me he was a doctor at St Mary's hospital on his way to help out at boxing" (YouTube, 2012b). Thus alongside the actual reparative qualities experienced by the doctor himself, this example also shows us the potentially reparative nature of contemporary television culture, as audiences were able to engage with and respond to this narrative of working through, in the hope perhaps of enacting some form of trans-formation for themselves and for others too (Yates, 2013).

Trying to stem the "flow" of television and therapy culture

So to conclude, what are we to make of the relationship between the notions of a therapeutic culture and the idea of television as an object that traverses the psycho-cultural boundaries of the inner and outer worlds of experience? I have argued that television can work therapeutically, facilitating the ongoing emotional processes of working through experience. As I have discussed, the meanings of "therapy" or "therapeutic" culture and its relationship to television are highly contested and fraught with questions. Yet it is worth noting that television researchers and therapy culture sceptics both share a form of cynicism, which may be rooted in a wish to distance themselves from the emphasis on feeling, emotion, and weakness, which is associated with femininity as an object of mistrust. For example, therapy culture sceptics, Lasch and Furedi, both see a link between the decline of paternal authority, and the feminising of Western culture and society. The picture they present is one of children placed carelessly in front of the television, mindlessly internalising its images, while the mother is out working, and where a father is no longer on the scene. Such scepticism about the value of therapy culture reflects, perhaps, an anxiety about the loss of paternal authority, and television crops up in the work of Lasch as a symbol of "dumbed-down" mass culture and feminine excess (Tyler, 2007; Yates, 2011). A similar motif of the lost father can also be found in Furedi's criticism of therapy culture. It may be that the maternal connotations of caring and nurturance associated with therapeutic discourse may also provoke anxieties related to the vulnerabilities of regressive dependency and fantasies of maternal engulfment (Layton, 2011; Yates, 2011).

The distrust of femininity as a signifier of engulfment is also present in critiques about the endless "flood" of television and popular culture, where fears of addiction, passivity, manipulation, and television as a form of "remote control" have been a recurring theme (Seiter, Borchers, Kreutzner & Warth, 1992). Concerns about the feminising aspects of television often emphasise the helpless, infantilising aspects of being caught in its thrall, and this same fear of regression echoes criticisms of therapy culture more generally. Given the domestic focus of those television studies, it is perhaps unsurprising that television has also been seen as the poor relation of film, and television-viewing as a low-status feminised activity. As Mimi White (2001) argues, the association between femininity and television in television studies is also related to the content, form, and scheduling of programmes, where the image presented in early studies of television is one of a constant and relentless "flow". As in therapy culture critiques, the notion of an endless flow of television into the home connotes feminine excess and a sense of being overwhelmed, which return us to the psychical realm of fantasy and the unconscious. Seen in this light, such concepts remind us of the need to develop a psycho-cultural approach to the study of television that draws on both the cultures of academia and the practices of psychotherapy. In developing such an approach, the aim should be to explore critically, yet also pay attention to and hold in mind the affects and fantasies that underpin the epistemologies of television studies past and present.

Notes

1. This work was first formulated in the 1970s in the work of Baudry (1970, 1975), Metz (1975), and Mulvey (1975).
2. Laplanche and Pontalis (1964, p. 19) define primary or "originary" fantasy as: "The primal scene pictures the origin of the individual; fantasies of seduction, the origin and upsurge of sexuality; the fantasies of castration, the origin of the differences between the sexes". Elizabeth Cowie (1984) applied Laplanche and Pontalis's theory of desire and fantasy to the processes of film spectatorship and the fantasy scenarios of cinema.
3. The concept of "intertextuality" refers to the ways in which "one text is marked by the sign of another" (Storey, 1996, p. 71).
4. For further details of *True Blood* Twitter accounts and related social networking activity, see: http://truebloodnet.com/true-blood-cast-crew-online/ (accessed on 29 November, 2012). Details of *The X Factor UK* Twitter activity can be found at: https://twitter.com/TheXFactorUK (accessed on 29 November, 2012).
5. Turner (2010, p. 156) defines the dual identity of the blogger who is both producer and user as the "prosumer".
6. Of course, the torch acted as a literal symbol of transformation in lighting the Olympic flames of the cauldron.
7. The popularity of reality shows which all use the emotional "back-stories" of their participants can also be seen in this light. See for example: *Big Brother* and *The X Factor* or makeover shows such as *How to Look Good Naked* (2006–present) and *What Not to Wear* (2001–2007).

References

Adorno, T. (1991). *The Culture Industry*. London: Routledge.
Adorno, T. & Horkeimer, M. (1976). *Dialectic of Enlightenment*. London: Continuum.

Bainbridge, C. (2011). From "The Freud Squad" to "The Good Freud Guide": a genealogy of media images of psychoanalysis and reflections on their role in the public imagination. *Free Associations: Psychoanalysis and Culture, Media, Groups, Politics, 62*: 31–58.

Bainbridge, C. Radstone, S., Rustin, M., & Yates, C. (Eds.) (2007). *Culture and the Unconscious*. Basingstoke, UK: Palgrave Macmillan.

Bainbridge, C. & Yates, C. (2010). On not being a fan: Masculine identity, DVD culture and the accidental collector. *Wide Screen, 2*(1): 1–22.

Bainbridge, C. & Yates, C. (2011). [Editorial.] Therapy culture/culture as therapy: Psycho-cultural studies of media and the inner world. *Free Associations: Psychoanalysis and Culture, Media, Groups, Politics, 62*: i–v.

Bainbridge, C. & Yates, C. (2012). Introduction to the special issue on media and the inner world: New perspectives on psychoanalysis and popular culture. *Psychoanalysis, Culture & Society, 17*(2): 113–119.

Baudry, J. L. (1970). Ideological effects of the basic cinematic apparatus. *Film Quarterly, 28*(2) (Winter, 1974–1975): 39–47. (Translated in 1975 by A. Williams.)

Baudry, J. L. (1975). The apparatus: Metaphysical approaches to the impression of reality in cinema. *Camera Obscura, 1* (Fall). (Translated in 1976 by J. Andrews & B. Augst.)

BBC (2012a). BBC Sport Olympic Ceremonies. Available at: www.bbc.co.uk/programmes/b00qf9wy/clips (accessed on 29 November, 2012).

BBC (2012b). Olympic Torch Relay—May 19th, Day 1, Land's End to Plymouth. Available at: www.bbc.co.uk/torchrelay/day1 (accessed on 29 November, 2012).

Billen, A. (2012). 30 Ultimate TV Box Sets. *The Times*. Available at: www.thetimes.co.uk/tto/arts/tv-radio/article3572691.ece (accessed on 20 October, 2012).

Biressi, A. & Nunn, H. (2005). *Reality TV, Realism and Revelation*. London: Wallflower Press.

Bollas, C. (1987). *The Shadow of the Object: Psychoanalysis of the Unthought Known*. London: Free Association.

Bollas, C. (1992). *Being a Character: Psychoanalysis and Self Experience*. London: Routledge.

Britton, R. (2007). Reality and unreality in fact and fiction. In: C. Bainbridge, S. Radstone, M. Rustin, & C. Yates (Eds.), *Culture and the Unconscious* (pp. 174–186). Basingstoke, UK: Palgrave Macmillan.

Brooker, W. & Jermyn, D. (Eds.) (2003). *The Audience Studies Reader*. London: Routledge.

Caldwell, J. T. (1995). *Televisuality: Style Crisis and Authority in American Television*. New Brunswick, NJ: Rutgers University Press.

Castells, M. (1996). *Rise of the Network Society* (Information Age Series: Vol. 1). Chichester, UK: Wiley-Blackwell.

Cottrell Boyce, F. (2012). London 2012: Opening ceremony saw all our mad dreams come true. *The Observer* online, 29 July. Available at: www.guardian.co.uk/commentisfree/2012/jul/29/frank-cottrell-boyce-olympics-opening-ceremony (accessed on 25 November, 2012).

Cowie, E. (1984). Fantasia. In: J. Evans & S. Hall (Eds.), *Visual Culture: The Reader* (pp. 356–369). London: Sage in association with the Open University, 1999.

Donald, J. (1985). Anxious moments in *The Sweeney* in 1975. In: M. Alvarado & J. Stewart (Eds.), *Made for Television: Euston Films Limited* (pp. 117–135). London: BFI.

Elliott, A. & Urry, J. (2010). *Mobile Lives*. London: Routledge.

Ellis, J. (1982). *Visible Fictions*. London: Routledge.

Ellis, J. (2000). *Seeing Things: Television in the Age of Uncertainty*. London: IB Taurus.

Evans, J. (2009). "As if" intimacy? Mediated persona, politics and gender. In: S. Day Sclater, D. W. Jones, H. Price, & C. Yates (Eds.), *Emotion: New Psychosocial Perspectives* (pp. 72–85). Basingstoke, UK: Palgrave Macmillan.

Evans, N. (2012). Pass the sick bag: BBC receives 2,500 complaints over Diamond Jubilee coverage. *Mirror Online*, 6 July. Available at: www.mirror.co.uk/news/,uk-news/diamond-jubilee-bbc-receive-2500-865284 (accessed on 20 November, 2012).

Ferguson, G. (2010). The family on reality television: Who's shaming whom? *Television & New Media, 11*(2): 87–104.

Fingeroth, D. (2004). *Superman on the Couch: What Superheroes Really Tell Us about Ourselves and Our Society*. New York: Springer.

Flitterman-Lewis, S. (1992). Psychoanalysis, film and television. In: R. C. Allen (Ed.), *Channels of Discourse Reassembled* (pp. 203–246). London: Routledge.

Freud, S. (1900a). The interpretation of dreams. *S. E., 4*: ix–627. London: Hogarth.

Freud, S. (1914g). Remembering, repeating and working-through (further recommendations on the technique of psycho-analysis II). *S. E., 12*: 145–156. London: Hogarth.

Freud, S. (1921c). Group psychology and the analysis of the ego. *S. E., 18*: 65–144. London: Hogarth.

Freud, S. (1927e). Fetishism. *S. E., 21*: 147–158. London: Hogarth.

Frosh, S. & Baraitser, L. (2008). Psychoanalysis and psychosocial studies. *Psychoanalysis, Culture & Society, 13*(2): 346–366.

Furedi, F. (2004). *Therapy Culture; Cultivating Vulnerability in an Uncertain Age*. London: Routledge.

Gray, J. (2006). *Watching the Simpsons, Television, Parody and Intertextuality*. London: Routledge.

Green, A. (2005). *Play in Donald Winnicott's Writings; The Donald Winnicott Lecture Given by Andre Green*. London: Karnac.

Greenberg, J. R. & Mitchell, S. A. (1984). *Object Relations in Psychoanalytic Theory*. Cambridge, MA: Harvard University Press.

Hall, S. (1979). The great moving right show. *Marxism Today*, January: 14–20.

Hills, M. (2002). *Fan Cultures*. London: Routledge.

Hudson, E. (2012). Paralympics: 7/7 survivor Martine Wrights makes debut. *BBC Sport—Paralympics*, 31 August. Available at: www.bbc.co.uk/sport/0/disability-sport/19440879 (accessed on 28 November, 2012).

Independent, The (2012). Leading article: Sit back and let the games cast their spell. *The Independent online*, 27 July. Available at: www.independent.co.uk/voices/editorials/leading-article-sit-back-and-let-the-games-cast-their-spell-7979511.html (accessed on 20 November, 2012).

Jayne, L. (2012). The Olympic Games, revealing British cynicism. 22 July. Available at: http://studyabroad.universiablogs.net/2012/07/27/the-olympic-games-revealing-british-cynicism/ (accessed on 25 November, 2012).

Kaplan, E. A. (Ed.) (1990). *Psychoanalysis & Cinema*. London: Routledge.

Kettle, M. (2012). London 2012: Repress your cynicism and let the games commence. *Guardian.co.uk*, 25 July. Available at: www.guardian.co.uk/commentisfree/2012/jul/25/london-2012-cynicism-games-commence (accessed 28 November, 2012).

Klein, M. (1988). *Envy and Gratitude and Other Works 1946–1963*. London: Virago Press.

Lacan, J. (1977). The subversion of the subject and the dialectic of desire in the Freudian unconscious. In: J. Lacan, *Ecrits: A Selection* (pp. 311–328). London: Tavistock/Routledge, 1989.

Lancaster, J. (2012). The Olympics descend on a grumbling London. *Bloomberg Business Week*, 12 July. Available at: www.businessweek.com/articles/2012-07-12/the-olympics-descend-on-a-grumbling-london (accessed on 12 November, 2012).

Laplanche, J. & Pontalis, J. -B. (1964). Fantasy and the origins of sexuality. In: V. Burgin, J. Donald, & C. Kaplan (Eds.), *Formations of Fantasy* (pp. 5–34). London: Routledge, 1986.

Lasch, C. (1979). *The Culture of Narcissism*. New York: W. W. Norton.

Layton, L. (2011). Something about a girl named Marla Singer: Capitalism, narcissism and therapeutic discourse in David Fincher's *Fight Club*. *Free Associations: Psychoanalysis and Culture, Media, Groups, Politics*, 62: 111–134.

Lebeau, V. (2001). *Psychoanalysis and Cinema. The Play of Shadows*. London: Wallflower Press.

Metz, C. (1975). The imaginary signifier. *Screen, 16*(2): 14–76.

Modleski, T. (1988). *The Women Who Knew Too Much: Hitchcock and Feminist Theory*. New York: Methuen.

Morley, D. (1992). Changing paradigms in audience studies. In: E. Seiter, H. Borchers, G. Kreutzner, & E. M. Warth (Eds.), *Remote Control: Television, Audiences and Cultural Power* (pp. 16–44). London: Routledge.

Mulvey, L. (1975). Visual pleasure and narrative cinema, *Screen, 16*(3): 6–18.

Mulvey, L. (1981). Afterthoughts on "Visual Pleasure and Narrative Cinema" inspired by "Duel in the Sun". *Framework, 16/17*(15): 12–15.

Newcom, H. (2000). *Television: The Critical View*. Oxford: Oxford University Press.

Radstone, S. (2007). Clinical and academic psychoanalytic criticism: Differences that matter. In: C. Bainbridge, S. Radstone, M. Rustin, & C. Yates (Eds.), *Culture and the Unconscious* (pp. 242–255). Basingstoke, UK: Palgrave Macmillan.

Richards, B. (2007). *Emotional Governance: Politics, Media and Terror*. Basingstoke, UK: Palgrave Macmillan.

Richards, B. & Brown, J. (2011). Media as drivers of a therapeutic trend? *Free Associations: Psychoanalysis and Culture, Media, Groups, Politics, 62*: 18–30.

Rieff, P. (1966). *The Triumph of the Therapeutic: Uses of Faith after Freud*. London: Chatto & Windus.

Rose, N. (1999). *Governing the Soul (2nd edition)*. London: Free Association.

Rubin, L. C. (2008). *Popular Culture in Counseling, Psychotherapy, and Play-Based Interventions*. New York: Springer.

Seiter, E., Borchers, H., Kreutzner, G., & Warth, E. M. (Eds.) (1992). *Remote Control: Television, Audiences and Cultural Power*. London: Routledge.

Silverstone, R. (1994). *Television and Everyday Life*. London: Routledge.

Storey, J. (1996). *Cultural Studies and the Study of Popular Culture: Theories and Methods*. Edinburgh, UK: Edinburgh University Press.

Storey, J. (2006). *Cultural Theory and Popular Culture, An Introduction (4th edition)*. Harlow, UK: Pearson, Prentice Hall.

Thornham, S. & Purvis, T. (2005). *Television Drama*. Basingstoke, UK: Palgrave Macmillan.

Tulloch, J. & Alvarado, M. (1983). *Doctor Who: The Unfolding Text*. London: Macmillan.

Turkle, S. (2011). *Alone Together: Why We Expect More from Technology and Less from Each Other*. New York: Basic.

Turner, G. (2010). *Ordinary People and the Media: The Demotic Turn*. London: Sage.

Tyler, I. (2007). From the "Me Decade" to the "Me Millenium". The cultural history of narcissism. *Journal of Cultural Studies, 10*(3): 343–363.

White, M. (2001). Flows and other close encounters with television. Electronic UNiSA Library Catalogue. Available at: http://newcatalogue.library.unisa.edu.au/vufind/Record/870780 (accessed on 28 November, 2012).

Wilde, C. (2012). How the Olympics changed British cynicism. 17 August. http://carolinewilde.com/2012/08/13/how-the-olympics-changed-british-cynicism/ (accessed on 29 November, 2012).

Winnicott, D. W. (1935). The manic defence. In: D. W. Winnicott, *Through Paediatrics to Psycho-Analysis* (pp. 129–145). London: Hogarth and the Institute of Psychoanalysis, 1975.

Winnicott, D. W. (1956). Primary maternal preoccupation. In: D. W. Winnicott, *Through Paediatrics to Psycho-Analysis* (pp. 300–305). London: Hogarth and the Institute of Psychoanalysis, 1975.

Winnicott, D. W. (1958). The capacity to be alone. *International Journal of Psychoanalysis, 39*: 416–420.

Winnicott, D. W. (1974). *Playing and Reality*. London: Pelican.

Wouters, C. (2007). *Informalization: Manners and Emotions since 1890*. London: Sage.

Wouters, C. (2011). How civilizing processes continued: Towards an informalization of manners and a third nature personality. In: N. Gabriel & S. Mennell (Eds.), *Norbert Elias and Figurational Research: Processual Thinking in Sociology* (pp. 140–159). Chichester, UK: Wiley-Blackwell.

Wright, E. (1998). *Psychoanalytic Criticism: A Reappraisal (second edition)*. Cambridge: Polity Press.

Yates, C. (2007). *Masculine Jealousy and Contemporary Cinema*. Basingstoke, UK: Palgrave Macmillan.

Yates, C. (2010a). "Video Replay—Families, Films and Fantasy" as a transformational text. *Psychoanalysis, Culture & Society, 15*(4): 404–411.

Yates, C. (2010b). Spinning, spooning and the seductions of flirtatious masculinity in contemporary politics. *Subjectivity, 3*(3): 282–302.

Yates, C. (2011). Charismatic therapy culture and the seductions of emotional well-being. *Free Associations: Psychoanalysis and Culture, Media, Groups, Politics, 62*: 59–84.

Yates, C. (2012). Fatherhood, political culture and the new politics. *Psychoanalysis, Culture & Society, 17*(2): 204–221.

Yates, C. (2013). *Playing with the Electorate: Political Culture, Emotion and Identity*. Basingstoke, UK: Palgrave Macmillan (forthcoming).

Young, R. M. (1994). *Mental Space*. London: Process Press.

YouTube (1987). Weather blooper by Michael Fish storm of 1987. Available at: http://www.youtube.com/watch?v=uqs1YXfdtGE (accessed on 29 November, 2012).

YouTube (1988). EastEnders Den and Angie anniversary. Available at: http://www.youtube.com/watch?v=HL-nYGKjhUw (accessed on 29 November, 2012).

YouTube (2012a). Emeli Sande—abide with me (with the Akram Kahn Dance Company, London 2012). Available at: www.youtube.com/watch?v=jj2 LqGvKsLw (accessed on 29 November, 2012).

YouTube (2012b). Closing ceremony—Paralympic Games—Sebastian Coe—London 2012 live 09/09/12. Available at: www.youtube.com/watch?v=9ovA5l4oGkQ (accessed on 29 November, 2012).

Žižek, S. (1992). *Looking Awry: An Introduction to Jacques Lacan through Popular Culture. Cambridge, MA*: MIT Press.

Žižek, S. & Daley, G. (2004). *Conversations with Zizek*. Chichester, UK: John Wiley & Sons.

List of television programmes and films cited

Big Brother (UK) (2000–2010). Broadcast on Channel 4, UK; (2011–present). Broadcast on Channel 5, UK.

Breaking Bad (2008–present). First broadcast on US cable channel AMC.

Doctor Who (1963–1986). Broadcast on BBC1, UK.

EastEnders (1985–present). Broadcast on BBC1, UK.

Honey We're Killing the Kids (2005–2007). Broadcast on BBC3, UK.

How to Look Good Naked (2006–present). Broadcast on Channel 4, UK.

In Treatment (2008–present). First broadcast on US network HBO.

Isles of Wonder (2012). Broadcast on BBC1, UK, 27 July.

Mad Men (2007–present). First broadcast on US cable channel AMC.

Mistresses (2008–present). Broadcast on BBC1, UK.

One Day in London (2012). Broadcast on BBC 2, UK, 2 July.

Play School (1964–1988). Broadcast on BBC1, UK.

Sherlock (2001–2012). Broadcast on BBC 1, UK.

Star Trek: The Original Series (1966–1969). First Broadcast on NBC, US.

Supernanny (2004–2011). Broadcast on Channel 4, UK.

The Bridge (2011). Broadcast on BBC4, UK.

The Jeremy Kyle Show (2005–present). Broadcast on ITV, UK.

The Jerry Springer Show (1991–present). Broadcast on NBC Universal, US.

The Killing (2011–2012). Broadcast on BBC4, UK.

The Marchioness: A Survivor's Story (2009). Broadcast on BBC 1, 5 December.

The Paralympics (2012). Broadcast on Channel 4, UK.

The Sopranos (1999–2007). First broadcast on US cable channel HBO.

The Sweeney (1975–1978). Broadcast on ITV, UK.
The X Factor (2004–present). Broadcast on ITV, UK.
True Blood (2008–present). First Broadcast on US cable channel HBO.
Twenty Twelve (2011–2012). Broadcast on BBC2, UK.
Waking the Dead (2000–2011). Broadcast on BBC1, UK.
What Not To Wear (2001–2007). Broadcast on BBC 1, UK.

PART I

THE VIEW FROM THE COUCH

CHAPTER TWO

Television as Rorschach: the unconscious use of the cathode nipple

Brett Kahr

What do suicide bombers watch on telly?

At precisely 8.50 a.m. on Thursday, 7 July, 2005, Mohammad Sidique Khan, a thirty-year-old al-Qaeda sympathiser, detonated an organic-peroxide bomb concealed in his rucksack, while riding on the London Underground, somewhere between Liverpool Street and Aldgate stations. He died instantly, killing six fellow passengers. During the next hour, three of Khan's comrades exploded their own home-made bombs, murdering a total of fifty-two women and men, and injuring approximately 700 others. Some three days before these atrocities, Mohammad Sidique Khan sent a poorly spelled text message to fellow conspirator, nineteen-year-old Germaine Maurice Lindsay, which stated, "I aint getting on no plain fool" (*sic*), a catchphrase used, apparently, by the television character "Sergeant Bosco Albert (B.A.) Baracus", portrayed by the actor, Mr T, in long-running American series *The A-Team* (1983–1987). After receiving this text message, Germaine Lindsay sent a reply, which read, "Fuck u bitch dats my line" (*sic*) (quoted in Godwin, 2010, p. 15).

In view of the horror that Khan, Lindsay, and their accomplices would perpetrate on London and the world some seventy-two hours later, one might have imagined that they would have had other preoccupations than spouting dialogue from a 1980s television programme. Richard Godwin (ibid., p. 15), a columnist for the *London Evening Standard* newspaper, reflected that the revelations of these text messages, and of the bombers' obsession with Mr T and *The A-Team*, would justify describing these young jihadists as "hapless goons", and that the carnage perpetrated by these assassins "was less to do with Islam, more to do with a group of dysfunctional, childish idiots", which Godwin noted rightly would be "no comfort at all for the families of the victims".

If anyone still harboured doubts about the way in which television and its discourse sears itself into the very fabric of our unconscious mind and into the labyrinth of our neuronal pathways, then this revelation of text messages, reported in the 7/7 coroner's inquest, dispels any questions in this respect. The mind and the media do, of course, enjoy a relationship of reciprocal influence, but how best might we describe this set of interconnections? Do the media merely reflect the contents of the human unconscious, or do they actually shape the nature of the unconscious over time?

No doubt educationalists, critics, politicians, religious leaders, and broadcasters alike will all have strong viewpoints on these vexing matters, as do mental health professionals. In the pages that follow, I hope to offer a clinician's perspective on the ways in which television seeps into the unconscious mind, as well as the way in which the unconscious mind filters, absorbs, edits, and identifies with the media and their offerings, in order to satisfy a series of very basic, often very primitive, wishes and desires.

Since its inception, practitioners of psychoanalysis have participated in many filmic and dramatic and television productions, even musical ones. As early as 1926, the Austrian cinema director Georg Wilhelm Pabst, a representative of the 1920s movement in German art known as *"Die neue Sachlichkeit"* ("The New Reality"), made a movie entitled *Geheimnisse einer Seele* (*Secrets of a Soul*) which débuted at the Gloria Palast, the lavish cinema-house in Berlin. Pabst's film has earned a beloved place in psychoanalytical history as the first film about the new psychology of Sigmund Freud, and it featured the German actor Werner Krauss in the role of a psychoanalytical patient who suffered from compulsions and from a knife phobia, with the Russian actor Pavel Pavlov portraying his psychoanalyst.

One might have thought that Freud would have welcomed such publicity for his new psychological science of psychoanalysis, but in fact, he expressed great displeasure over the vulgar popularisation and bastardisation of his discoveries, and in a private letter to his German colleague Ernst Simmel, Freud (1925, p. 99) wrote that, "In my opinion, psychoanalysis does not lend itself in any way whatever to the medium of the motion picture".

Freud's great suspicion towards the media also prompted to him to snub the Hollywood film mogul, Samuel Goldwyn, who, on a visit to Vienna, had hoped to recruit Freud as a psychological consultant to a movie about great lovers from history (Jones, 1957). Similarly, Freud turned down a lucrative series of offers to appear as an expert witness in the 1924 murder trial of the American juvenile killers Nathan Freudenthal Leopold, Jr. and Richard Albert Loeb (Jones, 1957; Kahr, 2005, 2007; cf. Marx, 1976).

And yet, in spite of Freud's reluctance to engage the media, the media certainly engaged Freud; and since Pavel Pavlov's portrayal of a compulsion-curing psychoanalyst in *Geheimnisse einer Seele*, psychoanalysts and other mental health professionals have appeared in numerous guises in films, novels, plays, and even Broadway musicals (Sievers, 1955; Fleming & Manvell, 1985; Conroy, 1986; Gabbard & Gabbard, 1987; McClung, 2007), ranging from the benign "Dr Alexander Brooks" in the Moss Hart/Ira Gershwin/Kurt Weill musical drama, *Lady in the Dark* (1944) (Kahr, 2000), to the more recent incarnation of "Dr Paul Weston" in the television programme *In Treatment* (2008–present) (Kahr, 2011).

In Chapter Three of this volume, Caroline Bainbridge discusses the portrayal of psychoanalysis in popular media, examining how the media might revere, celebrate, denigrate, or satirise both the analyst and the analytical process. I wish to approach the subject of media psychoanalysis from the other edge, exploring the ways in which television programmes, in particular, appear in the course of sessions with patients undergoing intensive psychoanalytical treatment. Apart from a very small number of communications, precious few psychoanalytical writings have yet explored how the patient's television viewing enters the consulting room (cf. Anonymous, 1927; Ekins, 1994; Kahr, 2011).

Television programmes in the consulting room

Thirty years ago, I began to treat my first case in three-times weekly psychotherapy, under the supervision of a senior psychoanalytically orientated psychiatrist. The patient, whom I shall call Mr A,[1] a middle-aged man who had spent more than twenty years in the back wards of a provincial hospital with a diagnosis of paranoid schizophrenia, used to scream in pain at night because he believed that the British Broadcasting Corporation would transmit his secret sexual thoughts to the nation each evening as part of the *Nine O'Clock News* (1970–2000). The patient would cry out, in German, "*Das BBC ist ein Scheisser*", which he translated as "The BBC is a shit-house", and he would hold his head and his anus, in agony, fearing that the news broadcast would somehow come to sodomise him. These ostensible paranoid delusions of persecution by the BBC made little sense to me, until one day, while reading through the patient's extensive case records in the hospital archives, I had come to learn that during Mr A's early childhood, his father had worked for the BBC as an employee. When I shared my archival discovery with the patient, he began to talk about a long history of sexual activity between himself and his father; and eventually, the references to the BBC as a "*Scheisser*" and sodomiser began to make infinitely more sense (cf. Kahr, 2012).

As I became a somewhat more experienced mental health practitioner, I began to notice more readily the many ways in which patients would introduce their television viewing into the fabric of the clinical encounter. Often, my analysands would present their television habits in a very offhand manner, explaining, for example, "Last night, while I was watching such-and-such a programme, I suddenly remembered …". They would often refer to television programmes in a disposable, throwaway manner. But as I became more savvy, I began to focus more fully on the nature of their programme choices, and what this might teach us about often underexplored, or indeed unexplored, aspects of their psychological life.

One of my patients, Miss B, a forty-five-year-old female, had never had a full sexual relationship with a man, despite her attractive appearance. Miss B used to watch the medical drama, *ER* (1994–2009), quite compulsively, again and again, and eventually she confessed to me that she harboured a huge crush on the actor who portrayed the chief medical resident. Sheepishly, Miss B reported that she would watch this telly doctor on video cassette, and would then rewind all the scenes in which he appeared, masturbating to a very pleasurable, if somewhat guilt-stricken, climax.

In our work, Miss B and I examined the multiple functions of *ER* within her mental life. Her overwhelming crush on the young doctor communicated, first and foremost, an important relational striving. In spite of her ongoing, multi-decade failure to have a sexual relationship with a real man in the non-television world, her crush on the telly doctor gave us some sense of hope that in spite of her fears, she craved masculine contact. We also explored the shadow side of this wish, however, examining the ways in which her masturbatory preoccupation with a television actor who probably lives in California might be a very safe way of having sex with a man without having to endure any of the risks attached to intimacy. But of course, as the intensity of the patient's crush on the doctor increased, I also wondered whether we might consider the fact that she found herself fantasising about a television *doctor*, as opposed to a lawyer, policeman, or cowboy; and that perhaps she hoped to find someone who could heal her. On one occasion, I even dared to make a transference interpretation, suggesting that her preoccupation with the television doctor might in fact provide some indication of her feelings towards me, a psychological doctor of sorts, who, by the way, had sometimes appeared on television. The patient replied, "Don't be ridiculous. The guy from *ER* looks nothing like you. And besides, he's hot!"

Some years later, I worked with a young male patient, Mr C, who had perpetrated many horrific sexual crimes against young girls, including rape and other forms of sexual assault. As a consequence of his forensic history, he lived in a secure institution outside London, which lacked any therapeutic resources such as art therapy and music therapy. Consequently, the patient spent virtually all day watching soap operas. He gorged himself on *Coronation Street* (1960–present), *EastEnders* (1985–present), *Hollyoaks* (1995–present), *Doctors* (2000–present), and any other regular drama serial, and he used to arrive at his session with me, under escort, and regale me with detailed plot summaries of each of the soaps. At first, I struggled to make arguably crude connections between certain characters in *EastEnders* and certain key figures in Mr C's early history; but eventually I realised that one could not reduce his television viewing to a simple *roman à clef*. Rather, I came to understand that the feast of television activities represented Mr C's very creative and yet very desperate attempt to deal with a life of extreme loneliness in a psychiatric institution, one whose naked corridors and chilly dormitories mirrored the desolation of his internal world. As a young, convicted rapist, Mr C felt that he had no future, and so he watched an endless parade of soap operas, not only as a means of soothing his chronic isolation, but also as an attempt to project his own hopelessness and despair into the plethora of miserable, tragedy-stricken characters who appeared daily and nightly on his tiny black-and-white hospital ward television screen.

Mrs D, a middle-aged woman who had sought treatment for depression, began to improve after one year of sustained analytical sessions. She soon became a zealot for the psychoanalytical process, and talked about our work with all her friends. One day, Mrs D told me that she had seen an episode of the American television drama, *Mad Men* (2007–present), set in the 1960s, and Mrs D had become very disturbed to see that the Freudian psychiatrist in the programme, who uses a couch, as I do, would often talk about one of his female patients, "Betty Draper", to her husband, "Don Draper", on the telephone, behind the patient's back. We explored Mrs D's anxieties about confidentiality, and whether she nursed a fear that I might breach her confidentiality with a third party. Consciously, she replied that she knew me to be too professional to do that. I then reminded Mrs D that only two or three days earlier she had asked me whether I might offer psychoanalysis to her best girlfriend, who, like she, also suffered from depression. I had refused to do so for obvious reasons; but in Mrs D's unconscious mind, she had already established a psychoanalytical *ménage à trois* in which she, and I, and her best friend, would all share secrets indiscriminately. In this instance, the reference to a television programme provided us with a clue to Mrs D's fear that I might break boundaries, which actually masked a wish that I might do so by treating her friend as well. This mirrored various blurry boundary situations across the generations in Mrs D's childhood and adolescent history. Certainly, the anxiety about whether I might resemble the psychiatrist in *Mad Men* served as a useful springboard for exploring these memories and fears.

Miss E, a young, unwed single mother, also suffered from depression and from co-morbid alcoholism. After she put her child to sleep at night, she would drink five or six whiskies on the trot while watching back-to-back episodes of the American police thriller *CSI: Crime Scene Investigation* (2000–present). In one teary session, Miss E confessed to me that she enjoyed the regular spate of bloody murders portrayed in *CSI* so much, and she had indeed become convinced that this programme allowed her to project her own murderous wishes towards her unwanted child, and towards the child's absconding father, thus freeing her, she felt, from perpetrating any gross child abuse. On one occasion, Miss E arrived at her session quite forlorn. She told me that on the previous evening, her television set had exploded, and that she could not enjoy her nightly fix of *CSI*. To her shock and horror, she became anxious, and aggressive, and in consequence, she had started to yell at her child who had in fact already gone to bed. In this respect, the television generally functioned as a sedative, and as a vehicle for the projection of murderous rage; and in the absence of this drug, the patient felt greatly at risk.

References to television programmes, and fantasies about television programmes, appear frequently not only in work with individual patients, but also with couples who attend for marital psychotherapy. Mr F and Mrs F, two former "hippies" from the 1960s, had a very fractious, sexless marriage, but as ex-"flower power" participants who had protested against the Vietnam War, they felt extremely ashamed to admit that they harboured murderous feelings of any kind, let alone towards each other. Every time I attempted to explore their unconscious hostility, my interpretations fell upon seemingly deaf ears. Fortunately, on one occasion, television came to our rescue. At the start of the session, Mrs F entered the consulting room first, while Mr F nipped into the toilet. While waiting for her husband to appear, Mrs F, ostensibly making "small talk", asked me if I had watched the aforementioned *Mad Men* on television the previous night. I did not reply. I waited, instead, for Mrs F's husband to join us, and then when both had taken their seats, they fell unusually silent. Mrs F asked, "Well, what shall we talk about today?" I opined that perhaps by having asked me about *Mad Men*, she had already begun the session while her husband had gone to pee. Perhaps, I queried, they both felt like "mad men" at times, but found it very hard to discuss these non-flower-powery feelings. To my surprise, the usually placid Mrs F unleashed a barrage of anguish, enumerating the many ways in which her seemingly peaceable husband Mr F resembled the duplicitous, schizoid, adulterous, corporate "Don Draper", underscoring that she hated her husband greatly. Mr F could not understand how his wife had arrived at such a formulation, and before long, the three of us entered a fuller, richer, deeper phase of the marital psychotherapy, in which the more "Mad Men-ish" features of their personalities could now emerge more wholeheartedly.

Other couples also presented television-related material, sometimes in a much more concrete way. Mr G, a television scriptwriter, and Mrs G, a housewife, attended for marital psychotherapy after Mr G, for many years a struggling author, had written a runaway success. In the wake of his newfound achievement as a television writer, he had received a flurry of very time-consuming commissions for further work, and had begun to meet some very glamorous actresses as a result. Mrs G became increasingly jealous and envious of her husband's newfound accomplishments and of his subsequent flirtations; and as a result, television literally became the third person in the marriage.

Ms H and Ms I, a long-standing lesbian couple, arrived at my office after Ms H., a budding television producer, had made her first feature-length documentary, and her girlfriend, Ms I, still had not bothered to take the time to watch a DVD of Ms H's film. Once again, television had become both a concrete and symbolic object that highlighted the ubiquitous themes of competition and sibling rivalry which scar many a marriage.[2]

Sometimes, television appears in analytical sessions not as a third party, and not as a piece of free associative material, but rather, as the very heart of a dream report. Mrs J, a multiply bereaved woman who has suffered for many years from a borderline personality formation, recently reported a dream in which she had attended the 2010 BAFTA awards ceremony, having watched the broadcast on her television the previous night. This patient, by the way, has no formal connection to the film or television industry. In her dream, she found herself dancing with Richard, Lord Attenborough, and she reported that the two of them had had a very nice time indeed. At first, the dream made very little sense; certainly it did not evoke any particular resonances. Mrs J told me that she had enjoyed the dream, as well as her dance with Lord Attenborough. Fortunately, I too had watched the BAFTA awards the previous night, something that I would not have done under ordinary circumstances, but I had a friend who had received a nomination for an award, and I watched the programme as a gesture of support. Having done so, I knew of course that Lord Attenborough had planned to attend the BAFTA ceremony in order to present a lifetime achievement award to the actress Vanessa Redgrave, but that owing to illness, he had had to pull out. At the last minute, His Royal Highness Prince William deputised, to great applause, and handed the prize to Miss Redgrave. I restrained myself from saying too much, as I wanted to ensure that I elicited the patient's associations, and not my own. In spite of Mrs J's reluctance to free associate to the dream narrative, I persevered, and I asked again about Lord Attenborough. Eventually, the patient told me what I already knew, namely, that Lord Attenborough had not appeared for the broadcast in real life, but that he did appear in her dream. This reminded her of her father who had died on the evening of her graduation from university, and who could not, therefore, watch her receive her prized parchment. Eventually, through further elaboration of the dream and its elements, and of the day residue of the BAFTA awards ceremony itself, broadcast on television, we both came to realise that all three of the celebrities involved in this segment of the programme, namely Lord Attenborough, Miss Redgrave, and Prince William, had lost very near and dear relatives in sudden, traumatic circumstances. Prince William, of course, endured the death of his mother, Diana, Princess of Wales, in a ghastly road traffic collision in Paris in 1997; Lord Attenborough had suffered the loss of both his daughter, Jane Holland, and his granddaughter, Lucy Holland, in the Asian tsunami of 2004; and more recently, Vanessa Redgrave lost her daughter, the actress Natasha Richardson, in a tragic skiing accident in Quebec, Canada, in 2009. Once we had realised these interconnections, the dream took on a very rich texture, and provided us with a wealth of analytical material for several sessions to come, exploring, *inter alia*, Mrs J's wish to bring back her dead father, as well as her propensity to hide her pain beneath glamour like a compulsive shopper who would drape herself in extremely expensive clothing whenever she felt depressed.

References to television programmes can also be very helpfully humbling for the psychotherapist. Mr K, a young man in his early twenties, spent a great deal of time watching the "fantasy fiction" television series, *Game of Thrones* (2011–present), based on the novels of George R. R. Martin. Mr K would often make reference to this programme, and he would speak about many of its characters in compelling detail. During one psychotherapy session, Mr K devoted at least ten or even fifteen minutes to a very elaborate description of a scene between two of the leading characters, namely "Tyrion Lannister", a dwarf, and "Jon Snow", the illegitimate son of one of the show's heroes. Mr K, a very tall young man, suffers, nonetheless, from feelings of pusillanimity and pronounced castration anxiety, manifested, in part, by his inability to forge a relationship with a woman. After he had finished reciting copious dialogue between "Tyrion Lannister", the dwarf, and "Jon Snow", the illegitimate son, I offered a very simple comment, noting that although Mr K stands over six feet tall, and though he has two long-standingly married parents, perhaps he often feels like both "Tyrion Lannister" and "Jon Snow", namely small and also lacking in parental love. Mr K agreed with my comment, but he admonished me, "You know, Brett, I am more of a bastard than you know. I think I never told you that my parents conceived me some months *before* they actually married. So, technically, I *am* a bastard, just like 'Jon Snow'". This interchange reminded me very powerfully that a tall man can still feel like a "dwarf", and a man with two married parents can still be a "bastard".

Tony Soprano's swimming pool

Thus far, I have provided a smattering of case material which offers some indication of the ways in which television imagery appears within the clinical psychoanalytical situation, ranging from television as a source of wish fulfilment, as a protection against loneliness, as a means of communicating internal psychic reality, as a means of obtaining sexual pleasure, as a source of rivalry between the members of a couple, as a means of communicating hitherto preconscious or unconscious material, and as a barometer of the transference. But television can also provide important information about structural change in a patient over a long period of time. Most patients who discuss television programmes, do so in an episodic or sporadic fashion, but I did work with one patient over a protracted period of time who had an obsession with the American television programme, *The Sopranos* (1998–2007), and who referred to the series in virtually every single one of her sessions. Let us explore the way in which Miss L's relationship to *The Sopranos* became transmogrified over the course of time.

In the first year of treatment, Miss L returned again and again and again to a key scene in *The Sopranos* in which the teenage son of the protagonist "Tony Soprano" attempts to drown himself in the family swimming pool. In the television version, the young son jumps into the pool, intent on suicide, but fortunately, "Tony Soprano" jumps in afterwards and rescues him. Miss L had made a very serious suicide attempt during her own adolescence, not by drowning, but rather with razor blades, but sadly, no one discovered her bleeding arms, and eventually, she had the presence of mind to take herself to casualty for emergency treatment.

In our second year of work, the patient no longer needed to rehearse the drowning scene in such a compulsive fashion. She had become much less destructive as a result of our five-times-weekly work, and she now told me that she knew that she wanted to live a long lifetime. Instead, she explained that her main anxiety concerned the forthcoming end of *The Sopranos*. Apparently, the series had come to an organic end, and no new episodes would be made. Miss L did not know how she would cope, as this family drama had become very much a substitute for her own. Partnerless, childless, and virtually friendless, Miss L lived a very bleak and arid existence, and *The Sopranos* had become very much a new family for her. At times, I actually found myself facilitating bereavement counselling for a fictional television character. In this respect, the television programme had become an object with which Miss L could enjoy a sort of intimacy, and it also served as a transitional object or linking object to help mollify feelings of loss and desolation.

By the time we embarked upon our third year of analysis, Miss L had now recovered from the fact that the American producers would be offering no more new episodes, but she took comfort from the fact that she could now purchase the entire series on DVD, and always have *The Sopranos* near to hand. Also during this year of further mourning work, Miss L began for the first time to recognise that although she grew up in Yorkshire, far from the Sicilian coast, she too had a Mafioso-like father who terrorised her in various ways, and that as a result, she also had a Mafioso-like aspect within her own character, which often caused violence in her relationships. This proved a particularly fruitful year of understanding in our work.

Hereafter, the analysis entered a fourth phase, in which *The Sopranos* had now become internalised. She had watched the complete series on DVD so many times that even she had begun to become a little bit bored by this; and eventually, she would attend sessions in which she would not mention *The Sopranos* at all. Towards the end of our fourth year of analysis, Miss L had now embarked on a fifth phase in relation to this iconic television programme. The patient told me that she had begun to host regular pizza and spaghetti evenings at her tiny flat for a newly found group of friends and neighbours. Previously, the patient had refused to let anybody into her bedsit under any circumstances, frightened of penetration or violence. When Miss L realised that she also feared that she might be violent herself to any strangers who knocked on the door, she became at once more available for social relationships, and now she began to fancy herself as "Mrs Soprano", cooking large Italian meals for the masses. Perhaps in this respect, Miss L had begun to internalise something of the more nurturant aspect of *The Sopranos*, as opposed to the violence, suicidality, and executions, which took place within this family on a regular basis.

We have now entered a sixth, and perhaps final, phase of the psychoanalysis, in which Miss L makes virtually no mention of the programme at all. For the first time in many years, she has begun to date a sweet young man, she has begun to hold down her first job, and she has started to think about returning to university, having dropped out of education first time round. Extraordinarily, she has also developed what strikes me as a very healthy and creative interest in Italian opera, especially the music of Giuseppe Verdi and Giacomo Puccini. The patient has intuited quite correctly that I have an appreciation for opera, and so she regales me with details of her new compact disc purchases. One day, I noted that she had a penchant for listening to compilations of the great female singers (e.g., Maria Callas, Leontyne Price, Joan Sutherland, and others), and wondered aloud whether she had now replaced *The Sopranos* with the *sopranos*.[3]

Conclusion: eleven years of television viewing

Television insinuates itself into the deepest recesses of our minds. It also serves as a cyber-Rorschach, which paints a picture of what lurks, perhaps, in our minds already. Today, we use television not only to entertain us, to inform us, and to soothe our loneliness, but also, we rely upon it in order to help our minds to work. Recently, a new patient had asked me whether I could recommend any really good books about the impact of parents on their children. As I work in a consulting room lined with books and journals, it seemed disingenuous to provide an evasive answer, or to wonder why the patient wanted to have such a recommendation. In fact, I recommended an excellent book written by the psychologist, Dr Oliver James (2010), *How Not to F*** Them Up: The First Three Years*. The patient became quite intrigued, and said, "Oliver James, Oliver James, ah, good, it sounds perfect. I shall have to buy a copy. But I don't have a pen. How will I remember that name? Oh, I know, I'll just think of Jamie Oliver, but backwards". Even basic cognitive information becomes communicated, processed, and remembered in the form of a television chef.

On 20 May, 2010, a documentary about the work of the Freud Museum of London appeared on BBC 4, broadcast as part of a four-part series entitled *Behind the Scenes at the Museum* (2010). A very pugnacious patient, Miss M, came to her session the following day, and told me how she had watched the programme about the Freud Museum, and how she had taken a great dislike to all the staff members portrayed therein. The calumniations of the Freud Museum became increasingly vitriolic, and I felt very torn between allowing the patient to use the session in a fully verbally unrestricted fashion, and my loyalty towards the Freud Museum and its staff members, some of whom I have known for more than twenty-five years. I listened patiently, without interruption, and then dared to wonder about the extreme vehemence of Miss M's hostility for the mild-mannered archivists who work at Maresfield Gardens. I also knew that Miss M, a compulsive Googler, knew that I myself had many ties to the Freud Museum, some of which could be found quite readily through a cursory search of the internet. In an effort to defend my friends at the Freud Museum, and to explore the deeper aspects of Miss M's feelings towards me, I suggested that her odium for the museum staffers might, in fact, represent a displacement of angry feelings towards me for all sorts of reasons, but principally, for not having cured her fully as yet. To my surprise, and to my secret delight, the patient returned for another session after the weekend break. She had told me that she had decided to watch the Freud Museum documentary once more on BBC iPlayer, and that she realised that she may have misjudged the staff. On second viewing, they did not seem quite so bizarre, and in fact, she even warmed to some of them. This gave me ample material to think with Miss M about all the relationships and opportunities that she has sabotaged in her life by executing people within seconds of meeting them, and sometimes even *before* she has met them. The patient, an English literature graduate with a detailed knowledge of the works of Jane Austen, then confessed that "first impressions" (a key supratext in *Pride and Prejudice: A Novel*) may often be inaccurate, and that she will now devote more time and energy to better reality-testing. It seemed extraordinary that Miss M and I needed to reach this discovery through the analysis of a television programme, but once again, such anecdotes provide powerful evidence of the way in which the remote control has begun, and continues, to structure our internal and external lives.

According to the October, 2010, statistics of BARB, the Broadcasters' Audience Research Board, the average Briton watches 27.15 hours of television per week. Over the course of a lifetime of seventy years, each of us devotes approximately eleven years, and sometimes more, to watching television! In view of this extraordinary fact, it should hardly surprise us that the content and the format of our psychoanalytical free associations, dreams, unconscious wishes, and sexual fantasies should be shaped and moulded by television. In this brief chapter, I do not propose to pass judgement on this piece of data, merely to report its existence, in the hope that subsequent discussion and reflection will help us to know quite what we might think about television, remote control, and the ways in which we communicate our lives and fully live them.

Notes

1. Throughout this chapter, I have taken considerable care and attention to anonymise the patients and couples to whom I make reference, in order to preserve confidentiality. I have adopted a sequential series of initials to describe all the patients (e.g., Mr A, Miss B, Mr C, and so forth), and I have removed any pieces of biographical data that would enable anyone else to identify these individuals.

2. Shortly after I had completed writing this chapter, yet another couple with whom I work shared some fascinating material about the television and its use within their marriage. Mr M. and Mrs M., an elderly couple, entered psychotherapy several years ago, in part because of Mr M.'s long-standing depression, which had a profound impact on their marital relations. Understandably, Mr M. had lost interest in sex, and Mrs M. became increasingly enraged, in spite of her efforts to be sympathetic. During one session, Mrs M. explained to me that she and her husband spend a lot of time watching television, but they do so in separate rooms. When I enquired what sorts of programmes they prefer to watch, Mrs M. replied that she loves the American mystery drama *Murder, She Wrote*, while Mr M. enjoys the American comedy-drama *Weeds*. Although I have little familiarity with either of these television programmes, I explored how the television serves to keep the couple apart, while also communicating something very palpable about Mrs M.'s *murder-she-wrote*-ish rage, and something about Mr M.'s depression, which he himself had once referred to as his *"weedy"* feelings. After discussing this subject in detail, the couple expressed a hope that they could spend more time together watching the same programme at the same time; and three weeks later, they reported their great pleasure at having purchased a new television which they

regarded as an improvement on their old *flat* screen (which, I suspect, represented the depression and flatness within the marriage).

3. Quite some time later, Miss L made yet one further reference to *The Sopranos*, not having talked about the series in the longest time. She had eventually married her boyfriend, and they had settled down into a reasonably happy and contented life together. However, shortly thereafter, Miss L's mother-in-law died very unexpectedly, and Miss L's new husband became somewhat depressed. Miss L encouraged him to seek psychotherapy of some sort, but he adamantly refused, thinking that it would not be "manly" to cry in front of a stranger. To her surprise, Miss L found herself returning to her box-set of DVDs of *The Sopranos*, and she began to watch the series over again. She took great comfort from the fact that even the rugged "Tony Soprano" had allowed himself to visit a psychiatrist, and she used this information as leverage in her discussions with her husband, who eventually relented and found psychotherapy to be a helpful experience.

References

Anonymous (1927). Proceedings of the British Psychological Society. *British Journal of Psychology: General Section, 17*: 266.

Conroy, P. (1986). *The Prince of Tides*. Boston, MA: Houghton Mifflin.

Ekins, R. (1994). Psychoanalysis, cinema, and the role of film in the psychoanalytic process. In: R. Ekins & R. Freeman (Eds.), *Centres and Peripheries of Psychoanalysis: An Introduction to Psychoanalysis* (pp. 193–213). London: Karnac.

Fleming, M. & Manvell, R. (1985). *Images of Madness: The Portrayal of Insanity in the Feature Film*. Madison, NJ: Fairleigh Dickinson University Press, and Cranbury, NJ: Associated University Presses.

Freud, S. (1925). Letter to Ernst Simmel. 26 October, p. 99. In: F. Deri & D. Brunswick (1964), Freud's Letters to Ernst Simmel. F. Deri & D. Brunswick (Trans.). *Journal of the American Psychoanalytic Association, 12*: 93–109.

Gabbard, K. & Gabbard, G. O. (1987). *Psychiatry and the Cinema*. Chicago, IL: University of Chicago Press.

Godwin, R. (2010). The 7/7 bombers were just a team of dangerous idiots. *Evening Standard*, 20 October, p. 15.

James, O. (2010). *How Not to F*** Them Up: The First Three Years*. London: Vermilion/Ebury/Random House.

Jones, E. (1957). *The Life and Work of Sigmund Freud: Volume 3. The Last Phase. 1919–1939*. New York: Basic.

Kahr, B. (2000). Psychoanalysis on stage: Moss Hart's *Lady in the Dark*. *Psychoanalytic Review, 87*: 377–383.

Kahr, B. (2005). Why Freud turned down $25,000: Mental health professionals in the witness box. *American Imago, 62*: 365–371.

Kahr, B. (2007). Why Freud turned down $25,000. In: J. Ryan (Ed.), *Tales of Psychotherapy* (pp. 5–9). London: Karnac.

Kahr, B. (2011). Dr Paul Weston and the bloodstained couch. *International Journal of Psychoanalysis, 92*: 1051–1058.

Kahr, B. (2012). The infanticidal origins of psychosis: The role of trauma in schizophrenia. In: J. Yellin & K. White (Eds.), *Shattered States: Disorganised Attachment and Its Repair. The John Bowlby Memorial Conference Monograph 2007* (pp. 7–126). London: Karnac.

Marx, A. (1976). *Goldwyn: A Biography of the Man Behind the Myth*. New York: W. W. Norton and Company.

McClung, B. D. (2007). *Lady in the Dark: Biography of a Musical*. New York: Oxford University Press.

Sievers, W. D. (1955). *Freud on Broadway: A History of Psychoanalysis and the American Drama*. New York: Hermitage House.

List of television programmes and films cited

Behind the Scenes at the Museum (2010). BBC4, UK.

Coronation Street (1960–present). Granada (ITV), UK.

CSI: Crime Scene Investigation (2000–present). First broadcast on US cable channel CBS.

Doctors (2000–present). BBC1, UK.

EastEnders (1995–present). BBC1, UK.

ER (1994–2009). First broadcast on US cable channel, NBC.

Game of Thrones (2011–present). First broadcast on US cable channel, HBO.

Geheimnisse einer Seele (*Secrets of a Soul*) (1926). Director, Georg Pabst, Germany.

Hollyoaks (1995–present). Channel 4, UK.

In Treatment (2008–present). First broadcast on US cable channel, HBO.

Lady in the Dark (1944). Director, Mitchell Leisen, US.

Mad Men (2007–present). First broadcast on US cable channel, AMC.

Nine O'Clock News (1970-2000). BBC1, UK.

The A Team (1983-1987). First broadcast on US cable channel, NBC.

The Sopranos (1997-2007). First broadcast on US cable channel, HBO.

CHAPTER THREE

Psychotherapy on the couch: exploring the fantasies of *In Treatment**

Caroline Bainbridge

In Treatment (2008–present) began airing in the UK in 2009 as the Media and the Inner World network was established. Its timeliness in relation to the concerns of the network was noteworthy. In particular, it chimed neatly with observations underpinning the network regarding the significance of an increasingly emotionalised cultural climate and the heightened visibility of talking therapies within popular culture. At a very obvious level, then, the appearance of *In Treatment* on television offered scope for reflecting on claims that we live in what has been variously described negatively as "therapy culture" (Furedi, 2004) or more positively as "therapeutic culture" (Richards, 2007; Richards & Brown, 2011; Yates, 2011). In its depiction of a psychotherapist engaging with different clients in his consulting room at the heart of the dramatic narrative, the series taps into our curiosity about the therapeutic exchange in a world where feelings are often seen as central to the shaping of our everyday experience. These feelings are frequently

*This chapter was first published as an original article in *Psychoanalysis, Culture and Society*, 17(2): 153–168. We are most grateful to Palgrave Macmillan for their permission to reprint it here in its original form.

aligned with anxieties linked to the ever-more fragmented nature of contemporary life with all its playful ideas about identity afforded by engagements with new technologies and so on, which raises interesting questions about our uses of media objects in relation to lived emotional experience.

Elsewhere, I argue that, in a highly media-shaped age, the media are internalised as objects of our inner worlds, with their representations providing a means of traversing the complexities and contradictions of contemporary emotional life (Bainbridge, 2011, p. 52). Similarly, Richards and Brown (2011, p. 29) contend that the contemporary media provide their consumers with "reflexive resources" that are used in the formation of more "therapeutic" selves. This chapter develops some of these ideas with reference to *In Treatment* and suggests that the programme provides a means of allaying the anxieties inherent in contemporary culture. Furthermore, in considering the fantasies circulating around the programme's international consumption, it demonstrates that, as internal objects, media can function as significant resources at a cultural level. They provide a means of rehearsing our psychological and emotional relationships to diverse socio-cultural figures of the contemporary imagination, ranging from the global notion of "America" through to the more localised (in)experience of psychotherapy as a means of self-healing/self-construction. The usefulness of a psychocultural approach to television specifically and to media more broadly is explicated here, enabling us to reflect further on the emotional and psychological investments we make in our media consumption.

Extrapolating from a psychological model of the mind to a psychocultural method of engagement with socio-cultural processes, this chapter illustrates the importance of our contemporary emotional relationship with media. It demonstrates that they act as a barometer of sorts, by which we are able to gauge the socio-political consequences of our increasingly emotionalised engagement with the world. Of central significance in relation to questions of cultural politics, of course, is that the HBO drama under scrutiny here is, in fact, an adaptation of the Israeli original, *Be' Tipul* (2005–2008). In itself, the complex structure of international origin, adaptation, and subsequent international distribution of this television series raises a number of pertinent political questions that can be scrutinised through the circulation of fantasies around this programme.

In the UK, television channels were comparatively slow to pick up the HBO version of *In Treatment*, which had enjoyed considerable success in the US (where it first aired in 2008). When it was eventually acquired for the UK market, it had already been subject to commentary by the likes of Gaby Wood (2009) in *The Observer* and Jonathan Bernstein (2008) in *The Guardian*, who anticipated the successful transition of this series and others such as *The Wire* (broadcast on HBO, 2002–2008) well in advance of UK channels adopting them. As Claire Birchall (2009) suggests, the British reluctance to pick up this drama series perhaps shows the extent to which "Britons are not as immersed in therapy culture as Stateside depressives". When it was eventually programmed in the UK, it appeared on a relatively niche cable channel (first Sky Arts 1 and subsequently Sky Atlantic), which meant that the target audience was comparatively small.[1]

In Treatment differs, then, in important ways from other HBO imports aired on a range of terrestrial and satellite/cable channels, which enjoy a more extensive reach. Nevertheless, the programme has garnered considerable critical attention both in print media and on online platforms, indicating the extent to which its themes are redolent of the contemporary cultural imagination grounded in concerns about psychological "well-being" and in the increasing emphasis on our highly fragmented and emotionalised experience of both interpersonal relationships and relationships to culture and society. As Paul Rixon (2011, pp. 13–14) suggests, the critical reception of television offers a useful means of gauging cultural attitudes, since "… while the critic is not all-powerful, he or she does play an important role in the way the public thinks and talks about television. How this interaction, between public and critic, has developed over time tells us something about the changing way a society values its popular culture".

Similarly, as Candida Yates (2007, p. 63) argues in her analysis of the usefulness of film reviews, critical evaluation of popular culture made by journalists "can tell us something about the cultural values and fantasies that circulate within a culture at any one time". The programme's contexts of reception are significant in helping us to understand how media objects work to circulate fantasies in and through culture, thereby revealing something of the anxieties and pleasures of popular culture. As John Caughie (1981, p. 10) has noted, "[Q]uestions of form on television (or anywhere else) must always be brought back to questions of institution, audience and conditions of viewing[;] at the same time it seems to me that we have to begin to specify the particular ways in which individual programmes work, how they produce their pleasures and address their viewers".

This chapter explores *In Treatment* as an exemplar of the uses made in television drama of the figure of psychotherapy and offers some reflections on their significance for viewers on the *living room* couch as opposed to the one in the consulting room. Taking a psycho-cultural studies approach, it also considers how television programmes can be read as symptomatic of the broader postmodern popular cultural climate in which we do our viewing. It is worth noting that there is remarkably little work that uses psychoanalysis to understand television when compared with the very extensive list of examples we could cite in relation to film and cinema studies. This chapter attempts to make an intervention into television studies to signal the usefulness of the object relations psychoanalytic approach for thinking through how best to theorise the pleasures of television and its role in shaping our relationships in and to the world at large. The work of Roger Silverstone (1994) on television as a transitional object, one that enables its viewers simultaneously to negotiate the threat of anxiety present in everyday life and also to meditate on creativity and responses to what we see and feel on the small screen is helpful here, and I draw on this work to argue that television drama functions as a psychological object within popular culture. To highlight the significance of such an approach, I build on Silverstone's ideas to raise questions of desire and its vicissitudes in relation to *In Treatment*; I also turn to the Kleinian notion of projection as a key psychological defence. This chapter illustrates how television objects can be used to facilitate an important (and perhaps therapeutic) space of working through in the broader socio-cultural context of therapeutic culture with its complex, and often contradictory array of emotionalised socio-political concerns (Yates, 2011).

Silverstone (1994) suggests that the role of television in everyday life can be understood through D. W. Winnicott's idea of transitional phenomena. Winnicott extended ideas about the unconscious functioning of the mind to theorise the importance of real, lived relationships and their formation inside our minds. For Winnicott (1953), transitional objects, transitional phenomena, and transitional space are fundamental to the subject's negotiation of individual identity and separation from the mother. They also constitute the first experience of symbol-making and are therefore linked to our capacity for playfulness, thought, and creativity. Hence, it is in the spheres of art, culture, and religion that our childhood capacity for play and creativity finds an outlet in adult life. Such spaces provide for experience that unites the inner and outer worlds, allowing us to live out a profound sense of enrichment that is uniquely personal and unable to be challenged by others. For Winnicott, therapy is just such a transitional space and requires a capacity for play and creativity in order to be effective.

Silverstone (1994) draws on these ideas to suggest that television has become fundamental to the subject's negotiation of individual identity and separation from the mother. As with transitional phenomena, television for Silverstone helps to constitute our experience of symbol-making. As he suggests (ibid., pp. 12–13) in his discussion of Winnicott's transitional object,

> [I]n the normal scheme of things the emotional significance of the early, intensely cathected object is reduced, eventually, to insignificance. The space it occupied is filled with other cultural activities and forms which continue the work of providing relief from the strain of relating inner and outer reality ... The cultural work continues with its consequent satisfactions and frustrations, and with the continuing reliance on objects and media to facilitate it. ... Our media, television perhaps pre-eminently, occupy the potential space released by blankets, teddy bears and breasts.

Thus, television helps us to negotiate the threat of anxiety present in everyday life and also allows us space to meditate on creativity and responses to what we see and feel every day. This observation seems especially pertinent given the widely acknowledged fragmentary nature of experience in a postmodern setting. How, then, does such a perspective enable us to think about *In Treatment* and its role as a television object of sorts, one that, by dint of its central narrative concerns, highlights our contemporary relationship with therapy culture?

Recently there has been a spate of television drama series in which psychotherapy is given a key place in the narrative—the most obvious US examples include *The Sopranos* (1999–2007), *Frasier* (1993–2004), and *Tell Me You Love Me* (2007–2008); in the UK, we might think about *Help* (2005), but this chapter takes as its sole focus *In Treatment* because that series presents the most sustained and therapy-focused narrative drive.

Its narrative focus centres on psychotherapy as practised by "Dr Paul Weston" (Gabriel Byrne) and on his relationships with a number of different patients over the course of each season, as well as on his own relationship with his supervisor(s). The narrative also explores the consequences of his work for his personal life.

The structure and format of the show, as well as its media reception, are significant in understanding the powerful fantasies it generates because these aspects of the programme work in tandem with its narrative content to engender fantasies particular to the distinct, culturally specific television flow in which any given broadcast takes place. There are a number of fantasies at play here. What is the function of such fantasies for viewers on the living room couch? First, it is important to note that, in the US, as in Israel, the scheduling of the programme was highly innovative. The first series comprised half-hour episodes screened at the same time on each night of the week,[2] simulating the regularity of the therapeutic contract and yet simultaneously repackaging it into shorter, more bearable half-hour slots. Most therapeutic "hours" last for fifty minutes, so it is interesting to think about what happens when this time period is telescoped in this way. In season one, at least, this scheduling helps to construct an obvious fantasy for viewers: they are witnessing what it would be like for them to be in therapy themselves. By committing to viewing the series for half an hour each weekday evening, viewers are entering into a kind of therapeutic contract of their own—a fact not lost on the reviewers who praised the show extensively for this experiment (Gilbert, 2009). Yet, despite the decision of the show's producers to design the schedule in this way and despite the reviewers' praise for its innovation, viewing figures suggest that audiences did not watch obediently. Instead they chose to view only selected characters/storylines or else to watch on their own terms (by DVD/download/online "catch-up" resources or by network personal recording technologies such as TIVO and Sky+ in the UK or Cablevision in the US) (Dichek, 2008; Rochlin, 2008; Wilson, 2009).

Of course, the original structure of the schedule also taps into the fantasy of what it would be like to be the partner/son/daughter of a therapist whose life is regimented in just such a way. As one critic noted, obviously "Dr Weston" must have other patients and the ones we see are the ones "who put salt in his wounds … reflecting problems he is going through" (Wilson, 2009, p. 16). Elsewhere, it was observed that the series amounted to "a marathon in TV terms, yet barely a dent on the amount of listening a real therapist has to do" (Wood, 2009). The programme, then, whose writers are required to have been in psychotherapy themselves, is seen to offer "an irresistible peek at the psychopathology of everyday life" (Stanley, 2008). It draws an audience of therapists and patients alike as well as members of the public whose curiosity about the therapeutic encounter is piqued by the show's main concepts. Therapists reportedly thanked the show's creator. They commented, "Finally, our families know what we are doing, what we have to deal with every day" (Wood, 2009). For therapists, too, then, the show prompts fantasies about a broader public understanding of the therapeutic process, albeit that therapists also express ambivalence about the programme as a valid representation of the work of psychotherapy in general and of psychotherapists in particular. As Brett Kahr (2011, p. 1056) has suggested,

> Viewers have watched *In Treatment* for all sorts of reasons, conscious as well as unconscious. For those curious about the art of psychotherapy, *In Treatment* provides an intimate glimpse into a clinical practice, albeit not necessarily our clinical practice. For others, the programme serves as a confirmation that one has to be mad to visit a psychological professional, and mad to be one as well. For those in the mental health field keen to damn all heretics who do not practise exactly as we do, *In Treatment* offers a field day of boundary violations that one can lambast.

As with other programmes, such as *The Sopranos*, there was anecdotal media comment on the effect of the programme in increasing the actual take-up of therapy in the real world. In Israel, the show's original creator, Hagai Levi, noted that a key effect was to increase the fees being charged by real-world psychotherapists: "In the series, patients paid 400 shekels—approximately $100—which is quite high in Israel, so automatically, almost every therapist raised his rate" (cited in Wood, 2009). Interestingly, despite the almost unanimous fervour of TV critics, for whom the seductiveness of the show produced expressions of love and addiction, audience numbers in the US fell very rapidly from 316,000 in week one to 196,000 in week four (Stelter, 2008). This decline suggests that, for viewers, the schedule was too demanding or perhaps too harrowing and viewers wanted to watch on their own terms. We have to pay some attention to the role of the reviewer in producing and circulating the kind of fantasies associated with the programme, and we need to think about how best to make sense of them, as discussed earlier (Rixon, 2011; Yates, 2007).

Academic approaches to psychoanalytic readings of television emphasise the importance of the fact that, as viewers, we do not identify with characters in television drama in singular, unified, or predictable ways. Instead, the conventions of television and its relay of looks through camera perspectives work to ensure that our identification patterns are fractured and broadly dispersed (Flitterman-Lewis, 1992). In other words, in our television viewing we tend not to identify uniquely with any given character in any given drama, as we are thought to do in cinema. As television viewers, we are positioned so that we move fluidly between different identifications and, indeed, hold a number of identifications in place simultaneously. From a psychoanalytic perspective, of course, identification is an intimate, personal, and often very private psychical mechanism of self-experience, one that is intricately bound up with identity itself. As Diana Fuss (1995, p. 2) suggests, "Identification is the psychical mechanism that produces self-recognition. Identification inhabits, organizes, and instantiates identity. It operates as a mark of self-difference, opening up a space for the self to relate to itself as a self. A self that is perpetually other".

Arguably, it is just such a process that is facilitated by our consumption of culture. Through our willingness to make multiple, fractured identifications with characters and scenarios depicted on-screen, we open up spaces for self-contemplation and reflection. This fluid viewer-positioning is particularly apparent in soap opera, that mode of television drama with a very open-ended structure and a distinct sense that imminent closure will not be forthcoming (there are clear echoes of the therapeutic situation here). For Sandy Flitterman-Lewis (1992), this viewer-positioning is central to television's particular conjunction of fantasy, desire, and belief; the fragmentary nature of our identification patterns in the experience of television drama intensifies the quality of our interest in it. By being able to slide between positions of identification, our viewing pleasure intensifies, and we become more bound up with the complexity of the lives of on-screen soap opera characters. The original writer of *In Treatment*, Hagai Levi, observes that the daily broadcast format of his programme places it squarely as an example of this genre, and he comments that he explicitly conceived the programme in this way in order to heighten its power (Wood, 2009). The implication here is that the success of *In Treatment* is based partly on its structure and form, enabling us to adopt several perspectives at once on the practice of psychotherapy. This plurality of perspective has consequences for the fantasies of psychotherapy that circulate around the programme as well as through it. It is worth noting that television viewing cannot be read as a "passive" activity; we are not mindless consumers of television fodder, as much of the work on audience demonstrates (Hall, 1973). Any effort to understand what is at stake in television viewing needs to account for the role of television consumption and enjoyment at both the conscious and the unconscious levels of psychological experience. It is important, too, to understand the active processes of spectatorship with all their capacity to evoke both self-reflective and dynamic creativity and unconscious impact on personal experience.

For example, in the representations of "Weston's" consulting room (based initially in his family home, and, subsequently, in his Brooklyn apartment), we see many personal effects, including an array of books, model boats, and pictures, as well as typical paraphernalia associated with a therapist's office: rugs, battered armchairs, comfortable couches, and, of course, a box of tissues. The *mise-en-scène* works to draw attention to the role of consumption in shaping our aspirations by aligning psychotherapy with a middle class social position and tapping into spaces that shape broader desires for upward social mobility.[3] It also works to enhance the pleasure of the gaze—the spaces are pleasant and the objects pleasing. At the same time, it encourages us to fantasise about who our therapist might be, a fantasy that aligns us, first, with the various patients on "Paul's" couch, who seek in various ways to get glimpses into his personal life. It also aligns us with "Gina" (Dianne Wiest) and, later, "Adele" (Amy Ryan), "Paul's" own therapists/ supervisors, who seek to help him to resolve the various dilemmas he faces in his therapeutic practice. By glancing in this voyeuristic way at "Paul's" work space inside his home and by being made privy, through the structure of the narrative, to various exchanges with members of his family, we are also at liberty to fantasise about "Paul's" role as a father/ husband/lover in ways that are not available to "Paul's" patients, who never actually meet members of his family or witness any aspect of his personal life, whereas we viewers do.

Thus, while the programme ostensibly offers us a representation of the therapeutic process and all its dramatic possibilities and consequences, it actually goes much further. As with *The Sopranos, In Treatment* offers us a vision of the psychotherapist that it would be impossible to gain through participation in therapy, as a patient, alone. What is more, by providing us with the voyeuristic opportunity to look in on the supervisory relationship between "Paul" and "Gina" and, in later seasons, between "Paul" and "Adele", the programme also offers us an opportunity to fantasise about ourselves as all-seeing and omnipotent. To cite one of the show's reviewers, "The first season was so riveting because it was so flattering; the viewer was the real supervisor in the room" (Stanley, 2009, p. 1). This fantasy of power can be seen as one of the key pleasures of watching this show. As Stanley goes on to note, "It's the *viewer* who gets to look at a watch and say 'I think our time is up'" (p. 1, italics added). There are resonances here with observations I have already discussed about the scheduling of this programme and the apparent refusal of the schedule by viewers in general. The omnipotent production decision to call time at thirty minutes instead of the traditional fifty is undercut by the viewer, as Stanley's perspective underscores. The practice of viewing on alternative platforms such as DVD or network personal recorders demonstrates an additional desire for mastery over the show on the part of viewers.

This desire for mastery and its attendant fantasies of omnipotence arguably emanate from the experiences of fragmentation and disintegration that characterise the contemporary age. At one level, the image of "Weston" and his troubled personal life mirrors the experience of viewers; it allows them room to contemplate the commonality of such experience and to fantasise about having more control. At another level, these images depict a familiar scenario of the breakdown of Western tropes of authority in the postmodern period. The chaos of "Paul's" emotional life is paralleled by his contempt for his job and his belief that he is unable, in the end, to help his patients. These concerns underpin the narratives that unfold with both "Gina" and "Adele" and present viewers with an opportunity to identify with "Weston" as well as to judge him as an archetypal example of a male authority figure plagued by "crisis".[4]

The fantasies that circulate around television programmes are related to more than narrative content. We also need to heed the cultural context in which a programme emerges, to see it as symptomatic of the popular cultural mood of any given moment (Bainbridge & Yates, 2005; Donald, 1985). *In Treatment* makes for a particularly interesting case study in this context owing to its origins not in America, but in Israel. *In Treatment* is a largely faithful but nevertheless altered re-visioning of the successful Israeli *Be' Tipul*. The Israeli original was bought by HBO, which also invited its creator, Levi, to act as a consultant writer on the programme. As many reviewers have remarked, the first two seasons of *In Treatment* are an extremely faithful (almost word-for-word) adaptation of its Israeli predecessor. Much of the dialogue is directly translated from the Hebrew, and it is only in the third season that American writers provide original narrative material.

Nevertheless, in the first two seasons of the show, there are crucial changes that have been made in translating the work for the American screen (and subsequently for those of many other countries importing the HBO version). First, the production values increase in the American version: "Everything looks and sounds richer" (Heffernan, 2008)—which also applies to the therapist himself. In the Israeli version, the therapist, "Reuven" (Assi Dayan), is "rumpled, sweaty and overweight"—a clearer contrast with the suave, attractive Gabriel Byrne could not be drawn. Here, then, the common fantasy of intimacy with on-screen characters may become confused with the clinical notion of sexual desire for the therapist (the erotic transference), which, in the psychoanalytic account, stems from the original relation to the parents and which shapes the therapeutic relationship.

In Treatment seems to create an erotic transference both within and beyond its textuality; there is a transference between the viewer and the television show, on one hand, and between the on-screen patients and "Paul Weston" on the other. Erotic transference provides a key running theme for the show. In season one, we see "Paul" struggle with the transference of his patient "Laura" (Melissa George); in season two, this theme surfaces once again in relation to "Mia" (Hope Davis), a patient from twenty years earlier who encounters "Weston" in the lawyer's office where she works when he finds himself seeking defence representation in a legal suit against him. For viewers of the US version of the drama, this thematic is, perhaps, further intensified by the star persona of Byrne, whose appeal to female viewers in particular is highlighted in reviews in the press (O'Driscoll, 2008). The programme exemplifies on many levels how sexualisation masks anxiety associated with the emotional dependence on the therapist. The therapist having been reduced to an object of desire, this anxiety can be held at bay. By articulating the complexities of erotic transference as a mechanism of therapeutic work, the television programme also opens up space for viewers to rework their relationships to television itself. In this way, opportunities are created for the contemplation of experiences of loss, dependency, and other difficult feelings that are made manifest in the characterisation of the patients on "Weston's" couch. There are important echoes here of Silverstone's (1994) argument that television can work as a transitional object for viewers in the living room. Here, television is used by its viewers as a form of therapeutic tool, one that is recognised by the very fact of its explicit articulation within the narrative of the programme itself.

Furthermore, the directness of the Israeli patients is tempered in the US version for fear that such directness would be perceived as "too violent". The cultural distinction between temperaments is decisive here; Levi observes, "In Israel, we don't have borders unfortunately, so you cross them all the time in personal situations" (Wood, 2009). HBO sought to adapt this aspect of the programme for the apparently more "restrained and polite" American culture. More substantively, in the opening season, one key storyline had to be changed. The story of "Yadin", a pilot who has dropped a bomb over Gaza and killed thirteen children, had, in Israel, huge political ramifications reaching well beyond the therapist's office, as it was based on a true story. Levi comments that this storyline was "deeply connected to the Israeli state of mind" (ibid.). In the US version, this storyline was seen as the most difficult to transpose culturally. In the end, it was replaced with the story of "Alex" (Blair Underwood), an African American navy pilot who drops a bomb on a *madrasah* in Iraq, killing children in the same way.

The nuances of the different political scenarios at the heart of the transposition are complex and telling, offering televisual perspectives on the political and cultural concerns prevalent in the respective nation states at the time of broadcast. Moreover, in the US transposition of the story, one can see the importance of several fantasies of American identity circulating, such as those related to discourses of imperial power, democratic forces for change, and issues of moral and cultural responsibility arising from the "war on terror". In addition, the complexity of ideas about "American" identity grounded in issues of race, ethnicity, and cultural difference is also condensed in the figure of "Alex", whose othering in the name of American war-mongering is all too apparent for viewers on the living room couch. "Alex" ends up dying in action after he has returned to flying for the navy in an attempt to make good his past actions. This situation raises many complex issues related to US history, cultural politics, and notions of identity. For American viewers, it provides a very distinctive matrix of allusion that demands self-reflection and active working through. Of course, for viewers watching in the UK or France or Spain, there is another layer of fantasy circulating here, one that relates to the global notion of "America" at play in all this. There are also fantasies about the ordinariness of therapy in everyday life in the US and the distinctions in comparison with the British/European cultural context, where, while counselling is not considered out of place, for some, psychotherapy and psychoanalysis still bear a hint of strangeness.

Symptomatically, then, what the first season of *In Treatment* offers us is a barometer of public feeling about the effects of America's decision to go to war in Iraq in response to attacks on the World Trade Centre and elsewhere in 2001. The public mood of disinclination for the war (which gathered momentum throughout the decade) and its ongoing consequences for the "American way of life" are given an outlet as the scene of television drama allows for a more nuanced exploration of the difficult issues at stake. In choosing to give prominence to this story with reference to the Iraq conflict rather than exploring the role of the US in relation to the ongoing conflict over the Gaza strip, there is also a cultural silencing, a refusal of responsibility that permeates our watching of the programme in the sea of media commentary and critical acclaim surrounding it. This silencing also taps into feelings of guilt and responsibility evoked by the war for viewers in nations with a culturally proximate experience of it. For viewers elsewhere on the planet, we might also reflect on what the successful sale of this US version of the show (rather than its adaptation for "local" culture, as happened in Holland and Serbia) suggests about the role of the US in our collective national psyches. Perhaps it functions as a suitable object into which international viewers can project their shame and anxiety about the participation of their nations in the war in Iraq?

Fantasies of what is to be understood on the global stage as "America" and the "American way of life", which were so frequently cited in defence of the war, are explored overtly in the third season of *In Treatment*, when "Sunil's" (Irrfan Khan) therapeutic work repeatedly advances themes of cultural alienation. The experience of what it means to be an American or in America is directly addressed in the narrative content of this storyline, leaving the conflicts and complexities of these debates writ large on the small screen. It is interesting that this particular season of the show is the first to be written solely by American writers. By choosing to portray such themes through this storyline, the writers reveal something of the discomfort with the notion of "Americanism" felt by ordinary citizens of the US after a decade of war and global unrest. Once again, we can see the potential of television to work therapeutically.

As is now clear, circulating around the programme is a complex array of fantasies that have been present since its inception. What is their function both for individual viewers and for the broader popular culture in which they are watching? It is important to keep in mind the now commonplace assumption that we are living in a therapy culture. Our everyday lives are closely bound up with the documentation of various emotional states and experiences in a variety of ways. This emotional turn has led to a more feeling-focused context for our engagement with others and with the world at large. At the same time, the media have become more closely implicated in our flailing sense of identity; how we are to manage our identities in an era of postmodern possibilities is a question that has attracted a great deal of comment. As Richards (2007) has suggested, the role of the media in helping to fashion the therapeutic turn in popular culture should not be underestimated.

Perhaps, in this context, television has a particularly intriguing function. Television's ability to allow us to adopt multiple positions of identification with its characters and structures allows us to experiment with a number of fantasies at the same time and to take pleasure in each or all of these simultaneously. *In Treatment* not only reflects these aspects of our popular culture but also becomes part of the cycle itself, helping to work "its ideological tensions, anxieties and fantasies into fictional forms" (Donald, 1985, p. 121). We may therefore see the programme as an exemplar of James Donald's concept of a "mapping fantasy"— "fantasy" because it gives shape to unconscious anxieties and wishes, "mapping" because its representations are drawn from a historically-specific period. Donald's position here is crucial in the formulation of any psycho-cultural approach to the media—psychoanalysis can be used to read media texts as symptoms of a broader cultural malaise.

His argument, however, does not go far enough, as it is also possible to use psychoanalysis to understand processes of mediatisation, consumption, and reception. It helps to explain how television itself provides us with objects that are internalised by viewers and that allow us to manipulate them through such psychical mechanisms as projection/ introjection/splitting/disavowal, providing us with a means of using the media as a means of regulating our emotional and psychological lives (Bainbridge, 2011). Following Donald (1985, p. 132), *In Treatment* can be seen as "a variation on a particular fantasy-structure, which both invites and must be capable of bearing the projections of viewers' desires and anxieties"; programmes such as this play out "in narrative form some of the political fears and resentments of the time" (ibid., p. 133). The programme also goes further. It opens up a space from which we can observe the many fractured and distinct positions it is possible to take up in relation to the pleasures and anxieties offered in such a programme. Such pleasures and anxieties are not limited to narrative content but stem from the experience of viewing the programme according to its formatting schedule (or otherwise) as well as from the extensive commentary provided by press reviews and magazine articles dealing with the appeal of such programmes.

We must also keep in mind that watching television is often a shared experience, and it is worth reflecting on how this particular programme's emphasis on the intimacy of the therapeutic encounter may underscore the validity of the wider cultural turn towards a feeling-focused cultural economy. Yet it may also be an example of a television programme that we work hard to ensure we can watch alone in order to take greater pleasure in the fantasies that its intimate setting allows. (There is a sense here that the programme enables us to replicate the dominant experience of therapy as an individual encounter.) In other words, the programme itself becomes an object that is circulated and exchanged, one that can be taken in or both found and created in our imaginations in a way that has parallels with the transitional object.

My contention is that for viewers on the living room couch, a television programme can easily take on such a guise, becoming a means by which we are able to play creatively with the complexities of our postmodern experience in a world that is moving at an ever-faster pace, in ever-more contradictory ways. In the specific case of *In Treatment*, a programme that offers a playful experience of therapy at arm's length, the show's therapeutic potential is arguably linked to the broader cultural experience that lacks intimacy and the kind of sincere connections we supposedly have available to us in therapy culture but that are increasingly hard to find. Programmes such as *In Treatment* may well provide reassurance for viewers by depicting this experience of isolation, disconnectedness, and emotional upheaval as commonplace and normative. It also provides viewers with new perspectives on possibilities for coping, proffering an otherwise impossible glimpse of what therapy entails, albeit one that is highly melodramatic. In the UK context, this raises a number of questions about the scheduling of this show on niche channels, which attract viewers with the requisite cultural capital to negotiate the complexity of intimacy required by the show's content. Such scheduling seemingly leads to a more limited reception of the programme in the UK, suggesting that the intimacies it demands may simply be too much for us in the end. It is also worth considering the difference that might have been made had HBO followed its policy implemented elsewhere in Europe to "remake" the show for a local audience. Would we have reacted differently to British patients on the couch?

By conceiving the programme as a psychological object in the way I have discussed here, we might enquire to what extent patients make reference to the media in their therapeutic spaces of exchange with clinicians. Anecdotal evidence from psychotherapists suggests that discussion of media images is indeed a prominent feature in work with specific patients who seize on media representations to represent key aspects of their personalities/desires/neuroses. There is scope here to map out a research project to follow this through, as it raises a number of interesting themes in relation to my claims about the use of the media as a psychological object. By suggesting that the media do indeed constitute objects of our inner worlds, we begin to move towards a more nuanced understanding of the function of the media in helping to shape our lives and our attendant senses of self. Arguments about socioculturally embedded media in the everyday infrastructures of twenty-first century life also suggest that such a perspective bears significance. I have sought here to show that television becomes a transitional object of the inner world, an object through which we can explore our identities and one that produces fantasies that open up spaces for all the projections, both bearable and unbearable, that such spaces may entail.

Notes

1. According to the UK Broadcasters' Audience Research Board, Sky Arts 1 and 2 enjoy only the most minimal audience share in the UK, such that the viewing figures for September–November 2009, when the first season of this programme aired, register as less than 0.1 per cent. The second season of *In Treatment* aired in the UK on Sky Atlantic

between April and June 2011, when the channel's audience share is recorded as 0.3 per cent (www.barb.co.uk/report/monthly-viewing-summary).

2. This innovation does not originate from the US studio. Instead, it follows the transmission schedule of its Israeli precursor, *Be' Tipul* (Oren, 2008). In the UK, transmission of the first season on Sky Arts 1 also followed this structure. In subsequent seasons, HBO varied this format in the US, so that episodes were split according to the day of the patient's session with "Paul" and broadcast back-to-back. In season two, the Monday and Tuesday episodes were broadcast one after the other on Sundays, with the remaining days of the week broadcast on Mondays. In season three, the number of episodes was reduced to four per week, with two episodes broadcast on Mondays and Tuesdays. In the UK, the second season moved to the new satellite channel, Sky Atlantic, and the broadcast structure followed the HBO model. Season three has recently (2013) begun to air in the UK on the same channel.

3. There are resonances here with the broader context of therapy culture, where care of the self is linked to the neoliberal fantasy of upward social mobility and its validation of a mode of possessive individualism that is largely intolerant of pain. The neoliberal fantasy also tends to make light of the reality of therapeutic work, which is often banal, repetitive, and fraught with difficulty and therefore incompatible with the economic drivers of the neoliberal agenda, where speed is of the essence.

4. For a psychoanalytic discussion of the "crisis in masculinity", see Bainbridge and Yates (2005), Layton (2011), and Yates (2007).

References

Bainbridge, C. (2011). From "The Freud Squad" to "The Good Freud Guide": A genealogy of media images of psychoanalysis and reflections on their role in the public imagination. *Free Associations: Psychoanalysis and Culture, Media, Groups, Politics, 62*: 31–58.

Bainbridge, C. & Yates, C. (2005). Cinematic symptoms of masculinity in transition: Memory, history and mythology in contemporary film. *Psychoanalysis, Culture & Society 10*(3): 299–318.

Bernstein, J. (2008). Aerial view of America. *The Guardian, The Guide*, 15 March, p. 14.

Birchall, C. (2009). *In Treatment*: Why can't UK networks commit to the hit show? *The Guardian* TV and Radio Blog, 11 June, http://www.guardian.co.uk/culture/tvandradioblog/2009/jun/11/in-treatment-uk-tv (accessed 1 November, 2010).

Caughie, J. (1981). Rhetoric, pleasure and "art television": Dreams of leaving. *Screen, 16*(3): 9–31.

Dichek, B. (2008). Close encounters of the therapeutic kind. *The Jerusalem Post,* 26 May, p. 34.

Donald, J. (1985). Anxious moments in *The Sweeney* in 1975. In: M. Alvarado & J. Stewart (Eds.), *Made for Television: Euston Films Limited* (pp. 117–135). London: BFI.

Flitterman-Lewis, S. (1992). Psychoanalysis, film and television. In: R. C. Allen (Ed.), *Channels of Discourse Reassembled* (pp. 203–246). London: Routledge.

Furedi, F. (2004). *Therapy Culture: Cultivating Vulnerability in an Uncertain Age.* London: Routledge.

Fuss, D. (1995). *Identification Papers.* London: Routledge.

Gilbert, G. (2009). Analyse this. *The Independent,* 26 September, p. 38.

Hall, S. (1973). Encoding/decoding. In: Centre for Contemporary Cultural Studies (Ed.), *Culture, Media, Language: Working Papers in Cultural Studies, 1972–79* (pp. 128–138). London: Hutchinson, 1980.

Heffernan, V. (2008). The rerun of the repressed. *New York Times,* 9 March, p. 24.

Kahr, B. (2011). Dr Paul Weston and the blood-stained couch. *International Journal of Psychoanalysis, 92*(4): 1051–1058.

Layton, L. (2011). Something about a girl named Marla Singer: Capitalism, narcissism and therapeutic discourse in David Fincher's *Fight Club. Free Associations: Psychoanalysis and Culture, Media, Groups, Politics, 62:* 111–134.

O'Driscoll, S. (2008). Has this shrink wrapped? *Irish Times,* 29 March, p. 5.

Oren, T. (2008). Therapy is complicated: HBO's foray into modular storytelling with *In Treatment. Flow* 7, http://flowtv.org/2008/01/therapy-is-complicated-hbo%E2%80%99s-foray-into-modular-storytelling-with-in-treatment/ (accessed 1 November, 2010).

Richards, B. (2007). *Emotional Governance: Politics, Media and Terror.* Basingstoke, UK: Palgrave Macmillan.

Richards, B. & Brown, J. (2011). Media as drivers of a therapeutic trend? *Free Associations: Psychoanalysis and Culture, Media, Groups, Politics, 62:* 18–30.

Rixon, P. (2011). *TV Critics and Popular Culture: A History of British Television Criticism.* London: IB Tauris.

Rochlin, M. (2008). On the couch on a Hollywood sound stage. *New York Times,* 27 January, p. 24.

Silverstone, R. (1994). *Television and Everyday Life.* London: Routledge.

Stanley, A. (2008). Four days, a therapist; fifth day, a patient. *New York Times,* 28 January, p. 1.

Stanley, A. (2009). Patients in therapy, therapist in trouble. *New York Times*, 3 April, p. 1.

Stelter, B. (2008). HBO puts episodes of a series online at no charge. *New York Times*, 3 March, p. 5.

Wilson, B. (2009). Is it TV or is it therapy? *Sunday Times*, 20 September, pp. 16–17.

Winnicott, D. W. (1953). Transitional objects and transitional phenomena: A study of the first not-me possession. In: *Playing and Reality* (pp. 1–25). New York: Basic, 2005.

Wood, G. (2009). How TV got inside the minds of America. *The Observer*, 19 April, p. 4.

Yates, C. (2007). *Masculine Jealousy and Contemporary Cinema*. Basingstoke, UK: Palgrave Macmillan.

Yates, C. (2011). Charismatic therapy culture and the seductions of emotional well-being. *Free Associations: Psychoanalysis and Culture, Media, Groups, Politics, 62*: 59–84.

List of television and radio programmes cited

Be' Tipul (2005–2008). HOT3, Israel.

Frasier (1993–2004). NBC, US.

Help (2005). BBC, UK.

In Treatment (2008–present). HBO, US.

Sopranos, The (1999–2007). HBO, US.

Tell Me You Love Me (2007–2008). HBO, US.

The Wire (2002–2008). HBO, US.

PART II

TELEVISION AS TRANSITIONAL OBJECT

CHAPTER FOUR

BBC *Play School*: playing with transitional, transitory, and transformational space

Carol Leader

Introduction

Do you remember *Play School*? Did you ever watch it? It was a classic BBC children's programme that ran on weekdays between 1962 and 1988, and was intended for pre-school children. Over the years, it came to have a large following of people of all ages. I understand that there were even daily bets taken on which of the windows—arched, square, or round—the camera would zoom through into a short outside film! The resident toys, "Humpty", "Hamble", "Jemima", "Big Ted", and "Little Ted", became famous. But *Play School*'s main audience and the one that it was primarily intended for were the under-fives and its production values were about making a tangible impact on young developing minds. The programme is therefore an interesting candidate to explore through a psychoanalytic lens. But there are also personal reasons for picking *Play School* as a subject of analytic scrutiny. Let me set the scene.

Setting the scene

Having left university in the early 1970s, a kind of fate led me to become one of five founders of a new theatre company called *Perspectives*, that nearly forty years later is still thriving as *New Perspectives* in the city of Nottingham. This was the beginning of my twenty-year career as a theatre, TV, and radio actor, presenter, and writer after which I trained and qualified as a psychoanalytic psychotherapist, firstly at the Association for Group and Individual Psychotherapy and then at the London Centre for Psychotherapy, now part of The British Psychotherapy Foundation. Although I was involved in a wide variety of work as an actor in the theatre and on television, it is as a BBC *Play School* presenter that I am still primarily remembered, such is the potent power of television, particularly in relation to the young child.

It is still, over a couple of decades later, not an uncommon experience to meet adults in their mid-twenties or so (I was one of the regular *Play School* presenters between 1974 and 1990) who immediately feel they know me, but have no idea how. Then a memory of their past, as a child sitting in front of the TV, suddenly comes back to them in a moment of "Aha!", and there is perhaps embarrassment but also surprise and delight that they have managed to lodge away so powerful a link with someone they have never actually met until now. Once a wrong number caller, on hearing me say, "I think you've got the wrong number", said, "It's Carol Leader, isn't it? I'd recognise your voice anywhere. I used to watch you as a child". The power of an experience that has been set down in the mind under prime conditions, where the child is fully mentally and emotionally engaged, is extraordinary.

Play School and psychotherapy have been two areas I have tended to keep separate in the past. I have not thought it helpful for patients to have to deal with outside aspects of their therapists' lives, although it is natural for them to be very interested in them. But the internet has changed that. Details of my career are available on the web, although I have no idea who put them up there. I have my own Wikipedia page, apparently created by a fan whom I do not know, but who appears to be highly informed as to my movements as a theatre and TV personality. I am also on a number of sites related to productions in which I have played leading parts. This sort of information is available to the world at the click of a Google search these days. So, I have been forced to face my former life in terms of some of my patients and have had to start allowing my two careers to exist together. This is something that has proved to be less worrying than I feared. I was always concerned about how I would deal with a patient who had looked me up on Google until it actually happened. I found I was able to work with the information and with my patient's reaction and put it to good use as part of the therapy. In fact it has helped me to integrate and see the parallels and similarities in these two careers: both are very much concerned with the fact that humans have an inner emotional world that has a profound effect on the individual's attempts to connect to the outer world.

Long before I knew anything about psychotherapy, let alone was considering having my own analysis and then training as a psychotherapist, I remember buying the theatre director, Peter Brook's, book *The Empty Space* (1968). At the time, I was twenty-four, and busily engaged in the early days of *Perspectives*. This book enabled me to recognise the empty or potential spaces in which powerful hypnotic and dreaming states could occur and which the theatre and all the arts offer. Brook's book explored how these potential spaces, while tending to be creative, can become dead and negative sometimes. The four sections of *The Empty Space* were entitled "The Deadly Theatre", "The Holy Theatre", "The Rough Theatre", and "The Immediate Theatre". It was clear that the writer was talking about *emotional experiences* far more than the actual physical space taken up by a stage—and that all four types of experience could sometimes be had as part of the same performance. In terms of this essay, these four categories can apply equally to television.

But it was only when I began my own analysis in the 1980s that I realised that these differing states could occur in the therapy space too and were to do with what Freudian and Jungian analysts call the transference. Later in my training, I encountered Donald Winnicott's theories of child development and his link between the experiences of infancy and childhood and our relationship to arts and culture.

The transitional object

It is important to note that Donald Winnicott's "transitional object" represents what he sees as "the most difficult thing, perhaps, in human development; or the most irksome of all the early failures that come for mending" (1971, p. 89). In fact the transitional object, in the first instance, usually a favourite piece of blanket or soft toy that the child takes everywhere, relates to a developmental and creative *process* that occurs in an intermediary space between a mother and a baby. The finding of a transitional object by the child indicates the beginnings of making a bridge between experiencing the world subjectively in terms of one's own omnipotent phantasies *and* experiencing the world as "other" and outside one's own omnipotence and omniscience. The former, subjective, omnipotent experience of the object, Winnicott terms as "relating" to the other, the m/other, and the breast, through projections. The latter experience, Winnicott terms "object usage". The achievement of "object usage" is never developmentally assured. It is a true achievement of both mother and baby stemming from the repeated risky destruction of mother, in phantasy, by the baby in moments of frustration and rage. This involves an inner narrative of "completely destroying the world" in terms of the baby's subjective experience at this stage. Yet, if after "world destruction" the baby repeatedly discovers a mother who is still devoted and understanding and cannot be destroyed by phantasy, then the baby can start to get a real sense of an "other", an objective object, who can survive rage and other seemingly overwhelming feelings, and is safe outside the omnipotence of the baby's projections. This discovery, that the world survives total destruction, evokes love, trust, and faith in the baby. The baby has surrendered their worst to the mother, yet she remains present and alive. More than that, the mother becomes a separate, objective reality who, while not being perfect because of her capacity to frustrate, is nevertheless "good enough", to use another Winnicottian term. The whole experience remains alive as a profound and real piece of living theatre.

However, if the mother is not "good enough", then she will not be able to play her part; she may not understand what the baby is experiencing, and too quickly may try to fix things before the baby gets angry or she may leave the baby to get on with it alone. This response, if repeated too often by the mother, is experienced as too concrete, too intrusive, or too absent by the baby who loses his or her sense of an emerging separate identity. The whole delicate vibrating *balance* of transitional space and process never really takes off or becomes disturbed and collapses. The mother/baby relationship may look similar from the outside to an unpractised eye, but the transitional space, the ability to play and experience something as becoming emotionally *real* and *useable* has gone. The baby is left with an *ersatz* experience that is deathly theatre.

> ... the triple misfortune is that the subjective object never becomes real but remains a bundle of projections, and externality is not discovered; as a corollary the subject is now made to feel that he or she *is* destructive; and finally, fear and hatred of the other develops, and with them, characterological destructiveness comes into being. (Ghent, 1990, p. 124)

The very first transitional object

It is the discovery and ownership of the very *first* transitional object that is such a significant landmark for Winnicott. He calls it the infant's "first possession": the mother is losing her total preoccupation with her baby but the baby is doing something too. The baby is detaching a nugget of attachment to mother and placing it into something usually soft, yet something that is "idiosyncratic and unsharable", (Phillips, 1988, p. 115), a first possession, that the child therefore owns and trails around with it wherever it goes.

Here, we are looking at preverbal development, but if the infant could speak to this first possession, she might say, "You are mine—I choose you and make you mine—but you are not exactly me—yet you are not other than me". Without this root, without this sense of *possession* that links the baby to mother through a transitional object that is *not* mother, the baby will not be able to mentally and emotionally *oscillate* (this is not a Winnicottian term) between reality and fantasy. This process of oscillation takes place between the baby and mother—enabling over time the flowering of experience into broader, more separated areas of creative play. But with this root, the child, the adolescent, and later the adult will be able to take part passionately in cultural activities, finding in them a way of experiencing being alive that feels deeply embodied and real. This is because they offer a *transitional space* or process that allows something chosen and external to become invested with deep inner subjective feeling and meaning that was once felt in relation to mother—something that Winnicott's work so potently illuminates.

As the area of transitional objects spreads out to include play and then adult culture, each of us gathers together our own personal array of objects and activities that the psychoanalyst, Christopher Bollas (1987), calls "genera". These are reminders of the transitional object and can reveal so much about the unique character and history of each person. The genera we collect about us allow us

> … to recollect an early object experience, to remember not cognitively but existentially—through intense affective experience—a relation-ship which was identified with cumulative transformational expe-riences of the self. (p. 17)

A child's favourite TV programme, particularly one that she or he watches each day, can form part of our personal genera.

For Bollas, the achievement of the transitional object is dependent on many previous experiences of mother, not yet personalised as a whole object, but taken in as a *process of transformation*. Later, the unconscious memory of this early transformational object "manifests itself in the person's search for an object (a person, place, event, ideology) that promises to transform the self" (ibid., p. 14). Bollas goes on to say:

> With the infant's creation of the transitional object, the transformational process is displaced from the mother-environment (where it originated) into countless subjective-objects, so that the transitional phase is heir to the transformational period .... (ibid., p. 15)

An oscillating world

The transitional space is where two separate but bridged elements are "oscillating", so that it is hard to see or know exactly who or how the experience is being created. It needs to have elements of reality *and* imagination. Is the breast something offered by mother or is it the baby who is creating it? Winnicott says that this is a question that we must not ask but it is important that mother is able to offer the breast at the same moment as the baby is imagining the breast—the two come together. But, as soon as you think it is one thing, you realise it is the other and then back again. As he wrote in a note within his paper, "The theory of the parent-infant relationship":

> I once said: "There is no such thing as an infant" meaning, of course, that wherever one finds an infant, one finds maternal care, and without maternal care there would be no infant. (Winnicott, 1960, p. 586)

The transitional space is therefore on the hinterland between an inner and an outer experience and can be felt very palpably at times in the silence of the consulting room—as long as there is not too much anxiety in the silence. The atmosphere is quiet but it "sings". There is a sense that something is going on between two people that is not fully conscious and that this must be protected and not mindlessly intruded upon. A great deal of the work of a therapist is growing to recognise when this *is not* happening. It is a dynamic that can be full of feeling and is related to early body and mind experiences that are preverbal and known in the soma, in the body, in such a way as to create dreaming images and phantasies in the mind. We are, for Carl Jung, in the realm of the *psychoid* archetype (1947, p. 213) and I will return to this theme later in the chapter.

Winnicott stresses that this process is *not symbolic*; it is on the way towards symbolism. It relies on something external and concrete. In the first instance, this is the mother's breast but there also needs to be the beginnings of an internal ego, a processing psychic element in the infant that is actively creating, "imaging" the external object, the breast, allowing a lively *experience* of that object at the same time as it arrives. Later on, the creativity of the psychoanalytic transitional space has a lot to do with finally getting deep and unknown states into images and words and thus symbolising, in the end, that which is rooted in the body as archaic feelings and experience. But these experiences can also be available to us through cultural experience that is shared with others.

On those wonderful occasions when we go to the theatre or watch a great film and become fully absorbed in the drama of it, we ignore the fact that we are watching actors playing characters in a made-up story and are swept up in the illusion that what we are watching is *real*. We accept the illusory and playful nature of the transitional space that theatre, opera, art, film, and television, and the rest of our so-called "high culture" and "popular culture" can provide. And at certain unplanned and unknowable moments, we experience moments of insight and change. But it is perhaps only in the last few decades that cultural input for children seems to have been given more priority. With all this in mind, I now want to turn to the BBC programme, *Play School*, and what its originators set out to offer young children.

BBC Play School

Play School was devised by Joy Whitby, the former producer of BBC radio's *Listen with Mother* (1950–1982) and, according to her (Jackson, 2011), it came into existence as a direct response to concerns about the perceived poor standard of British pre-school education. Something more human and relational was required during the vital time when, for Winnicott, a child learns through play. Although the programme looks somewhat outdated now, it has elements that are much needed perennials for creative experience, and, for its time, *Play School* was trying to do something rather radical: it was very different in tone from the more conservative BBC television programme, *Watch with Mother* (1952–1973), that had been broadcast since 1952 and that for four days out of five was about listening usually to a woman's voice, telling the story that was being played out by a number of different puppets. If you are of a certain age, you may remember some of the characters. My favourite day was Monday with *Picture Book*, because although the presenter, Patricia Driscoll, spent a lot of time talking to a wooden marionette dog that I never liked and that noisily clattered about on the table top next to her, she did also relate directly to the child at home. She would read stories out loud and demonstrated a wide range of interesting craft activities. Tuesday was *Andy Pandy* (1950–1970), Wednesday, *The Flowerpot Men* (1953–1971), Thursday, *Rag, Tag and Bobtail* (1953–1975), and Friday, *The Woodentops* (1952–1973), a family of string puppets that like the *Picture Book* dog I always found rather spookily wooden (especially the walk of the *Woodentops* dog called "Spotty Dog".) When *Play School* began in 1964, the educational advisor for the programme, Nancy Quale, did away with string puppets and they were hardly ever part of the programme.

Play School's beginnings were suitably auspicious: it was actually the first ever programme to be shown on the fledgling BBC 2 as the channel's opening night had to be cancelled due to a power cut. *Play School* then ran for twenty-four years until 1988 and became something of a national treasure. In fact it still has fan clubs and publications. In 2010, I attended a book launch at BAFTA of the first of a two-part compendium about *Play School* written by *Play School's* researcher and archivist, Paul Jackson (2010). In 2010, Sue McGregor also presented a reunion programme about *Play School* on Radio 4. At the time of writing, in 2012, there has been a number of articles in certain sections of the tabloid and more serious press claiming that the *Play School* presenters spent a good deal of time having sex and smoking dope in their dressing rooms (Gardner, 2012; Robertson, 2012; Wardrop, 2012; Williams, 2012). This was not quite my experience! However, what this press coverage shows is the continued fascination with *Play School*, which appears to be still embedded as part of the genera of British cultural memory and imagination. I presume that the programme would have been showing when more than a number of those reading this chapter were either children or parents watching with children.

Having trained as a psychotherapist, I find myself wondering whether Joy Whitby was familiar with a series of lectures by Winnicott that were broadcast on BBC radio during the 1940s and 1950s and that have since been collected and published (Winnicott, Greenspan, Spock, & Berry Brazelton, 2002). In these lectures, Winnicott documented his ideas about the "good enough mother" for the first time. Here was a mother, who alongside "doing things right", was also allowed to fail in order that she could become *real* and not magical. This was certainly part of the presenting style of *Play School*. *Play School* was not trying to be clever, perfect or slick, and Winnicott's (1960) theory of the good enough mother also reflected this view when he argued that an attitude of maternal perfection was also one that invades and collapses the transitional space. *Play School* was very simple, direct, and relatively slow enough to leave space for the child's own response. It was made clear that presenters were required to talk to the camera as if they were talking to one child, face to face, who was watching at home. The programme aims were put into written form in 1979 by the current producer, Anne Gobey (Jackson, 2010). I would argue that these aims sit well with the theories and ideas of Winnicott as discussed above. Here are just a few extracts:

> In any one year of *Play School*—two hundred and sixty programmes—all aspects of a young child's play are reflected and encouraged on the basis that play is the child's first school … We offer to this child a daily television programme that may, by becoming part of his life, enrich his experience. There may not be a caring adult around to bring him to the programme regularly and therefore he is spoken to directly and encouraged to want to watch and participate. For this reason *Play School* is called an entertainment, a source of enjoyment. … Formal education cannot start until the foundations have been laid—before writing and reading, there must be vocabulary; before maths—an understanding of number; before expression—experience … In every programme, the child is invited to participate in movement or singing, counting or guessing and left with stimulus for play and new facts and ideas to explore. There is a team of presenters, all of whom are professional actors, actresses, singers or comedians. They are chosen for their ability to present the material lightly and with directness that avoids condescension. Their backgrounds, accents and personalities are varied and help to accustom a child to the international nature of life in the Twentieth Century. (Jackson (2010) pp. 424–425)

Play School was reliably familiar but with differences. This is exactly what the ordinary loving mother who is "good enough" represents and we can see from the programme aims that the producers of *Play School* recognised that a child may not necessarily have a good enough carer: "There may not be a caring adult around to bring him to the programme regularly and therefore he is spoken to directly and encouraged to want to watch and participate" (Jackson, 2010).

But *Play School* also brought "the third" onto the scene, as there was always a man as well as a woman presenter to relate to the child. The presenters changed each week and were often back about six weeks later. This appeared to be a good time for the children to form favourites for whom they could watch out, but this strategy also allowed children to get used to change and diversity. Unlike on *Watch With Mother*, a full range of British dialects was represented with occasional presenters from Europe and Australia. Nevertheless, as the shot below (in which I can be seen holding "Little Ted") shows, in the late 1970s, the programme's representation of racial diversity was still very much in its infancy.

Figure 1: *Play School* presenters—group shot.
All photos copyright BBC and with thanks to *Play School* author and archivist Paul R. Jackson.

Importantly for maintaining familiarity for the viewers, there were regular features such as the house itself with its door, and the famous windows. The daily ritual of going through a different one each day to watch a film about the outside world also provided a familiar pattern for the children watching. (The famous pause before the announcement of which window had been selected on any given day became a daily guessing game but, pragmatically, it was as much to do with giving the camera person time to zoom in from a full studio shot with the presenter in frame to a single shot of the windows in close-up, and then into a fade. This was a very tricky technical move.)

Figure 2: *Play School* window set.

Figure 3: *Play School* toys.

There were also always the clock and the five toys: "Humpty", "Jemima", "Big Ted" and "Little Ted", and the much-despised "Hamble"—a bad tempered, hard, old fashioned and ugly doll that none of the presenters liked and whom I think may have been much happier in *Watch with Mother* with the puppets! She was the object that had a lot of bad stuff projected into her.

Each toy had its very different character in a highly scripted pro-gramme that nevertheless had an easy casual familiarity about it—so much so, that mothers would often write in and ask to present the programme themselves. Spontaneity was encouraged. In my audi-tion on camera, my sailing ships made out of walnut shells with paper sails that had behaved perfectly in the rehearsal all sank one by one. In desperation, I said, "I think I've put too much plasticene in to hold up the sails ... I know, I'll take the sails out and they can be rowing boats instead". I did not know it at the time but this "failure with an experiment" and the recovery from it, probably got me the job. Here was the need for the "good enough" presenter who certainly was not perfect, but who could manage mistakes creatively and spontaneously, without too much anxiety. (I suspect these qualities are also similar to what is required of a therapist.) Here is also an environment where the adult will take responsibility for his or her mistakes. This is the area of a facilitating environment where someone is free to join in with it or not. "Here's a song about a train, join in if you like", or "Do you want to be a dragon with me?" or "Clap your hands with us if you'd like to". These are the ways the presenter would invite the child to participate.

Play School was not just used by toddlers, as it also allowed a kind of regression for older children coming home from school. It was shown daily in the morning on BBC2 to infants and their carers, and then repeated on BBC1 at 4.20 p.m. and was remarkably popular. The need for something familiar to hang out with and be non-purposeful after a busy day at school, or as something to idly watch when ill at home—was not only popular with many real children but also was seemingly an essential element in the life of the fictional teenager, "Adrian Mole"—aged thirteen and three-quarters. On 26 June he writes:

Doctor said our thermometer is faulty. I feel slightly better.

Got up for twenty minutes today. Watched *Play School*; it was Carol Leader's turn, she is my favourite presenter. (Townsend, 1982, p. 86)

Television as a transitory *object*

It is important when thinking about television as possibly therapeutic to note that it all depends on the *way* television is being used both by the broadcaster and by the viewer. What has the potential for being a transitional object—or more accurately a transitional *process*—can become what psychoanalyst, Joyce McDougall (1985), helpfully defines as a *transitory object* (or process), which is linked to addiction: psychological needs have to be met *physically* with drink, food, drugs, money, or over-working. But the idea of the transitory object would, I suggest, apply to *any* concrete activity that gets mindlessly stuffed into the potential oscillating transitional space in order to prevent the feelings of loss and emptiness that are an uncomfortable but natural part of this process, just as feeling hungry and empty is a good way of knowing when to eat healthily. If small amounts of loss can be tolerated when one is an infant, with the help of a "good enough" mother using games such as "peek-a-boo" or not jumping in to help or feed her child immediately in an over-anxious way, then a real life dialogue can begin. Eventually, there grows the faith of finding the mother as a separate responsive "other" and the subsequent ability to begin to think symbolically. This is in contrast to a merged, two-dimensional, addictive relationship that resists a healthy amount of loss and the growth and change that then arises from it. I will return to this subject in the last section of this essay, which is about the connection between the work of Jung and Winnicott and their experience with their own mothers.

The transitory object, like a sweetie, comforts only surface needs by offering a quick fix and that is fine occasionally. But it does not soothe, contain, or make a connection with either the deep anxiety or the deep safety at the core of a person which eventually allows separation from another to take place—in fact it anaesthetises all the difficult feelings that are part of this process. Instead the child gets the sense that there is something "wrong" with difficult feelings rather than a sense that they are a part of life with which we all need help in order to be able to handle them.

Clinical example—"Sam"

As Brett Kahr discusses elsewhere in this volume, television is a regular visitor into the consulting room both as a transitional object and as a transitory one. One of my patients, whom I shall call "Sam", has internal relationships that are so conflicted that he struggles to find benign external relationships of his own. He regularly brings in something from a television drama or film that is about a difficult family relationship that he has been watching on the box the night before. The transitional nugget from an interaction with the outside television enables him to bring back into the analytic container additional understanding of his own behaviours and difficulties with relating to people, in a way that is often therapeutic: he starts to get a sense of how he projects his own difficulties and feelings into situations and people "out there". In this respect, television is used in the service of communicating painful feelings to the therapist, helping him or her to make new links between feelings and thoughts.

But Sam is also a patient who regularly has radio and television on at the same time as he plays computer games and who goes to sleep with these mechanical versions of the mother still on, because the *feelings* generated in his internal space in which he might hope to play and think are felt to be unsafe and intolerable. The dreaming space therefore has to be crowded out and collapsed with noise and constant activity to shut out the prospect of some necessary painful feelings. This is the use of television as a manic defence, an addictive *transitory* object that will only ever provide short-term comfort and never real creative satisfaction and development.

Winnicott and Jung

In this last section, by way of offering an additional theoretical viewpoint, I will briefly look at Jung's theory of the "transcendent function" (1959a) which predates the work of both Winnicott and Bollas and operates in a comparable psychological arena to the transitional *process* and "transformational object" (Bollas, 1987). But I am also including Jung for the powerful influence his autobiography, *Memories, Dreams, Reflections* (1982) most likely had on Winnicott's addressing of his own childhood difficulties and how this also informed his theoretical work. Jung's dominant preoccupations hover, like Winnicott's, around an earlier developmental stage than Freud's Oedipus complex with its personal repressed unconscious and the challenge from the father (Freud, 1924d).

The classic Oedipus complex centres on the repressed and therefore murderous phantasies that the child of around three to six years of age experiences towards the father. Father is seen as a threat because he comes between the imagined exclusivity of the mother/child twosome. Freud saw the successful moving through the Oedipus complex as the increasing ability of the child to identify with the parent of the same sex, rather than clinging to a regressive infantile relationship with mother with its related neurotic symptoms. Accepting the presence and superior authority of "the father"—the father's "No"—allows the child's mind to take on a third position in relationships, of being sometimes the excluded one in a threesome. This promotes a reflective ability that assists the toleration of feelings of loss and anger without going into immediate retaliatory reaction: it becomes possible to think symbolically as an alternative to concrete action, a vital aspect in the development of mature thinking.

However, much of post-Freudian theory has placed an increasing importance on pre-Oedipal development where the child has initially to grow out of a merged relationship with mother where the boundaries between *two* individuals are not distinct, before there can be any real sense of the third coming into play (see Kohut & Wolf, 1978). As far as Jung and Winnicott are concerned, they have both written about having mothers who were not psychologically "good enough" for their developmental needs.

Jung's parents separated while he was a young child and his mother spent several unexplained periods in hospital. He wrote of her strange moods in his autobiography:

> I was sure she consisted of two personalities, one innocuous and human, the other uncanny. This other emerged only now and then, but each time it was unexpected and frightening. She would then speak as if talking to herself, but what she said was aimed at me and usually struck me to the core of my being, so that I was stunned into silence … . (Jung, 1982, p. 66)

> There was an enormous difference between my mother's two personalities. That was why as a child I often had anxiety dreams about her. By day she was a loving mother, but at night she seemed uncanny. (Jung, ibid., p. 67)

Jung went on to understand himself through the recognition of two very distinct number one and number two personalities. His "complex theory" (1934) emphasised the tendency of the primitive psyche to split defensively or to *dissociate* into a number of discrete archetypal complexes when faced with overwhelming experiences. He also suggested that these underlie the later Oedipus complex stressed in Freud's work and that they result from repression rather than dissociation. Therefore, although Jung wrote very little about infancy and childhood, he saw the central developmental challenge of life as separation from the mother. As with Winnicott's work, we are accordingly dealing with processes that are earlier than the unconscious fight against and subsequent healthy "surrender" to the father. Developmentally, one could say that the individual is "on their way to symbolism" but still requires aspects of the concrete. We are not looking at fully whole and separated objects. We have not yet arrived at multidimensional symbolic thinking that is linked with the father. The earlier space of the mother and the meeting between mind and concrete matter—where mind sinks into matter or arises from it—is what Jung called the *psychoid*, as I have already mentioned. It is the place where the "living symbols" from the deep collective unconscious are birthed into actual images appropriate to the culture and personal experience of the receiver of the images. As Jung was forever pointing out, there is no such thing as imprinted archetypal images in the unconscious, only a predisposition for certain archetypal motifs, a central one being "the mother complex".

As for Winnicott, his biographer Rodman draws attention to a poem, "The Tree" (Rodman, 2003, p. 290) that Winnicott, who never consummated his first marriage of over twenty years, wrote at the age of sixty-seven. His poignant words clearly suggest the lasting influence that his severely depressed mother had on his development: in the poem he writes about being stretched out on her lap like a dead tree, learning to make her smile, assuaging her guilt; that enlivening her being was what his living was about. It is striking that Winnicott's whole vocation appears to have represented his attempt to enliven his inner maternal object.

Winnicott's review of Jung's Memories, Dreams, Reflections

It was during the period when he was deeply preoccupied with writing his now famous review of Jung's autobiography (Winnicott, 1964) that Winnicott had a dream of world destruction where he felt something fundamental in his mind mend: he was able to symbolise his destructive ruthless impulses in a way that had been impossible in the relationship with his depressed mother. The dream was in three parts: first, there was total destruction and he was destroyed; next, he was the agent of destruction and destroyed everything; finally, he dreamt that he was waking up and as he did so he recognised his role in all three sections of the dream *without any dissociation*. It was an immensely satisfying dream for him (Meredith-Owen, 2011). He was clearly in a symbiotic space with Jung's childhood damage as a result of immersing himself in Jung's autobiography. Winnicott wrote that it was a dream, "for Jung and for some of my patients, as well as for myself" (cited in Sedgwick, 2008, p. 548).

The birthing of the deep archetypal image within the individual, in the manner that Winnicott "birthed" his dream, is central not only to the individual but to artistic and scientific endeavour in wider cultural activities. The collective dream comes from deep within but is also a response to the external world and the collective aspects of the psyche. This cultural phenomenon has its beginnings in the earliest moments of childhood, beginning within the containment and privacy of the transitional space between mother and child and later with the extension of this private space into lively and non-addictive relationships with books, television, radio, and theatre, for example, or with the artist's studio, rehearsal room, laboratory, or therapy session.

Jung and alchemy

For Jung, "psyche *is* image" (1983, para. 75) and image represents both the pre- *and* post-verbal: the space of the past but also the space of future developments that have yet to be verbalised. The *psychoid*, I suggest, makes a parallel with Winnicott's transitional space and with much of Jung's later work on medieval alchemy with its so-called search to make gold. Jung rediscovered with delight that the so-called *concrete* experiments of these early chemists were in fact mostly an attempt to discover psychological gold: the meanings and workings of the mind. The beautiful artwork that the alchemists produced represented an attempt to use a transitional space between the concrete and the ephemeral to "image" the unseeable, to represent it in some way (Henderson & Sherwood, 2003). This suggests that the actual chemical experiments were a type of transitional processing, linking emotional states to the symbolic, to mind. The powerful images that the alchemists produced represent the deep potential of the non-separated and therefore *collective* unconscious meeting with consciousness through the birthing of a "living symbol", a process that Jung called "the transcendent function" (1959a).

In clashing together to produce an image, the "opposites" of conscious and unconscious process and psyche and soma are transcended. When this happens they give birth to a psychological third, which the father also represents.

The third, the 3D symbolic function of the mind, evolves for Jung in this sensory, fully experienced way. Jung wrote:

> In psychology one possesses nothing, unless one has experienced it in reality. Hence a purely intellectual insight is not enough, because *one knows only the words* and not the substance of the thing from inside. (1951, para. 61; my emphasis)

Conclusion

This chapter has set out to make links between the profound effects that the outer world of media, alongside parenting, can have on the inner world of the child and how television can be a force of help or hindrance in this respect. This medium can play its part as a transitional object, or alternatively can be used as a transitory object that leads or holds back the child and, later, the adult within the context of the separate, wider cultural world. I have used *Play School* as a specific lens through which to explore these themes and ideas, making links between Winnicott's and Jung's theoretical preoccupations and their own childhoods with failing mothers unable to offer a vibrant transitional space.

As with Winnicott and Jung and also, I imagine, for many other psychotherapists, my own childhood disturbances have led me to reach for an understanding of the unconscious generational burden a child can be left with. I believe that this understanding is particularly pressing if this child has a parent who is depressed or disturbed over too long a period of time when they are young. A parent who is not able to reach a meaningful mental connection with their own archaic feeling core will unconsciously pass on this problem and the need for solutions to the next generation. Yet I have also become increasingly impressed by the psyche's ability to seek out environments that might keep things psychologically alive for the time being. The discovery of personal genera is an important aspect of this process. In this respect, my years presenting *Play School* played their part in my own psychological journey even though I was ignorant of this at the time.

To this day, I have a very strong memory from my childhood of watching Patricia Driscoll, the presenter of *Picture Book*, do potato printing. I would have been about five years old. Retrospectively, I think I must have been linking up to even earlier unconscious memories that the programme was triggering, memories of the transformational object as experienced through my own mother. Watching Patricia Driscoll pouring different coloured paints into saucers and then cutting up potatoes with a knife ("You must ask mummy to help you with this ..."), and dipping halves in the different colours before making different prints on a piece of paper, was just out of this world for me. It was like watching gold being made. The vividness with which I remember this moment with the television and its links with other artistic activities, including when I became a mother and had a child of my own, defines it as an aesthetic experience that was real, lively, and meaningful for me. I think this aesthetic moment was also somewhere in the background when, having become an actor soon after leaving university, I approached the producer of *Play School* to request an audition.

In bringing my two different professions together, I have been able to see that the fundamental aspects of life that I was exploring through being an actor and presenter and have carried on exploring as a psychoanalytic psychotherapist are not a million miles away from Jung's passion for alchemy, or Winnicott's theories on the transitional space, or from that nice lady showing me all the different patterns I could make with potatoes and paints.

References

Bollas, C. (1987). *The Shadow of the Object: Psychoanalysis of the Unthought Known*. London: Free Association.

Brook, P. (1968). *The Empty Space*. London: Penguin.

Freud, S. (1924d). The dissolution of the Oedipus complex. *S. E., 19*: 171–180. London: Hogarth.

Gardner, T. (2012). And today, children, Play School's going to pot. *Daily Mail*, 3 May. Available at: http://www.dailymail.co.uk/news/article-2138825/ And-today-children-Play-Schools-going-pot-Presenters-stoned-minds-reveals-Johnny-Ball.html. Accessed 28 October 2012.

Ghent, E. (1990). Masochism, submission, surrender—masochism as a perversion of surrender. *Contemporary Psychoanalysis, 26*: 108–136.

Henderson, J. L. & Sherwood, D. N. (2003). *Transformation of the Psyche: The Symbolic Alchemy of the Splendor Solis*. New York: Brunner-Routledge.

Jackson, P. R. (2010). *Here's a House—A Celebration of Play School, Vol. 1 & 2*. Birmingham, UK: Kaleidoscope.

Jung, C. G. (1934). A review of the complex theory. *Collected Works VIII*. London: Routledge & Kegan Paul, 1948.

Jung, C. G. (1947). The nature of the psyche. *The Collected Works of C. G. Jung, volume VIII*. London: Routledge and Kegan Paul, 1960.

Jung, C. G. (1951). The self. *Collected Works IX ii, Aion*. London: Routledge & Kegan Paul, 1959.

Jung, C. G. (1959a). The transcendent function. *Collected Works VIII, The Structure and Dynamics of the Psyche*. London: Routledge.

Jung, C. G. (1982). *Memories, Dreams, Reflections*. London: Flamingo.

Jung, C. G. (1983). Commentary on "The secret of the golden flower". *Collected Works XIII, Alchemical Studies*. New York: Bollingen Foundation.

Kohut, H. & Wolf, E. S. (1978). The disorders of the self and their treatment: an outline. *International Journal of Psychoanalysis, 59*: 413–425.

McDougall, J. (1985). *Theatres of the Mind*. London: Free Association.

Meredith-Owen, M. (2011). Winnicott on Jung: destruction, creativity and the unrepressed unconscious. *Journal of Analytical Psychology, 56*: 56–75.

Phillips, A. (1988). *Winnicott*. London: Fontana.

Robertson, C. (2012). This is a house. This is a door. Here's the presenter stoned on the floor. *Sun*, 3 May. Available at: http://www.thesun.co.uk/sol/homepage/showbiz/tv/4294187/Presenters-on-BBC-kids-show-Play-School-went-on-stoned.html. Accessed 28 October 2012.

Rodman, F. R. (2003). *Winnicott: The Life and Work*. Cambridge, MA: Da Capo Lifelong.

Sedgwick, D. (2008). Winnicott's dream: some reflections on D. W. Winnicott and C. G. Jung. *Journal of Analytical Psychology, 53*: 543–560.

Townsend, S. (1982). *The Secret Diary of Adrian Mole Aged Thirteen and Three-Quarters*. London: Methuen.

Wardrop, M. (2012). BBC Play School presenter "went on-air stoned". *Telegraph*, 3 May. Available at: http://www.telegraph.co.uk/culture/tvandradio/bbc/9242648/BBC-Play-School-presenters-went-on-air-stoned.html. Accessed 28 October 2012.

Williams, R. (2012). Sex in dressing rooms: Play School presenters "stoned out of their minds"—inside BBC Television Centre. *Independent*, 3 May. Available at: http://www.independent.co.uk/arts-entertainment/arts-well-look-whos-here-1303876.html. Accessed 28 October 2012.

Winnicott, D. W. (1960). The theory of the parent-infant relationship. *International Journal of Psychoanalysis, 41*: 585–595.

Winnicott. D. W. (1964). Review of Memories, Dreams, Reflections, by C. G. Jung (London: Collins and Routledge, 1963). *International Journal of Psychoanalysis, 45*: 450–455.

Winnicott, D. W. (1971). *Playing and Reality*. London: Routledge.

Winnicott, D. W., Greenspan, S. I., Spock, B., & Berry Brazelton, T. (2002). *Winnicott on the Child*. New York: Perseus.

List of television and radio programmes cited

Andy Pandy (1950–1970). BBC, UK.
Bill and Ben (1953–1971). BBC, UK.
Listen with Mother (1950–1982). BBC Radio, UK.
Picture Book (1955–1973). BBC, UK.
Play School (1964–1988). BBC, UK.
Rag, Tag and Bobtail (1953–1965). BBC, UK.
The Reunion (2010). BBC Radio, UK.
The Woodentops (1952–1973). BBC, UK.
Watch with Mother (1952–1973). BBC, UK.

CHAPTER FIVE

Family romances in Jack Rosenthal's television drama

Sue Vice

J ack Rosenthal's writing for television is often seen to typify the "golden age" of British television drama, and his plays are viewed with nostalgia as an example of the era's gentle social comedy (Purser, 2004). However, a psychoanalytic perspective on his work reveals that the "gentleness" of the comedy, and the "taken for granted" (Silverstone, 1994, p. x) nature of the televisual medium itself, often relies upon unexpectedly disturbing and challenging elements. The narratives of Rosenthal's best-known television plays centre on individual and familial rites of passage, revealing how psychic conflict takes on dramatic form in his writing, while the psyche's formations are fleshed out in the form of individual characters. Such moments in Rosenthal's work include that of first love in *P'tang Yang Kipperbang* (1982), courtship in *The Lovers* (1970), parents becoming "empty-nesters" in *Eskimo Day* (1996) and *Cold Enough for Snow* (1997), and redundancy and retirement in *Sadie, It's Cold Outside* (1975). The source of this comedy is often far from gentle, as is clear in the examples I discuss here, which centre on religious and historical rites of passage that accompany the separation anxiety of acceding to adolescence. Rosenthal's award-winning works in the "Play for Today" series, *Bar Mitzvah Boy* (1976) and *The Evacuees* (1975) represent, respectively, a startling instance of the televisual trope of the "Oedipal dilemma", in Candida Yates's phrase from the opening chapter in the present collection, and efforts by young brothers to rid themselves of a false mother and return to one who offers love and acceptance. In each case, comedy is integral to persuading audiences to consider disruptive and uncomfortable psychoanalytic truths.

Bar Mitzvah Boy: *"today I am a man"*

Rosenthal's remark about this play, "The original idea had nothing specifically to do with Jews" (quoted in *Heathman's Diary*, 1976), may seem at first sight disingenuous, given the detailed representation of its subject and the nature of audience responses to it. The Jewish content of *Bar Mitzvah Boy* seems inextricable from the plot. Thirteen-year-old "Eliot Green" has Friday night dinner with his family, during which his mother "Rita" worries about the dinner-dance for the following day's bar mitzvah celebrations, while his father, "Victor", wishes the whole event were already over. "Eliot" flees from the synagogue during the service the next day, to the horror of his family, but his recitation of his Torah portion in a playground is judged by the rabbi to mean that he is bar mitzvah after all. The evening's dinner-dance goes ahead as planned. Contemporary audience members who wrote to Rosenthal after the play was broadcast were divided between those—mostly non-Jewish viewers—who applauded its touching and funny representation of Jewish family life, and those—almost all self-identifying Jews themselves—who saw it as inaccurate and shaming (Dunn, 2011; Vice, 2009). Yet despite the play's encapsulation of the detail of lower-middle-class British-Jewish life in the mid-1970s, its fidelity is as much to the psychoanalytic as to the cultural or religious meaning of a bar mitzvah. Indeed, the play echoes the psychic structure of the ritual itself: ostensibly, it is about a young man acceding to the tenets of Judaism, but its unconscious importance is developmental and concerns what it means to become a man.

The dramatic irony in Rosenthal's play centres on the fact that "Eliot" takes the religious significance of his bar mitzvah much more seriously than his family does. Although his parents have invested both affect and money in the bar mitzvah, which his older sister, "Lesley", describes as, "The biggest day of their lives" (Rosenthal, 1987, p. 45), it has lost its content. "Eliot" is provoked into an outburst at the dinner table by his parents' unswerving focus on the outer trappings of the event, particularly his mother's new hairstyle and whether he will have a haircut in the morning:

ELIOT: I thought I was supposed to read the blessings, and the portion of the law ... The Torah doesn't mention it's a hair-dressing contest! (ibid., p. 25)

Even "Lesley" is surprised that her brother has bothered to learn the ten commandments when he is not required to recite them, and, like her parents, misunderstands what "Eliot" means in implying that it is not just "people" who will be watching his performance, or for whom it might be an affront to break the fourth commandment to "honour the Sabbath day" by driving to the synagogue. Such a transcendent or judgemental being is not explicitly identified: "What else *is* there? Giraffes?" (ibid., p. 20), as "Lesley" asks. It seems to be an idealised parental as much as a godlike figure that "Eliot" invokes, one who is not swayed by propriety or convenience in relation to the traditions that are affirmed.

"Eliot" also takes seriously the nature of the bar mitzvah as a rite of passage, although he does not acknowledge it as such, and it is as if his religious concerns are in fact a screen for anxieties about attaining intellectual and sexual maturity. Although he calls out, "Naked women! Les femmes nues! Nudae feminae!" (ibid., p. 11) when he gets home from school, his "bravado" in so doing is due to the fact that no one else is in the house to hear him. His habit of repeating even these phrases in the three languages of school lessons reveals his liminal position, between child and adult. When she tries to comfort him after an evening of parental angst, "Lesley" tells him to sleep without dreaming: "Except about football or cricket or Olivia Newton-John. It is still Olivia Newton-John, isn't it?" (ibid., p. 45). For "Eliot", as "Lesley's" list of acceptable dream images shows, sexual behaviour takes the transitional form of images of celebrities, or the use of risqué words, amid the interests of schoolboy life.

Although she too is thirteen, "Eliot's" school friend, the non-Jewish "Denise", sees more directly than he does the sexual significance of the rite that awaits him, as the play's opening reveals:

ELIOT: You know what tomorrow is, don't you? ... Only the day that marks my passage, isn't it! ...
DENISE: What's he mean? "Marks his passage"? Is it rude?
SQUIDGE: It's something Jewish. What Jewish boys do. You wouldn't understand.
DENISE
(*suspicious*):   It *sounds* rude. (ibid., p. 10)

Despite what "Squidge" says, "Denise's" suspicion that something "rude" will take place shows that she does indeed understand "what Jewish boys do"—which is to undergo a ritual that implicitly recognises the assumption of sexual maturity. Later, after "Eliot" has fled the synagogue and meets "Denise" in a café, she reveals once more her understanding of the unacknowledged meaning of the bar mitzvah's "ordeal by recitation" (Arlow, 1951, p. 194):

DENISE: It's nothing, standing up saying prayers ... Christian girls have an even worse day. Of an intimate nature ... Anyway, then you're a woman. Official. (Rosenthal, 1987, p. 62)

"Denise's" description of girls' entry into puberty does away with the idea of a ritual altogether, and likens the "day" of the boy's bar mitzvah directly to the "sudden shock" that is the girl's experience of menarche. Her apparent conflation of religion and gender, in invoking "Christian girls" in contrast to "Jewish boys", might sound like an acknowledgement of the patriarchal nature of orthodox Judaism. The starkly differentiated gender roles, and indeed the family plot, in the world of *Bar Mitzvah Boy*, according to which "Lesley" claims that Hebrew is "all Chinese" to her and is, along with her mother, a spectator in the women's gallery at the synagogue rather than a participant in the service, would not obtain were the Greens members of a more egalitarian Reform synagogue where bar mitzvah takes place when the individual, at sixteen, is already beyond puberty. However, "Denise's" phrase registers instead her awareness that the religious adjective is simply a cover for the gendered reality of becoming adult. In both cases, a sudden transfer to biological and sexual maturity takes place. For this reason, the bar mitzvah is associated with marriage, and even confused with it when "Rita" is at the hairdresser's discussing the dinner-dance menu: "A wedding, is it?", asks another customer (ibid., p. 14). The unexpected similarity of the two states is emphasised if we consider the origins of "Rita's" expressions of concern that the bar mitzvah dinner-dance might not go ahead. These lie in Rosenthal's 1966 Armchair Theatre play, *The Night Before the Morning After*, where a mother worries about the possible danger to the wedding dinner caused by her daughter's pre-ceremony nerves. The fact that the dialogue has been almost seamlessly transferred from the earlier, marital context to that of the ostensibly religious rite-of-passage once more reveals their likeness.

The accession to adulthood that the bar mitzvah marks is one in which the boy is released from the authority of his father in a way sanctioned and literally witnessed by the community. As Jacob Arlow argues, the group loyalty of the superego replaces the Oedipal rivalry and fear of castration experienced by the id (1951, p. 214). However, this process in *Bar Mitzvah Boy* is not smooth, but riven with ambivalence on "Eliot's" part. The conversation between "Lesley" and her brother in Jackson Street playground, where he takes refuge after bolting from the synagogue, implies that "Eliot" ran away because he could not identify with his father. Yet "Eliot" does not express conventional Oedipal wishes towards him. Indeed, "Victor" appears distant and self-absorbed, confusing his memories of "Eliot's" childhood with "Lesley's" and being distracted by the newspaper or television instead of participating in "Rita's" planning for their son's bar mitzvah. When "Eliot" has vanished, "Rita" laments her husband's distance:

RITA: You're his father.
VICTOR: So what am I supposed to do? (Rosenthal, 1987, p. 71)

In a generational extension of this distance, "Grandad" misrecognises "Eliot" as a much younger boy and invites him to "sit on your Zaidy's knee" (ibid., p. 33). Neither man exhibits overt sexual affect. While "Grandad" is a widower, "Victor" repeatedly interrupts the barber "Solly's" attempt to tell a smutty joke, about a "Yiddishe feller" and a "dolly bird" in a miniskirt, to tell his own, more innocent one. It is as if they are both, although adults, located in a pre-Oedipal world and cannot offer a role model of adult masculinity to "Eliot". Like much of the visual imagery of the play, the *mise-en-scène* of the playground, and "Eliot's" failed disguise in the form of a "Mickey Mouse" mask, suggests his nostalgia for childhood. Although we see him on the eve of his bar mitzvah taking down posters from the wall of his bedroom and putting them along with his toys into the waste-paper basket, just before he goes to sleep he retrieves them all.

Yet while he is ambivalent about leaving childhood behind, "Eliot" also takes on the adult stance of looking down on and judging the men of his family. When "Lesley" reminds him that "Every Jewish boy gets bar mitzvah'd. Every single one. For thousands of years," including their father, their grandfather, and her boyfriend "Harold", "Eliot" responds, "They're not men, Lesley" (ibid., p. 68). The scene in the playground, in which he lays out the detail of his dissatisfaction with the menfolk, is crosscut with brief scenes back at home that include "Victor", "Grandad", and "Harold", each of which bears out "Eliot's" comments. "Eliot's" father is "a big spoilt kid", his grandfather an infantile narcissist who wants "everyone to think the world of him … like babies do", while "Harold" is "scared all the time" in case he fails to please everybody. No explicit criticism is made of his mother or of "Lesley" herself; this is partly because "Lesley" is her brother's confidante, but also because this is a play about boys and men, and accession to adult masculinity. It is as if "Rita's" role in reducing the bar mitzvah to an empty social ritual is insignificant by contrast to that of her husband. However, it is revealing that the only part of his Torah portion that "Eliot" gets "stuck on" in his playground recital is the "bit about Esther" (ibid., p. 77), one of the Hebrew Bible's most prominent female prophets for her role in saving the Jews from massacre by the Persian prince, Haman. In Rosenthal's play, "Eliot" eventually takes his own part in ensuring the continuity of the Jewish people, as if subliminally determined not to be bested by a woman. "Lesley" does not exhibit Oedipal rivalry towards her brother since she is sufficiently older to take on the role of surrogate mother as much as a sibling, as she demonstrates in offering to pacify their parents by telling the necessary lies about "Eliot's" behaviour: "I've had the practice. I've been grown-up for years" (ibid., p. 74). "Lesley" is, in any case, caught up in her own project of reluctantly accepting an adult female role in relation to "Harold", whose over-eager courtship she deflects throughout the play, resulting in "Eliot's" censure of "Harold" rather than his sister, to whom she is, as she puts it in terms that distance as much as affirm, "nearly bloody engaged!"

Viewers of the play may wonder, like "Lesley", who accuses him of fearing he would "make a nudnik" of himself (ibid., p. 70), whether "Eliot's" stated reasons for abandoning his bar mitzvah tell the whole story. "Eliot" seems to wish for such extreme individuation and separation from his family that he cannot take the sanctioned step to achieve it. The play's resolution may seem surprising—an act of rebellion is recuperated and the enormity of a boy fleeing his own bar mitzvah is resolved by "Rabbi Sherman's" Talmudic reasoning—but it reflects both the inevitability of growing up and "Eliot's" ambivalence in relation to it. During a bar mitzvah ceremony, the father casts off his son and is no longer morally responsible for his sins. However, we have seen that "Eliot" fears the reverse: that he may be held responsible for his father's transgressions. During "Eliot's" recitation of the commandments to "Lesley", the scene changed to one in which "Victor" was having "a short back and sides" at the barber's. As "Victor" watches his reflection in the mirror while "Solly" cuts his hair, we hear "Eliot's" voice-over, reading out the second commandment:

ELIOT: "For I the Lord thy God am a jealous God, visiting the iniquity of the fathers upon the children … and showing loving kindness to the thousandth generation, unto them that love me and keep my commandments". (ibid., p. 19)

"Eliot's" ventriloquising God's utterance in this way represents the harsh judgement he makes of his father, whose "iniquity" in "Eliot's" eyes consists of not honouring the sabbath and not caring "tuppence what other people want" (ibid., p. 71). It is as if "Eliot" is rejecting generational inheritance itself. As Rosenthal comments on such judgement, which marks a breach in the identification of the television audience with the play's protagonist, "a thirteen-year-old is, after all, thirteen. The age when he knows everything and no one else knows anything. Particularly his parents" (Rosenthal, 2006, p. 217). This moment of recognising "Eliot's" partial view is also signalled by his reading aloud the fifth commandment, of whose relevance to his own behaviour he appears oblivious: "Honour thy father and thy mother, that thy days—", until he is interrupted by "Lesley" "commanding" him to get a haircut.

It is perhaps an expression of "Eliot's" rivalry with his father—who is significantly called "Victor"—that he rejects the moment at which he would become responsible for his own transgressions. When he is summoned by his Hebrew name and patronymic, "Eliayhu bereb Velvel … 'Eliot' son of 'Victor'", "Eliot" stands up obediently—in order to leave the synagogue, rather than to go up to the bimah to read his portion of the law. Yet punishing his father in this way is paradoxical, since it means that "Eliot" must remain infantilised. It does, however, at last provoke a reaction in his father, who expresses recognition of the specifically paternal nature of rage against one's children:

VICTOR: I'll murder him. I will. I've spent thirteen years bringing him up; and now I've done it, I'll bloody strangle him! … My *father* said it. "Children break your heart". [Pause] I'll break every bone in his body. (Rosenthal, 1987, pp. 58–62)

The first encounter that "Eliot" has when he leaves the synagogue is with a group of men "looking at the merchandise in the window of a girlie-magazine shop" (ibid., p. 54). This seems to contrast jarringly with the scene of religious initiation that we have just been witnessing: but in fact it is a continuation of it, representing the world of male adulthood that "Eliot" both wishes for and fears. His ambivalence about such adulthood is made clear almost immediately in the terms of his teenage world, when "Denise" tells him that "Squidge" went home early from the swimming pool, crying because he had stubbed his toe:

ELIOT: "Crying?" [*puzzled*] He's over thirteen, though, is Squidge. (ibid., p. 56)

This response demonstrates a childlike view of adulthood and a restricted one of masculinity. "Eliot's" perspective is both judgemental and conservative. On Friday evening, he showed his disapproval of the spectacle of "Harold" wearing an apron to do the washing up:

ELIOT: I thought that was a woman's job? Or is that just a theory put about by chauvinist pigs? (ibid., p. 28)

Ultimately, we learn that it is not individual men of whom "Eliot" disapproves, but human frailty itself: "I'm not saying they're the only ones. That's the trouble. It's every feller you ...", until he is once more interrupted by "Lesley": "It's all an excuse!" (ibid., p. 69).

Throughout *Bar Mitzvah Boy*, "Eliot's" disdain for his family's disavowal of the ceremony's religious significance masks his own ambivalence about adulthood. Even his indignation that his bar mitzvah is treated as "a hair-dressing contest", and his refusal to have a haircut at his mother's request, shares in this duality. As he puts it to "Lesley":

ELIOT: Do you know why I wouldn't go for a haircut yesterday? Because everybody wanted me to. I was being a stupid kid. Awkward. Like dad. (ibid., p. 69)

This is an over-determined confession. It reveals "Eliot's" knowledge that cultural and psychic inheritance is inescapable, as well as his wish to be the adult in relation to his "stupid kid" of a father. It is here that the Oedipal rivalry is made clear, in "Eliot's" conviction that he can supersede not just "Victor" himself, but his community as well. Yet the constant refrain about haircuts is not just the occasion for comedy, since it is the site of "Eliot's" judgement as well as his refusal. "Rita" seems unwittingly to perceive something of the truth in her mistake at the dinner table:

RITA: Victor, he's not standing in a synagogue, on the greatest day of his life looking like Kojak. [They all stare at her, puzzled.]
LESLEY: Kojak's *bald*. (ibid., p. 25)

The bar mitzvah is the second Oedipally orientated rite in Jewish tradition for boys, the first being circumcision, conducted when the child is eight days old. Like the bar mitzvah, circumcision is a religious ritual with an unconscious dimension. Although Mortimer Ostow argues that being circumcised is never "relegated" to the unconscious of the individual (1982, p. 169), it does have an unconscious meaning for the community. As Freud puts it, circumcision is "a symbolical substitute for castration", and a sign that the initiate is "ready to submit to his father's will" (1939a, p. 91). "Eliot's" refusal of the haircut that his father successfully undergoes, is another rebellion on his part against psychic as well as cultural strictures: he does not wish to "submit to his father's will". It is the earlier rite of circumcision that "Rita" unwittingly invokes in her Freudian slip about Kojak (Freud, 1900a, sees unconscious fear of castration in the manifest dream image of cutting hair). "Rita's" concern that her son might appear "bald" in the synagogue reveals her anxiety that failing to appear appropriately at a bar mitzvah might also result in the incomplete resolution of the Oedipus complex represented by the threat of castration, with circumcision as its latent counterpart.

However, the play succeeds in resolving "Eliot's" fantasy that he owes nothing to his father and his consequent rejection of his father's community. Through the intermediary parental figures of "Rabbi Sherman" and "Lesley", "Eliot" is able to exercise adult judgement to be both "the first man since 'Adam'", as "Lesley" puts it, "since there are no others", and a member of the community. "Lesley's" judgement on her brother's flight from the synagogue is that it is "probably the most grown-up thing I've ever heard of" (Rosenthal, 1987, p. 74).

The Evacuees: *"I bet she's a witch. Any money"*

Rosenthal's "Play for Today" from 1975 is, as its title suggests, about childhood and enforced separation, in contrast to the individuation rite represented in *Bar Mitzvah Boy*. In 1939, brothers "Danny" and "Neville

Miller" are evacuated from urban Cheetham Hill in Manchester to seaside Lytham St Annes near Blackpool. They are taken in by a child-less couple whose Victorian approach to child-rearing contrasts with that of the boys' loving, working-class family life. Eventually, "Danny" lets his mother know how unhappy the brothers are, and she takes them back to bomb-damaged Manchester. In *The Evacuees*, we see the psychic effects of a historically specific experience, rather than, as in *Bar Mitzvah Boy*, a religious ritual whose unconscious underpinning is revealed. While both plays concern the growing up of young boys, the important family relations in *The Evacuees* are, in contrast to *Bar Mitzvah Boy*, those with women.

The *Evacuees* also fuses its narrative of growing up with one that draws on Jewish tradition. In *Bar Mitzvah Boy* when "Lesley" leaves the house to retrieve her errant brother from the playground, "Victor" mut-ters in exasperation: "First him. Now her. It's like the bloody exodus from Egypt. [*To the rabbi*] No disrespect" (ibid., p. 66). In *The Evacuees*, the wartime experience of evacuation is likened to the biblical Exodus in a more sustained allegory, in which the boys' return is akin to the Israelites' coming upon the Promised Land after their years of wander-ing in the wilderness. The first scene we see after their arrival back home from evacuation is set during the festival of Chanukah, and "Neville" demonstrates his familiarity with the story by gabbling a summary:

NEVILLE
[*parrot-fashion*]:   The festival of Chanukah commemorates the return of the Israelites to the Temple after forty years in the wilderness ... (ibid., p. 138)

While there is little evidence of the children in Rosenthal's play uncon-sciously believing that their being evacuated is punishment for the "hatred and jealousy" of their Oedipal conflicts, as Susan Isaacs claims in the *Cambridge Evacuation Survey* (1941) was the situation for very young evacuees (quoted in Shapira, 2012, p. 22), the parallel bibli-cal narrative implies that the exile does have a retributive cause—in the Israelites' case, for doubting God's promise. In Rosenthal's play, although the boys delay calling upon their mother's love in order not to worry her, "Mrs Miller's" "promise" of love does not fail them.

Despite the fact that their "bleak" home surroundings are empha-sised in the film's *mise-en-scène*, and the boys undergo frequent air raids on their return to Manchester, these factors are viewed by "Danny" and "Neville" with relief in contrast to the warlike threat embodied by their foster-parents. On their first evening at their foster-home, the boys enter "the Grahams'" dining room to the sound of one of Hitler's speeches. Although it is "Mr Graham" whom "Danny" suspects of being a German spy for listening to the speech, the camera movement suggests otherwise: we hear a shout of "*Sieg Heil*" as the camera pans across the room and focuses on his wife. "Danny" revealingly mispronounces the dictator's name as "Her Hitler", transforming "Herr", the masculine address in German, into a feminine pronoun. Later, "Danny" makes this association between dictator and dictatorial foster-mother explicit in his evening prayer that Hitler "die slowly with toothache and horrible gashes. [*Pause.*] And the same goes for Mrs Graham. Only double" (Rosenthal, 1987, p. 118). Hitler is blamed for having caused the children to end up with this surrogate parent.

The progress of the war itself is linked to the children's fate, and we see a poster about the evacuation of Dunkirk accompanying their doomed effort to evacuate themselves by roller skating back to Manchester. While this, like the parallel between "Mrs Graham" and Hitler, represents a comic hyperbole, it also emphasises the fact that the real threat for evacuated children came not so much from the war as from those measures taken to protect against it. Contemporary commentators feared that the anxious, aggressive evacuees (Shapira, 2008, p. 21), particularly those who lived in hostels rather than foster-homes, would come to take on the fascistic attributes of Britain's foe; while later analysis suggested that "urban evacuees, primarily working-class, were often unwelcome in middle-class homes" (Kanter, 2004, p. 14). Both truisms are reversed in *The Evacuees*, where it is "Mrs Graham's" behaviour that takes an authoritarian form, precisely because she "welcomes" the children too definitively: the boys have to stand up at table for their spartan meals and clean the house every day. "Danny" finally writes down their woes for his mother to read during a children's game—"She is dead cruel to us ... She hates us. And we hate her back" (Rosenthal, 1987, p. 137)—but his characterisation of "Mrs Graham's" behaviour is partly a misrecognition. Their foster-mother later describes her feelings rather differently, in conversation with her husband:

MRS GRAHAM: I taught them respect, yes. Agreed. To respect their elders and betters. I wouldn't say that was cruel ... I'd say that was love. That's the word I'd give it. (ibid., p. 139)

Indeed, it is clear that "Mrs Graham's" tragedy is to love the children in a way that exceeds her fostering role at the same time as being insufficient to it. She is "embarrassed" to be caught by her husband surreptitiously pressing "Danny's" jacket to her cheek (ibid., p. 119), and "Mrs Miller" is disconcerted in turn to see "Mrs Graham" smoothing the younger boy's hair in a *"maternal"* way (ibid., p. 134). In his complaint to his mother, "Danny" adds that, "She steals your letters and whatever you send us" (ibid., p. 137), acts of apparent acquisitiveness and greed. However, such behaviour represents an effort to steal the children's affection as part of a campaign, one that even "Mr Graham" finds emotionally sinister, to remove any reminders of their mother:

MRS GRAHAM
(*fighting the tears*):   I had to make them try and forget her, Gordon, hadn't I?

(*He looks at her uneasily.*)

    MR GRAHAM: Their own *mother*?
    MRS GRAHAM: *I* was their mother! (ibid., p. 139)

"Mrs Graham's" plunder includes parcels of food that link "Danny" and "Neville" to their past, not only in terms of familial affection but as a specifically Jewish past: in one parcel that the boys never see, their mother sends "cooked chicken with helzel, and marzipan cake" (ibid., p. 110). Their grandmother also expresses this fusion of individual and communal love when she gives the boys chopped liver for their train journey to Blackpool, and during one of her visits "Mrs Miller" offers the same "intermediate object" of food (Kestenberg & Weinstein, 1988, p. 91) in the form of a salt beef sandwich. In her analysis of the case history of an adopted boy whose belongings from home were taken from him, Clare Britton argues that the "transitional" objects of a teddy bear and clothing "stood for everything he brought with him" from the past, and were things that he "could not afford to lose" (1950, p. 179). The cost of "Mrs Graham's" theft of gifts from home is similar for "Danny" and "Neville", even though the perishable items of food, as "a bridge to mother herself" (Farrell, n.d.), are "intermediate" rather than transitional objects. The gentile nature of this foster-home and "Mrs Graham's" campaign to separate the children from their mother coalesce in her provision of forbidden food:

DANNY: I don't like cold sausage, Mrs Graham.
MRS GRAHAM: Of course you do! It's real pork. (Rosenthal, 1987, p. 106)

Only the threat of getting "no tea" altogether on another occasion prompts "Danny" to ask, "Not even a pork sausage, 'Mrs Graham?'" (ibid., p. 116). This time it is not wartime hardship or evacuation to non-Jewish families that makes it acceptable to eat non-kosher food, as the boys' teacher, "Mr Goldstone", assures them (ibid., p. 96), but "Mrs Graham's" regime of punishment and control.

In contrast to D. W. Winnicott's "good-enough" mother, "almost complete adaptation" (Winnicott, 1953) is what "Mrs Graham" demands from the children, instead of offering it herself. In this reversal, rather than exhibiting the regression often exhibited by young evacuees, the children are made to act as adults. They do so also in protecting their mother from their unhappiness by keeping it secret, in an attempt to manage her emotions; as "Neville" puts it, "She's got enough to worry about" (Rosenthal, 1987, p. 117). Yet the boys are old enough that the "false selves" (Winnicott, 1956) they develop in order to keep "Mrs Graham" at bay remain simply behavioural. At their first meal, partly in order to offset the effect of having to eat non-kosher food, "Danny" copies "Neville" in enacting the Jewish ritual of covering his head and reciting a Hebrew prayer covertly, by pretending to scratch his head and cough; at other times, the boys withdraw into silence or, in their shared bedroom, pretend to be asleep. After the boys have gone home to Manchester, "Mrs Graham" reveals that she asked to adopt them officially, emphasising the gap in her understanding of the designation and the reality of mothering. Her verdict on "Mrs Miller's" warmth towards her sons is that "Her love isn't love at all. Too *much* love" (Rosenthal, 1987, p. 139). The division between the children's perspective on "Mrs Graham's" cruelty and hatred, and that of "Mrs Graham" herself, who describes it as "love", is part of what makes the play not simply a work of memory on Rosenthal's part, despite its basis in his autobiography (Rosenthal, 2006). The scene between "Mr and Mrs Graham" that we witness after the boys' departure represents an adult view of events characterised by "unusual sympathy" (Fenwick, 1975), since it takes place outside the boys' viewpoint.

In *The Evacuees*, the plight of "Danny" and "Neville" exemplifies the fact that children evacuated from large cities were "on the whole much less upset by bombing than by evacuation to the country as a protection against it" (Shapira, 2008). External dangers were easier to deal with than the internal ones of separation and loss (A. Freud & Burlingham, 1973, p. 24). Lisa Farley analyses what the boys in Rosenthal's play experience as the "terrible conflict of the evacuation: a helping hand that was felt as deprivation" (Farley, 2012, p. 40). She argues that the code name for the evacuation scheme, "Operation Pied Piper", reveals the planners' unconscious awareness of the likelihood of its resulting in "loss, betrayal and abandonment" (ibid., p. 30), malign effects that are implied by the legend itself, in which the disgruntled Piper took revenge on untrustworthy townspeople by luring away their children, who were never seen again. The legend's subtextual link to the experience of evacuation is hinted at in Rosenthal's play in terms of both the *mise-en-scène* and its plot. When the pupils of "Derby Street School" arrive in Blackpool, where householders have to be persuaded on the spot to foster, we see the boys in silhouette running along a grassy headland behind their teacher, "Mr Goldstone", as if he is the piper luring them away to an ominous end. Winnicott's concerns about the fate of the young evacuees with whom he worked during the war included the fear that, separated from their parents, children might become susceptible to the "idealised authority" of fascism (Winnicott, 1984, pp. 26–27). His wish that the evacuees' carers might be "free-minded people" who offer "local adaptation" is an ironic one in view of "Mrs Graham's" child-rearing attitudes, while "Danny" and "Neville" exhibit not only the "resilience" of sibling solidarity (Young & Mitchell, 2005, p. 48) but also "the defiance of the unconscious" that Winnicott advocated, and need little assistance in withstanding the allure of a charismatic leader gone bad (Winnicott, 1984, p. 27).

Although "Danny" and "Neville" are older than the evacuated children for whom "physical separation from the mother was seen to be a pathogenic effect in its own right" (Davis, 2012), we see the age-specific results of their developing maturity in these circumstances. At first, both boys mistake romantic for war-related determination, and are disappointed that a teenage girl turns out to be on her way to a tryst in the dunes rather than on a mission as a German spy. "Neville", two years older than his nine-year-old brother, later tries to comfort "Danny" after they are sent to bed without any dinner by showing him a pin-up photograph, with which the younger boy is *"unimpressed"*:

DANNY

(*not at all sure why he's been invited to look at it*):   It's a lady in a bathing costume. (Rosenthal, 1987, p. 117)

The divided role the photograph of this "lady" plays is clear when, in the boys' bedroom after one of their mother's visits, "Neville" slips the pin-up back into its hiding-place inside his comic. This suggests not only a retreat from the images of impending adulthood back to the boy-ish world of comics, but "Neville's" inability to separate himself from his mother and take up a sexual identity of his own: the comforting role of the pin-up is unsuccessful and, *"for the first time ... Neville quietly starts to cry"* (ibid., p. 126). The photograph alternates between being a reassuring maternal image, or a token of impending puberty, depend-ing on "Neville's" emotional state.

As if as a result of his time away from home, and significantly when he is in the company of his mother, "Neville", unlike "Danny", can nego-tiate the signs of the adult sexual world. This includes his recognition of the pregnant state of a line of women, one of whom is the young girl of the mis-identified romantic tryst, sitting and knitting on Blackpool Pier. We learn that by this time the boys have been in Lytham for nine months, as if "Neville's" awareness has had the same gestation period as that of a human child. The nine months' anniversary has an uncon-scious resonance for the boys' mother too. Although she is "shocked" that "Neville" exhibits knowledge of pregnancy, "Mrs Miller" also iden-tifies her sons with the unborn children: "They've come here so's the babies won't get bombed", as she puts it of the pregnant women (ibid., p. 121). This statement reveals a need on "Mrs Miller's" part to reas-sure herself that, despite the "deprivation" (Winnicott, 1984, p. 31) she has suffered, she is doing the best for her own "babies", as if partaking of the guilty fantasy identified by Winnicott on the part of mothers of evacuated children, who might blame her own unworthiness for their absence, and imagine that it is her "own self that fails to provide them with the home they ought to have" (ibid., p. 32). Back in Manchester, where it is "Danny" who is now old enough to keep the talisman in his satchel, another boy recognises the pin-up photograph's transitional significance by asking, "Who's this?" (Rosenthal, 1987, p. 144).

Conclusion

Jack Rosenthal's concerns in these two plays, with generational and Oedipal conflict, male adolescence, and the nature of good-enough parenting, are represented through visual and verbal comedy. The plays' dialogue reveals Rosenthal's uncanny ear not just for everyday speech, but specifically for the utterances of schoolchildren. His ability to capture the social meaning of an era in tiny detail shows the accuracy of Roger Silverstone's evaluation of television's important transitional function in a potential space: "Everyday life becomes the site for, and the product of, the working out of significance" (Silverstone, 1994, p. 164). Rosenthal relies in particular on the technique of "everyday surrealism", that is, the comic use of non-sequitur and the failure of people to understand or reply to each other, combined with a mixture of classical with down-to-earth discourse that is reminiscent, for instance, of Samuel Beckett's plays. Everyday surrealism is also a way of registering those moments where, as in the Freudian slip or dream-work, the unconscious speaks.

It is this imbrication of the psyche and the everyday that is distinctive about those of Rosenthal's plays that I have analysed here, as well as constituting the very source of television's significance as a medium. As "Plays for Today", *Bar Mitzvah Boy* and *The Evacuees* were dramas within a television strand that had a self-selecting but significant audience, averaging four million viewers and often attracting considerably larger numbers. Such viewing figures reveal the wide reach of challenging material that both called upon and reflected what Candida Yates, in this volume, describes as "the conscious and unconscious dynamics of [the] family groups or friends" that made up the audience.

The television writer, Peter Bowker (2012), has described Rosenthal and Alan Plater as "two of the most influential" writers of the "golden generation that produced Alan Bleasdale, Troy Kennedy Martin and Dennis Potter", and I would argue that Rosenthal's influence is perceptible in terms of "everyday surrealism", and its televisual appositeness, even in the most contemporary generation of writers, including Simon Amstell, whose work I will mention below, as well as Robert Popper, author of *Friday Night Dinner* (2011–2012), in which brothers, "Adam" and "Jonny Goodman", return to, and regress in the company of, their parents at a Sabbath evening meal. In Amstell's *Grandma's House* (Amstell & Swimer, 2010/2012), we see the same conflict between generations as in Rosenthal's *Bar Mitzvah Boy*, in terms of both class and register, again often acted out around the dinner table. As in *Bar Mitzvah Boy*, "Simon" has conversations at cross purposes with his mother, "Tanya", in which spiritual values clash with materialistic ones.

However, such conflict in *Grandma's House* does not always follow the pattern established by "Eliot Green", whose religious questions were met with his parents' secular observations. In the former, "Simon's" mother "Tanya" responds with defiant scepticism to her son's use of a therapeutic discourse. His wish that his mother "complete" with her past in relation to his father "Richard", "Tanya's" estranged husband, is met with her riposte, turning his verb into an adjective: "He's already complete: a complete prick!", while "Simon's" question to his mother about his father's canoeing trips with another woman, "Why do you think he was like that?", is greeted with "Tanya's" exasperated reply, "I don't know: maybe he liked rowing!" These non sequiturs and over-literal rejoinders are the result of different registers, in which "trite questions are met with existential answers" (*Metro*, 2012); yet audience members are not invited simply to identify with "Simon's" viewpoint, just as "Eliot's" perspective in *Bar Mitzvah Boy* was shown to rely on the extremity of youth. "Simon's" effort to reconcile his parents fails partly due to his own inability to free himself from the patterns of the past in relation to his father. In a reverse formation, "Tanya" takes her son to task about the high psychic and physical cost of mothering, which her son greets with determinedly literal responses:

TANYA: How can you lie to your mother? You came out of my womb!
SIMON: I know, but I live in Hampstead now.
TANYA: Eleven stitches I had for you!
SIMON: All right, but they must have healed by now, no?

"Simon's" effort to establish his present state of adulthood is a version of "Eliot Green's", even if it is not one marked by religious ritual.

Jack Rosenthal was, as an obituary described him, one of a "new breed" of playwrights who wrote "almost exclusively for television" (BBC, 2004) and drew on its specific resources. A psychoanalytic approach to Rosenthal's plays demonstrates the source of their success in what might be called a comedy of the unconscious, by means of which the viewer is sutured into narratives about family relations and life milestones. In *Bar Mitzvah Boy*, the adolescent drama of individuation is given the comic form of a religious ritual that is refused; while in *The Evacuees*, we see in fictional form something of the wartime experience that gave British child psychologists an abundance of data on bonding, parenting, and separation (Kanter, 2004 p. 70). Rosenthal's legacy in these terms is made clear in contemporary examples of

British-Jewish television drama, such as *Grandma's House*, that include their own Oedipal and "revisionary" (Bloom, 1973, p. 10) versions of his psychoanalytic dramas.

References

Amstell, S. & Swimer, D. (2010–2012). *Grandma's House*. Two series, originally broadcast 9 August–13 September, 2010, and 19 April–24 May, 2012.

Arlow, J. (1951). A psychoanalytic study of a religious initiation rite: bar mitzvah. In: M. Ostow (Ed.), *Judaism and Psychoanalysis* (pp. 187–218). London: Karnac, 1997.

BBC (2004). Obituary: Jack Rosenthal. http://news.bbc.co.uk/1/hi/entertainment/3040267.stm#top (visited 19 October, 2012).

Bloom, H. (1973). *The Anxiety of Influence: A Theory of Poetry (2nd edn.)*. Oxford: Oxford University Press, 1997.

Bowker, P. (2012). Don't denigrate mainstream drama writers. [Talk given at the BBC Television Writers' Festival.] http://scriptangel.wordpress.com/2012/07/13/dont-denigrate-mainstream-drama-writers-peter-bowker/ (visited 25 July, 2012).

Britton, C. (1950). Child care. In: C. Morris (Ed.), *Social Case-work in Great Britain* (pp. 164–188). London: Faber.

Davis, A. (2012). "Evacuation is a story of tragedies" (D. W. Winnicott): World War Two and British Child Psychology. [Seminar paper, Centre for History in Public Health, London.] January.

Dunn, K. (2011). Responses to Rosenthal. *Journal of British Cinema and Television*, 8: 272–282.

Farley, L. (2012). "Operation Pied Piper": A psychoanalytic narrative of authority in a time of war. *Psychoanalysis and History*, 14: 29–52.

Farrell, E. (n.d.). The psychoanalysis of anorexia and bulimia. http://www.psychoanalysis-and-therapy.com/human_nature/farrell/chap3.html (visited 25 July, 2012).

Fenwick, H. (1975). The war that Jack relived. *Radio Times*, 27 February.

Freud, A. & Burlingham, D. T. (1973). *Infants without Families: Reports on the Hampstead Nurseries, 1939–1945*. Madison, CT: International Universities Press.

Freud, S. (1900a). *The Interpretation of Dreams*. S. E., 5: 633–685. London: Hogarth.

Freud, S. (1939a). *Moses and Monotheism*. S. E., 23: 3–137. London: Hogarth.

Heathman's Diary (1976). Jack Rosenthal Drama Scripts Collection. Sheffield, UK: University of Sheffield, BARB/b.

Isaacs, S. (Ed.) (1941). *The Cambridge Evacuation Survey*. London: Methuen.

Kanter, J. (2004). *Face to Face with Children: The Life and Work of Clare Winnicott*. London: Karnac.

Kestenberg, J. & Weinstein, J. (1988). Transitional objects and body-image formation. In: S. A. Grolnick, L. S. Barkin, & W. Muensterberger (Eds.), *Between Reality and Phantasy: Winnicott's Concepts of Transitional Objects and Phenomena* (pp. 75–97). New York: Jason Aronson.

Metro (2012). *Grandma's House* is a prim and prickly triumph. [Review.] 27 April.

Ostow, M. (1982). The psychological determinants of Jewish identity. In: M. Ostow (Ed.), *Judaism and Psychoanalysis (2nd edn.)* (pp. 157–186). London: Karnac, 1997.

Popper, R. (2011–2012). *Friday Night Dinner*. Two series, originally broadcast 25 February–8 April, 2011, and 7 October–11 November, 2012.

Purser, P. (2004). Jack Rosenthal: Award-winning dramatist with a humorous and gentle take on life. [Obituary.] *The Guardian*, 31 May.

Rosenthal, J. (1966). *The Night Before the Morning After*. Originally broadcast 2 April.

Rosenthal, J. (1970). *The Lovers*. Series one originally broadcast 27 October–1 December.

Rosenthal, J. (1975). *The Evacuees*. Originally broadcast 5 March.

Rosenthal, J. (1975). *Sadie, It's Cold Outside*. One series, originally broadcast 21 April–26 May.

Rosenthal, J. (1976). *Bar Mitzvah Boy*. Originally broadcast 14 September.

Rosenthal, J. (1982). *P'tang, Yang, Kipperbang*. Originally broadcast 3 November.

Rosenthal, J. (1987). *Bar Mitzvah Boy and Other Television Plays*. Penguin Harmondsworth.

Rosenthal, J. (1996). *Eskimo Day*. Originally broadcast 5 April.

Rosenthal, J. (1997). *Cold Enough for Snow*. Originally broadcast 31 December.

Rosenthal, J. (2006). *By Jack Rosenthal: an Autobiography in Six Acts*. London: Robson.

Shapira, M. (2008). The war inside: child psychoanalysis and remaking the self in Britain, 1930–1960. [Unpublished PhD dissertation.] http://hdl.rutgers.edu/1782.2/rucore10001600001.ETD.17567 (visited 7 September, 2012).

Silverstone, R. (1994). *Television and Everyday Life*. London: Routledge.

Vice, S. (2009). *Jack Rosenthal*. Manchester, UK: Manchester University Press.

Winnicott, D. W. (1953). Transitional objects and transitional phenomena. *International Journal of Psychoanalysis*, 34: 89–97.

Winnicott, D. W. (1956). Clinical varieties of transference. *International Journal of Psychoanalysis*, 37: 386.

Winnicott, D. W. (1984). *Deprivation and Delinquency*. C. Winnicott, R. Shepherd, & M. Davis (Eds.). London: Tavistock.

Young, L. S. & Mitchell, J. (2005). Looking for the siblings: A critical narrative of child evacuation during World War II. *Critical Psychology*, 15: 42–63.

List of television programmes and films cited

Bar Mitzvah Boy (1976). BBC1, UK.

Cold Enough For Snow (1997). BBC1, UK.

Eskimo Day (1996). BBC1, UK.

Friday Night Dinner (2011–present). Channel 4, UK.

Grandma's House (2010-2012). BBC2, UK.

P'tang Yang Kipperbang (1982). Channel 4, UK.

Sadie, It's Cold Outside (1975). Thames Television (ITV), UK.

The Evacuees (1975). BBC1, UK.

The Lovers (1970-1971). Granada (ITV), UK.

The Night Before The Morning After (1966). Thames Television (ITV), UK.

CHAPTER SIX

Spending too much time watching TV?

Jo Whitehouse-Hart

Television and domestic viewing

The postwar twentieth and twenty-first century living room may have displayed an array of changing fashion, styles, and designs, but, for the most part, domestic spaces for relaxation contain a television, which remains an enduring and important entertainment technology embedded in everyday life. Understanding television's role in daily life and the way in which audiences respond to and use television has been a central concern of the academic fields of media and television studies. Perspectives have been divided between text-reader-interpretation and product-user-context approaches, with sociological paradigms dominating the various methods. Such divisions have also resulted in the relative lack of studies which take into account the text being watched, the audience (as located historically and socially), the viewing context, and associated practices (see Lacey, 1997 and Wood, 2009 for exceptions).[1] Psychoanalysis has, for the most part, been rejected by television researchers, but has had considerable impact within film theory where it has been applied principally to the cinematic scenario. Such approaches have not been effectively developed to understand the viewing of films on television.[2] This chapter will show that it is possible to bridge these restrictive

111

theoretical and methodological gaps by arguing that television viewing should be explored as a *psychosocial* activity.[3]

The psychosocial approach I use here, starts from the position that the outer (sociological) and inner (psychic) worlds are mutually constitutive in that they have effects on each other. Whilst it is essential to consider the effects of discourse and the hierarchical organisation of the social world for instance, it is of equal importance to understand the way in which the unconscious, as something dynamic and conflictual, presses upon everyday life (Evans, 2000, p. 13). The meanings audiences make in relation to what they watch, their patterns of identification, and the practices that constitute their viewing habits must be understood in light of this two-way traffic between inner and outer worlds.

This chapter will use an original approach developed from ideas from object relations psychoanalysis to highlight some of the complex psychosocial processes that previous studies have missed, because of this reluctance to address both social and psychic processes. Object relations theories are pertinent to audience research as they point to the significance of attachments to, and relationships with non-human objects or "things" which also include a range of cultural experiences such as cinema and television viewing (Bollas, 1992, 1995; Winnicott, 1971). My approach is also significant in that it takes into account both the text being viewed (which is often a pre-recorded film or programme), and the nature of the experience and the particular viewing practices audiences adopt in relation to viewing significant texts. (This includes the significance of viewing texts in distinct spaces such as bedrooms.) While the focus of this chapter is television, it is important to note that when viewers talk about watching television, they might not always be discussing conventional broadcast television. Often, they are referring to the use of television to watch films, which might be pre-recorded from a television broadcast or a purchased DVD, and films have always been part of television's "flow" (Williams, 1974).

The research on which this chapter is based, adopted Hollway and Jefferson's (2012) Free Association Narrative Interview (FANI) method in an in-depth, interview-based research project that explored something previously neglected: the biographical, emotional, and social significance of "favourite" television programmes and films.[4] This psychoanalytically informed method is based on the idea that research subjects unconsciously defend against difficult thoughts, feelings, and ideas that might be generated in any research situation. As a consequence, conventional interview techniques often produce "defended" answers that miss the emotional significance for the interviewee. FANI draws on techniques from narrative research where the interviewee is asked open-ended questions designed to elicit emotionally and biographically significant narratives. In the spirit of free association, the interviewer follows the respondent's ordering of events and examines the data as a "whole". Of course, the use of psychoanalysis in both method and data interpretation is not straightforward and concern has been expressed about the ethical implications of adopting a set of ideas and techniques designed for a specific use—the treatment of emotional problems in a clinical setting (see Frosh, 2010). Whilst it is clearly important that ethical concerns should remain paramount in research design, I will not discuss this here, as I have explored this theme extensively elsewhere (see Whitehouse-Hart, 2010 and 2013).[5]

My research suggested that, for viewers, "favourites" referred to those texts that has particular significance for them. At times this was linked to biographical experience, but sometimes it also related to the fact that they had generated unexpected and powerful emotional responses. Some viewers would repeatedly view such "favourites" and *films* were often given as examples of such selections. What was significant was that, in most cases, the films in question, were those that had been first encountered on television, often leading the viewer to purchase a pre-recorded DVD of the text which could then be viewed again. This suggests that the domestic setting and experience might be significant in understanding the way a text is interpreted and used. It was also found that sometimes, viewers have particular texts that they periodically choose to watch, but which they actually find "difficult". This begs the question: if watching television is for leisure and pleasure, why would someone choose to watch something that they find unpleasant? It is my contention that psychoanalysis can help explain such processes and I use the case studies below to illuminate this, thereby showing the complexity of viewing.

In the past, empirical audience research has tended to focus predominantly on "family viewing" (see Morley, 1992). This can be seen as a response to the notion that the predominant audience unit was the "average nuclear family", which, in itself, was conceived by the broadcasting institutions themselves and partly grounded in fantasy. Prior to the emergence of digital television, broadcasters provided a programming schedule that was said to correspond to the rhythms and domestic routines of the family, whilst at the same time constructing particular times of the day, especially evenings, when television viewing became established as an entertaining means of passing the increasing leisure time associated with postwar societies (Ellis, 1989; Lopate, 1977; Spigel, 1992).

In the days of single television set ownership and restricted channel choice, it is fair to say that most viewers experienced communal viewing (with their families), and how this now exists as a memory for contemporary audiences will be addressed below. The viewing landscape has now changed. In recent years, television has been revolutionised by the development of time-shift/record-replay technologies such as DVD and digital technology. The most significant effect of this has been the growth of programme choice and the ability to sidestep the broadcast schedule and create what has been called a "user-flow" (Caldwell, 2003)—a personalised navigation through the broadcast schedules and across different technological platforms. This also allows television to be used by audiences to watch programmes and films on demand on their televisions and other platforms in a way that had previously been impossible. These developments raise questions about how we might understand the experience of viewing different types of *content*, particularly when theories of television and film viewing have differed so sharply in the past. As Klinger (2006) has argued, today, the film industry and also film studies academics recognise that that most film viewing takes place in the home on a television set and films are an important part of many viewers' own user-flows. (This is explored further in my two case studies below).

If the social experience of watching television is changing and becoming more *individualised*, then this is taking place against the backdrop of a range of wider social developments, with the idea of the nuclear family being replaced by the reality of a range of reconfigured relational and domestic structures. In this chapter, I concentrate on one neglected but significant and increasing group: single men who live alone.[6] I present an account of twenty-first century domestic television viewing and leisure time in the lives of two single men—Chris (twenty-nine) and Daniel (thirty-seven). New patterns of work involving the often pressing demands of relocating for employment purposes mean that the idea of spending one's entire working life in the community in which one grew up and with family in close proximity is now anachronistic. Chris and Daniel both hail from working class backgrounds and have experienced a degree of social mobility. They now live alone and are engaged in earning a living and building a career. As I have discussed elsewhere, changes in work patterns, familial relationships, and social mobility have been theorised in relation to men and what has been deemed the "crisis" of masculinity (see Beynon, 2002; Whitehead, 2002; Whitehouse-Hart, 2010) and, as my case studies show, some of the anxieties that emerge out of these changes and ensuing responses could be viewed as gender specific. The relationship between the experience of loss associated with the "crisis" of masculinity and the repeated use of DVD technologies has been discussed in depth elsewhere by Bainbridge and Yates (2007).

It has been suggested that the twenty-first century is characterised by the use of technologies that allow people to lead new forms of "connected lives" (Elliott & Urry, 2010). Members of the Facebook and iPhone generation are thought to be able to conduct emotional and affective lives successfully through the use of digital technologies (ibid.,). But what about those people who live alone and are *not* logged or plugged into virtual and networked worlds? In contrast to popular views of the communicative lives of single people, Chris and Daniel do not spend all their time in a digitalised world of socialising and friendships. In fact, they both experience some degree of social isolation from their families and friendship groups as a result of changing employment and life patterns associated with late modernity. Both men like to watch television as a means of filling "leisure time" when they are not working. They would be considered by audience researchers as "active" audiences,[7] creating their own unique viewing practices using digital, time-shift, and record-replay technology, as the reader will see. However, this issue of *time* and how to spend it, is complex and can, for some, like Chris and Daniel, weigh heavily on the psyche, in particular provoking forms of anxiety. It is possible to understand in part why this might be the case by briefly reviewing the way in which television has featured in prevailing discourses and popular thought.

On the one hand, television is thought of as ordinary and quotidian, a bit of "harmless" entertainment; yet on the other, television has been a source of social anxiety, with fears expressed around the moral and intellectual welfare of audiences. The nature of this anxiety is two-fold, revolving around both the activity of watching television and the content. Prevailing discourses, supported by medical and "effects" research, see television viewing as lowbrow and banal, with concerns frequently expressed that spending *time* watching television is a "problem" and "bad for you".[8] So television is both a harmless object *and* an object of anxiety. To spend too much time watching television is a marker of bad taste, lack of culture, and idleness. These contradictory ideas about television permeate and become a feature of the viewing experience for the men in this study.

Discourses featuring television do not exist in isolation, intersecting for instance with other discourses that structure taste, gender, and class in a complex mix. Discourses are lived both performatively (externally) and subjectively (internally) and television discourse can be negative and evaluative, provoking anxiety in viewers. Both Chris and Daniel express anxiety about the *amount of time* spent watching TV. They are concerned that some of their viewing practices, such as repetitive and long sessions of time-shift viewing, are both "bad" and "sad". Both men enjoy watching television and films at home, but they worry about "time-wasting". It is a fact that both men have leisure time to fill, yet why should television be both a compelling and yet problematic activity for them? What is it about television and time that might provoke anxiety and what does it mean for these men? Questions arise about identity and conflict out of the particular neo-liberal social organisation of late capitalism in which audiences exist and watch TV. Whilst I have pointed to the limitations of some existing approaches to audience research, I think it is possible to productively revisit one prominent but much maligned paradigm, known as "uses and gratifications" theory (Katz, Blumer & Gurevitch, 1974), as a means of exploring what these conflicts and issues might be.

This now rather outdated paradigm conceived of the audience as goal-directed, and considered the way television was used to meet pre-existing social needs, arising as consequences of the social organisation of modernity. An example of this view is the idea that television is a friend to those who are socially isolated and can be used as a form of escape, to help audiences to forget about the difficulties of everyday life. McQuail's (1987, p. 73) account also states that audiences use television as a "means to engage with one's own identity, emotional issues and conflicts". Accused of behaviouralism and functionalism, this approach proposed that television may be used as a form of problem solving. Katz, Blumer, and Gurevitch (1974) noted that uses and gratifications theory relies on an undeveloped view of "needs" and their point of origin (which may be in the individual, in the social, or in both) and that it also gets caught up in asking what kinds of "problem-solving" might be done. Elliott (1974) deemed this approach individualistic, not sufficiently sociological and "mentalistic", concentrating on the mental states of individuals. For Elliott, the latter is especially problematic as it is impossible for researchers to know anything other than superficially about the mental state of audiences.

It seems that far from being simplistic, however, this idea about what audiences do with television emotionally and in response to the social world, actually raises important psychosocial questions about the role played by this commonplace entertainment technology in contemporary societies. If we take on board these criticisms, then the psychosocial approach proposed here can address this issue of needs and the mental states of individuals, utilising psychoanalysis methodologically and interpretively to offer a more nuanced and layered understanding of the needs, goals, and "problem-solving" activities of viewers, as the case-studies will show.

As I have noted, object relations theory shows how individuals invest in and put objects to important psychic and emotional uses. These uses are in keeping somewhat with the "use-value" of the objects, a function that is inherent and embedded in the "character" of the object/activity (Bollas, 1992, 1995). Like film, television is designed to take viewers through a range of emotions and mental activities, and individuals seek out television to experience its unique character. If one aspect of this concerns the use of television as a means of "escape", or as a way to "pass the time", as uses and gratifications proposed, what kind of "need" is this? And how should we understand it? As my case studies show, television plays a significant but contradictory role in the lives of my interviewees, Chris and Daniel. Their viewing practices indicate that the idea of uses and needs can only be understood as part of a series of complex psychosocial processes that constitute "viewing".

Daniel: filling time

For Daniel, "there is always something good to watch" on television. He is a quintessential modern active viewer, creating his own user-flow through his Sky Plus box, video, and DVD player. Daniel has adopted a practice of delayed gratification, frequently saving up entire series to view in one go at weekends. ("I Sky Plussed every episode and watched it from beginning to end, just getting up to pause it". This prompted him to say: "I'm very sad aren't I?") Daniel refers frequently to viewing as a child with his parents and siblings as "happy times" and this memory stands in sharp contrast to his contemporary viewing environment at home alone. Television was associated with his first taste of power as he recalls that, as the youngest child, he usually "got his own way" when the family debated what to watch. Television viewing also featured at a key moment in Daniel's life, when, as a teenager, he was presented with the unique opportunity for independence when his parents went on holiday and left him alone at home for the first time. He spent the entire week watching the television series *Twin Peaks* (1990). He explains:

> I got a week off work and it was the time before I had a mobile phone and then the phone wasn't likely to ring at home and I wasn't going to be disturbed. So literally I would get up, sit and watch and watch and watch until bedtime. Get up the next day, watch and watch and watch and that's what I did. … You lose yourself in the plot.

Here, it is possible to see something of the dreamlike quality Raymond Williams (1974) ascribed to the continual "flow" of images and sounds that characterises television. (The particular series mentioned in this instance is also recognised as having a dreamlike and surreal quality.) It is interesting that at this moment, when Daniel had his first taste of independence, he made a choice to stay home and exercise control over his viewing using television fully to structure his time. Clearly the mixture of viewing, getting lost in the plot, and his sense of autonomy, provided Daniel with something pleasurable, but he is also aware that his choice was different to the activities of most of his peer group and perceived as odd. He recalls that people at work found his story of a week of *Twin Peaks* as odd and colleagues asked, "Is he weird or something?"

If at eighteen, television viewing stood in opposition to being with his parents, now it stands in opposition to work. As the extract below shows, despite work being "torture", Daniel has made himself indispensable. Time is strictly divided into "pleasurable" and "non-pleasurable" aspects, corresponding to a typical work/leisure divide of modernity which sees work as the space of alienation and leisure as the realm of freedom and creativity.

> I haven't had more than a day's holiday off work in more than two years. I do overtime on Saturdays. I normally leave for work at

6.30 a.m. and get home at 6.30 p.m. … A good film or television programme, whatever makes it worth going to work, it's what you've treated yourself to do. You know you've *tortured* yourself for that many hours, so you think "right I'm gonna make the most of my viewing time".

Daniel told me that he "doesn't know why", but he is no longer taking holidays with or seeing friends as often as he used to. This seems odd, as Daniel is a friendly, personable, and intelligent man. It is possible to see work and television as filling up the large chunks of time which holidays and weekends generate particularly in response to his increasing isolation.

It is useful here to work towards a psychosocial view of time to understand the uses of television for Daniel. Zygmunt Bauman (1999) has argued that the separation of work and leisure associated with modernity can be used to explain particular attitudes to "time". The future, for example, can be seen as a "target" towards which the individual travels in a movement "towards another present distinct from" and "more desirable than" the current present' (p. 3). To achieve this, Bauman suggests, individuals attempt to *manipulate* time, and time is evaluated between modalities of the present of "differing quality and varying value". Advances in technology such as Sky Plus offer the viewer immense power to control time and restructure various "presents", in a way that was previously in the hands of the broadcasters.

One trend that Bauman (ibid., p. 4) notes is that work becomes "an activity that derives its value from what it is not: preparing the ground for non-work and leisure time". Daniel's expression of work as "torture" might be perceived as a contemporary expression of the Marxist concept of alienation. However, free time is not some utopian space for this single man, who for whatever reason, is spending more and more time alone—it is a space that must be filled. Conversely, Daniel has made himself indispensable at work, rarely taking time off and this feeds what Bauman calls an "opposing tendency" of "work for work's sake" (ibid., p. 4). Work provides the justification for filling his leisure time with viewing. This pattern of work and viewing has become the rhythm of Daniel's life but he is also anxious about this, as he frequently worries he is a "sad case", indicating a degree of interpellation by negative viewing discourses, where watching TV is wasted time.

Time and time-travelling is also a feature in a number of Daniel's favourite texts, including television programmes such as *Doctor Who* (1963–present). However, he spent a long time discussing one particular emotive and compelling film text which he first encountered on television and has since purchased on DVD: *Simon Birch* (1998). He watches this film often and it frequently makes him cry. It is possible to see the repeated viewing of this film (which for Daniel is part of "watching TV") as an example of the way in which emotional concerns affect the construction of a user-flow. It tells the story of a life-limited child and his attempts to circumvent this by achieving goals and attempting to do something heroic before he dies. The film explores the limits of time, the idea of time passing too quickly and as something that is "under threat". During the interview, he produced a copy of the DVD and I was struck by the remarkable physical resemblance between the actor who plays Simon Birch's friend and father figure and Daniel. This suggests that there might be some biographical events or questions around parent-child identification, loss, and desire that make the film so evocative and emotional. He also explains this character is a "nice guy" and I found myself feeling sad that a "nice guy" like Daniel was single, and felt sadness in our unspoken communication.[9]

I think that it is possible to understand this issue of time in relation to television and its uses more fully by using insights from post-Kleinian object relations. It has been suggested that television functions as a transitional object due to its constancy and its ability to soothe anxiety and survive aggressive onslaughts (Silverstone, 1994). Transitional phenomena are internalised into psychic structures that, in health, one can draw on for "comfort" in anxiety-provoking situations (Grolnick, 1990). As I have noted, Daniel talked about family viewing and he explained that television had been an important object used for entertainment, communication, and intimacy. It is possible to think of television as an "evocative object" (Bollas, 1992, 1995) that links Daniel with family and childhood, even if this is idealised and coloured by phantasy, in response to the solitary life he currently leads.

Winnicott's (1971) ontological concept of "holding" can help us to examine the nature of being and its relationship to *time* more effectively. It is used to explore the "experience of being alive" and the means by which a "sense of continuity of being is sustained over time" (Ogden, 2004, p. 1350) which Winnicott calls "going on being" (1965b, p. 44). In earliest infancy, prior to the child becoming aware of itself as a subject, time is "other" to the infant. The world of clocks, schedules, routine, and calendars is profoundly threatening at this stage where what is "not me" is extremely disrupting to the child's continuity of being. One important function of "maternal preoccupation" sees the mother, forgoing her needs, for sleep for example, to absorb the impact of man-made time as she attunes herself to the infant's rhythms and needs. The mother provides a setting in which the child can gather together the various "bits", which eventually allow the child to feel integrated.

Transitional phenomena occur in a "third space", an area of experience between reality and fantasy. It is in this space that the child learns to experience and tolerate being alone as well as how to manage the anxieties associated with this. Here time becomes a symbol or mark of the external world beyond the child's control but, at the same time, it is connected to the child's physical and psychological rhythms (Ogden, 2004, p. 1353). Time is other to the infant but she copes with this as she learns to experience a continuity of self over time. Another primitive form associated with holding is known as the "autistic contiguous" (Ogden, 1989). This primitive sensory mode of experience is concerned with the infant's relationship to "surfaces", such as the mother's skin, the rhythm of her breathing, and changes in temperature at the skin surface that sustain the child in a "non-reflexive state of sensory 'going on being'" (ibid., p. 32). The soothing relationships with sounds and shapes and surfaces are important as they are the most primitive forms of holding that the child experiences, and anxiety can be reduced in later life by allowing oneself to become "moulded" (ibid., p. 33) to surface and sensory environment. This offers an explanation for why lying on the sofa in the dark watching the flickering lights of the television performs a holding function for Daniel as a response to living alone. Television viewing also becomes a setting, which Daniel can experience as a holding environment, because it allows him, through his manipulation of time, some sense of control around the demands placed upon him by time in the social world.

Object relations theories emphasise the value of creative living in emotional well-being. This begins in infancy and involves being open to the unique qualities of the world of objects, responding to desires, allowing oneself to become *immersed* and *absorbed* in objects, which Winnicott (1965a, 1971) associated with the freedom he assigned to the "true", rather than an adaptive "false" self. However, the social demands of material need and the workplace put limits on freedom, which Daniel recognises and, as an active and creative viewer, subverts by using technology to manipulate time. Daniel opens himself up to and absorbs himself in the sensory dreamlike qualities of television viewing, which can be seen as a creative act that should enrich the unconscious. Bollas (1995, p. 92) proposed that creative living is not possible without unconscious freedom and it is impossible to achieve this creativity in any meaningful way without "variety", "difference", and "uniqueness". Daniel however, has chosen to engage with a narrow colony of objects consistent with what has been called "conservative object use" (Bollas, 1995; Mann, 2002). Such objects are symptomatic of the barriers that some individuals may (unwittingly) construct, which hinder the development of openness, but as I am suggesting here, they are also an unconscious response to the social. While Daniel is open to the viewing "object", his viewing is contradictory as he expresses concerns about "not seeing people" and says that he spends "too much time watching TV". It is this contradiction that can explain in part the melancholic tone that tinted the interviews.

Is it possible that Daniel's absorption in television might make him an example of what Bollas (1995) has called a "preoccupied" or "passionate" person? Here the individual "conjures up a mental space into which he can bring all of his interests to the exclusion of all else" (ibid., p. 79). In passionate object relating, the experience of getting "hooked" or "lost" (as Daniel did at a significant biographical moment with *Twin Peaks*) is compelling and the subject is changed by the experience, providing scope for creative thought and living. However, where there is anxiety, perhaps as a result of a social situation such as living alone, the individual "conjures up an object of such interest in order to preoccupy the potential space of a more liberated object use" and this "betrays the anxieties that generate such a move on the part of the ego" (ibid., p. 88).

The subject often lacks insight into how habits and practices became established. It is not possible to know fully what motivated the initial decision almost twenty years previously, to spend his first week of independence watching television continuously, but this powerful sensory experience undoubtedly had an impact on Daniel. At that time, Daniel found that television viewing met a range of desires affectively and intellectually, while, at the same time, being "held" in time, and serving transitional functions. At the same time, this retreat set in motion a gradual but steady move over the next two decades that see Daniel become socially isolated. His time became split between a starkly dichotomous understanding of "work" and "home", and it is interesting to note here that, for Bollas (1995), "home" can be seen as referring to a restricted set of objects and activities. It is possible that, for whatever reason, the world outside his home provokes anxiety. By filling his time with something "pleasurable", it is possible that he does not have to confront the anxiety and difficulties associated with venturing into the world and trying to make relationships and face possible rejection. Here we are reminded once more of Bauman's (1999) suggestion that the future exists like a "target", towards which the individual travels, hoping for fulfilment. If you are single, live alone, and are getting older, the future can also provoke anxiety. Television technology allows Daniel to manipulate time, filling non-work time and keeping him "occupied". He is able to use this to weather the consequences of his decision not to socialise and the demands of time passing as he approaches middle age. This makes the demands of the future temporarily disappear as he is able to exist in a world of the present in which he has some control over how he "passes time". However, it is this that accounts for the feeling of sadness which coloured the interviews.

Chris: "twitchy" viewing

For Chris, viewing is also a contradictory experience. Leisure time also presents a challenge and viewing often generates anxiety. Unlike Daniel, who clearly delineates his work and leisure time, for Chris, the worlds of leisure and work overlap and this presents him with dilemmas. Chris is in the early stages of a career in information services within academia, specialising in film. His professional and personal interests overlap as Chris could be described as a cineaste. The disciplinary demands of developing a professional identity in contemporary neo-liberal economies influence Chris, as he continually feels that he should be working. The thought of watching television is appealing but makes him "feel guilty". As a cineaste with an intellectual interest in films and also as part of his work identity he spends a lot of time recording, collecting, and cataloguing videos and DVDs of films and television shows, rather than sitting down to watch them. Chris explains that he adopted this practice in response to a time of change involving living alone, worries about his career, and the end of a relationship:

> … because I was having a bit of a ropey time and I needed something to do. I was kind of *pushing things away* and getting a little bit *obsessed* about stuff. I got really *obsessed* about recording films.

> I ended up with mountains of videos and all these films I never
> have a chance to watch. I'm *really anal* about stuff like that you
> know.

He explains that when he watches television or films at home the experience of viewing alone generates anxiety. He is unable to relax as he is wasting time and always feels he should be working or "or doing something productive". Chris explains that when he sits down to watch a film he "gets twitchy" (anxious and feeling "guilty about not work-ing" *and* his inability to relax). He thinks that this is something gener-ated in response to being on his own:

> Well instead of sitting watching the film I'd be worried I should be
> doing the washing up or something. And I'd get up and do it half
> way through the film. And there have been times when … I haven't
> even watched the end of the film. I can't relax if I'm on my own.
> I find that a bit frustrating really because I come home from work
> and all I want to do is *slob out* and watch a film, not necessarily to
> totally engage with it—but to *switch off*.

Unlike Daniel, it seems that Chris is not able or is reluctant to lose him-self in viewing. He cannot allow himself to become fully absorbed and, at times, maintains what might be described as a tangential relation-ship to the act of concentrated viewing through his cataloguing and collecting. With his knowledge of cinematic theory, Chris would know that pleasurable film viewing is usually associated with an intense absorbing "gaze", rather than the distracted "glance" of television viewing (Ellis, 1989). However, even this potential absorption seems to be a pressure for Chris as his desire is to "switch off" and "slob out". Partly this relates to the *choice* of text, as he actively seeks out films to watch that frequently generate an unpleasant viewing experience. He describes such films as "threatening" because they are something he "doesn't intellectually *understand*". Following a viewing of a diffi-cult film that he does not feel he understands, he then has a new set of demands to "chase it up and read around it and *make myself* understand it", presumably like the academics he deals with on a daily basis, whom he assumes *do* understand difficult films.

Rather than a form of relaxation then, his viewing is an important part of the intellectual labour he associates with his professional and personal identity. The interview, however, is peppered with statements about Chris's lack of confidence in his professional abilities. He worries that he is a "loser" in his professional life and in relationships. Discourses of taste converge around the concept of intellect. This is particularly prominent for someone who works in an environment based on intellectual ability and questions of "good taste", which have been linked to questions of differential social power (Bourdieu, 1984).

Chris is the middle child of a working class manual labourer and a housewife and represents an example of widening participation in higher education. He is a first generation university graduate who has entered a profession and achieved what would be deemed upward social mobility. As the child of working class parents, however, he does not benefit from inculcation into the bourgeois world in which he now operates. One way that this translates for Chris is into anxiety generated by the dilemmas posed by relaxation versus intellectual viewing. At the same time, he is constantly trying to deal with difficult feelings about not using his time "productively", which can be seen as symptomatic of the pressures of life in neo-liberal societies to achieve, financially and professionally.

Chris lists a number of films as "favourites" that he acknowledges are paradoxically also "threatening" to him, as they are recognised for complex storylines, plot, unconventional dialogue, and characters whose psychological motivation is difficult to understand. He feels a sense of fulfilment only after he has mastered these films intellectually. One theme that emerged in relation to a number of these films is that they contain characters he perceives as "losers". I want to suggest that it is possible to look more closely at specific points of identification with some of these texts to understand the conflicts and anxiety generated by solitary domestic viewing.

Barton Fink (1991) was first viewed at the cinema and Chris now owns this film on DVD. This text is deemed a favourite, but it is one that creates a contradictory and conflictual experience when viewed on TV at home, as it generates anxiety and threat. This suggests something about the way in which viewers can use the domestic television set and viewing experience to address emotional concerns.

Chris says:

> … *Barton Fink*, which I really like, but it is *gut wrenching* and *sick making*, because he was such a *fake, weak-willed* guy. I find that a bit

disturbing really. I *hate* seeing really fake people, really *weak-willed* people who are really unsuccessful and to see that on film it gives me the *shivers* because I would so hate to be in their position—it's almost *scary*.

The tone of this extract suggests a level of fear that is in excess of anything suggested by the text and implies, given the biographical information Chris offered in the interview, that the fear revolves around points of identification for Chris. The film concerns a man's struggles with "intelligence", failure in professional life, relationships with women, and feelings of discomfort and aggression towards his working class neighbour. "Barton Fink" is a moderately successful screenwriter who is contracted to write a screenplay for a large Hollywood studio but develops writer's block. When he eventually finishes the script, it is not well received and he is devastated to be accused of lacking talent. There are numerous scenes in the film where Barton struggles to pass the time and to find a way through his problem. He is often curled up on his bed with a pillow over his head to shut everything out, evoking Chris's desire to "slob out" and not keep working.

There are points in the film where the viewer sees close-up shots of Fink feeling *extremely uncomfor*table *as he views films*. The sight of a weak, unsuccessful, fake, intellectual man on screen is very difficult for Chris because it presents him with a number of his own fears around exposure of his professional limitations and difficulties with relationships. However, what is "gut wrenching" for Chris is not simply that the film presents him with an image of his own fears, but, more specifically, that it evokes his identification with this flawed character who tries to portray himself as a cultured intellectual.

Neo-liberal subjectivities are formed in relation to the demands to "perform" and "achieve", particularly for professionals in highly-pressured arenas, but this generates anxiety (see Elliott & Lemert, 2006; Layton, 2003). Chris has not been immune to the demands to perform and be successful and it is possible to see the pressures he faces as part of the lived experience of social mobility. Social and physical mobility also change familial relationships. Layton (2003) describes painful processes associated with moving from being working class into the middle class and one distressing aspect sees the upwardly mobile individual find aspects of the self and others abhorrent (for example, those associated with being working class such as taste and disposition). The character, "Fink", finds his working class neighbour disgusting and I have proposed that it is Chris's identification with the character that is problematic for him. This aspect of contemporary upwardly mobile subjectivity can be explored further by examining identification in the light of Chris's biography and by returning to the theme of "threatening" viewing.

We have seen such threatening viewing for Chris associated with being alone ("watching on my own I find quite challenging"). In contrast, he explains what he calls "harmless" viewing:

> My family would always be about ... if I was sitting watching my dad would probably just be coming home from work and he'd come in when I was watching, for example. And Mum'd be buzzin' about doin' somethin'. ... Television definitely does bring back that sort of memory, that homely safe feeling.

This "safe", distracted viewing is associated with childhood, home, family, and the rhythm of the day (Lacey, 1997). Chris also tells a heartwarming story of watching films with his father who would fall asleep, tired after a day's work, describing the intimacy as "bliss". This indicates something of the complex ways in which memories become significant in response to the present or that television functions in some instances as a "mnemic" object (Bollas, 1992, p. 34), enabling Chris to touch base with previous positive self-states in a way that reduces anxiety. However, his viewing is also entwined in complex processes of loss associated with his social mobility, which is felt most acutely around his painful loss of intimacy with his father and in a particular form of sibling rivalry:

> I've got a younger brother who is just the total opposite to me and he lives about two hundred yards from my parents, and has never been away, never does anythin'. It sounds really harsh on him but, erm, he's married and really conservative and went to work with my dad. He's just really quite different to me.

Chris's brother really is his opposite; as he is working class, married, unambitious. Despite this, he retains a form of intimacy and commonality with his much loved father that "successful" Chris will never experience again in the same way.

Staying with the specific but contradictory ways in which this plays out in relation to his television viewing, I want to return to the idea that television operates as a transitional object. While viewing can be conflictual and anxiety provoking for Chris, he still manages to find a viewing space and adopts what I will call an "evocative transitional text" that helps to resolve some of these conflicts. The US comedy, *Frasier* (1993–2004) was already well established before he "discovered" it and he instantly became hooked. Once discovered, it became subject to the usual treatment: "I started recording them every night, I got really obsessed with recording those". This is a text that Chris *can* and *does* watch "over and over again". He uses the text as "wallpaper", explaining. "I have it as background noise or whatever". His use is in keeping with the idea of a sensationally based transitional phenomenon, used to manage separation anxiety, felt most acutely by the child at bedtime (Winnicott, 1971). Significantly, then, this is a text that is repeatedly watched in his bedroom:

> What I do which is a bit sad, is when I go to bed, I've got a video in my room. And I'll put on *Frasier*. I'm not necessarily watching it, it's just background noise really, *harmless* [my emphasis], I do that a lot, although I try to phase myself out of doing that. I should go up there and I should *read*, or do something more stimulating, but to be honest, I go to bed to slob out.

Clearly, even this soothing text that allows him to slob out, still provokes a degree of anxiety about his use of time. Chris is constantly dealing with conflict between "working", intellectual study, and doing chores, etc., and the desire to relax and do nothing. He associates self-discipline with dynamism and is constantly disappointed by his indolence. The final sentence of the extract calls to mind the image of a frustrated, "weak" "Barton Fink" lying across his bed struggling with his inability to write. In *Frasier* however, he has found a text that helps him deal with the contradictions and conflicts between his inner and outer worlds and its transitional qualities allow him permission to use the text in an anxiety reducing setting.

If we examine character and storyline in *Frasier*, it is easy to see the points of identification but also, I think more significantly, the way in which this text helps resolve contradictions for Chris. The comedy revolves around sibling rivalry and an unconventional domestic arrangement. "Frasier Crane" is a psychiatrist and a cultured intellectual and despite his supposed superior knowledge about "women", he is unlucky in love. He is, however, the son of "Martin", a working class man who now lives with him. While "Frasier" prefers high culture, his father sits in a tatty old recliner chair, drinks beer, and watches TV. His father's carer, "Daphne", is a northern English working class woman who, like Chris's own mother "buzzes" about the apartment. The comedy is generated around the themes of class and familial conflicts. "Martin" and "Daphne" frequently undermine "Frasier's" posturing with blue-collar values. There are constant clashes emerging out of their intellectual and class differences, which they must negotiate. However, the relationships are held together by a deep bond of love. Despite their differences, there are scenes of love and intimacy between father and his sons. The "Frasier" family live together happily despite their class differences.

"Frasier" is Chris's favourite character:

> He's really *calming*. Because he's a buffoon, really. He's obviously really intelligent but he's also a bit of a buffoon. So it's quite heartening to know that even these people who are super intelligent aren't perfect, they can be a bit flaky or whatever.

"Frasier" is a "buffoon" but Chris finds him calming, identifying with his flakiness, while sending up intelligent people as one way of coping with his anxieties about his professional and intellectual identity.

Aspects of the characters' lives, plot settings, plot development, and comedy make "Frasier" an "evocative transitional object". For Bollas (1992), object selection is a form of evidence, which articulates something about the subject's self-experience allowing the self to "speak". Evocative objects carry a history and bear the marks of parental provision and internal object relations. Bollas argues that "the decision to use an object rests with the unconscious aims of the person" (1992, p. 36) and crucially this builds on the importance Winnicott placed on an individual's use of subjective and transitional objects for psychic survival and growth. "Evocative objects" are distinguished by the way in which they contribute to psychic growth and creative living and they are not static as they stimulate "use". For this reason, a text cannot be "read" or analysed as a singular bounded object, it is something that is put to use—in this case by Chris—in a specific setting in particular ways, holding potential transformative functions for Chris. However, this must be qualified because evocative objects can also be "born of conflict" (ibid., p. 79), which suggests something of the difficult situation in which this text was discovered and put to use. The soothing transitional aspects of the text concern the ways in which the "family" resolve conflicts and continue to love each other and experience intimacy. The humour also helps Chris to manage the anxiety associated with his professional life. *Frasier* evokes memories of family viewing as a child to help him to manage anxiety as well as helping him to come to terms with issues of loss associated with social mobility.

Conclusion

This chapter has outlined some of the ways that television use has changed from a shared activity to a more individualised practice following the advances associated with time-shift and digital technologies. I have suggested that the idea of family viewing is partly a construction and cannot automatically be associated with communication, intimacy, and emotional security. However, as the case studies have shown, this idealised notion is evoked by these viewers in response to the difficulties associated with being single and living alone. It should not surprise us then that for some viewers, like those described here, television should exist both consciously and unconsciously as a site where feelings of loss and desire are evoked, experienced, and opened up to the possibility of emotional change. The studies attest to the psychosocial significance of domestic television in the pre-digital era and the psychic possibilities that have emerged in relation to the developments of digital and time-shift technologies. Such developments are also significant when applied to the idea of audiences using the television set in combination with other technologies to construct a gendered, emotionally germane user-flow.

Television viewing is also a socio-cultural activity, and I have described some of the ways that television has been understood academically and how these approaches have been taken up and translated into some commonsense, moral, and even dystopian discourses. I broadened the idea of "uses" and "needs" to think about the emotional experiences of television as an object with specific uses, as an activity, and the relationship with specific texts. I have explored one prominent and specific discourse around the notion of television as a leisure time or "time passing" activity, which in different ways can generate anxiety, as the examples above show. Such studies have the potential to illuminate aspects of increasingly complex relationships to work and leisure time in neo-liberal capitalist societies. These accounts illustrate complex psychosocial relationships between individual biographies, discourse, and social organisation, and internal psychic conflicts and imaginative lives. Psychoanalysis also helps us to think about the emotional consequences of social organisation and change.

Television viewing as an activity is contradictory, which is why established schools of thought that concentrate on "pleasures", "uses", and "needs" must also acknowledge that the meaning of such terms are not transparent and that they mask complex emotional and affective processes. My case studies also show that while the practice of viewing can be examined as a specific activity, it is important not to neglect the *content* of the text being viewed. This focus on content and its meaning suggests the significance of holding on to and developing textual analysis methods within television research.

Watching television to pass the time or relax, then, involves complex psychosocial processes and this chapter has used the idea of evocative transitional objects, suggesting that they perform important but contradictory holding and anxiety management functions to illuminate this. Perhaps those much maligned uses and gratifications theorists, with their focus on television as a problem solving activity, were right to note that viewers use television to engage with emotional conflicts both consciously and unconsciously. Psychoanalysis provides an important set of theories and concepts to supplement sociological approaches that have dominated television study and therefore helps to improve our understanding of the role, place, and experience of television for contemporary audiences.

Notes

1. "Reception" studies, including those concerned with the way audiences decode texts in social settings, have largely adopted sociological interpretive frameworks to understand the ideological and social effects of texts. In contrast, film studies embraced Freudian and Lacanian ideas to explain the affective and identificatory pleasures of the cinematic experience. For accounts of these developments, see Lapsley and Westlake (1998) and Morley (1992).
2. Notable exceptions include Roger Silverstone's (1994) object relations influenced account of television as a transitional object and Tania Modleski's (1982) discussion of fantasy to understand women's psychic investments in soap operas.

3. Valerie Walkerdine's (1986) "Video Replay" essay stands as a landmark psychosocial study as it took account of the social, historical, and cultural specificity of the working class family she studied, whilst utilising the psychoanalytic concept of fantasy, to show how and why investments of fantasy in the film *Rocky II*, repeatedly watched on a video recorder, could not be divorced from the family and the relational context in which the viewing takes place.

4. The study was based on twelve long, in-depth interviews and a series of letters. The respondents' names have been changed and personal details removed to ensure anonymity. For a detailed account of the FANI method and critical evaluation, see Hollway and Jefferson (2012).

5. I have explored this elsewhere, in particular the role and impact of the researcher in the joint production of data (see Whitehouse-Hart, 2013, forthcoming). However, I would argue that it is still possible to exercise the same care of the subject required of all research with human subjects (see previous note). While psychoanalytic research utilises a language borrowed from clinical practice, it is used to enhance understanding about affective and emotional processes, not to diagnose. In this sense, it is no different from any research paradigm, which uses technical and academic language to interpret data in which the interviewee may not recognise his or her representation in the data.

6. The Office of National Statistics Labour Force Survey 2012 states that the number of people living alone without spouse, partners, or family rose from 6.6 million in 1996 to 7.6 million in 2012.

7. Politically, the imperative has been to look for the "active", "critical" audience. Yet this goal has contributed to a reluctance to accept a view that television viewing could in any way be conflictual or present emotional difficulties for viewers, which from a psychoanalytic perspective, is an inevitable aspect of everyday life.

8. It is not uncommon, periodically, to find television associated with dystopian visions of modernity. See recent examples linking TV viewing with poor IQ, physical and emotional health (Parker-Pope, 2008; Walsh, 2011).

9. See Whitehouse-Hart (2013, forthcoming) for account of unconscious dynamics in research situations.

References

Bainbridge, C. & Yates, C. (2007). Everything to play for: Masculinities, trauma and the pleasures of DVD technology. In: C. Bainbridge, S. Radstone, M. Rustin, & C. Yates (Eds.), *Culture and the Unconscious* (pp. 107–122). London: Palgrave Macmillan.

Bauman, Z. (1999). Modern adventures of procrastination. *Parallax*, 5(1): 3–6.

Beynon, J. (2002). *Masculinities and Culture*. Buckingham, UK: Open University Press.

Bollas, C. (1992). *Being a Character: Psychoanalysis and Self Experience*. London: Routledge.

Bollas, C. (1995). *Cracking Up: the Work of Unconscious Experience*. London: Routledge.

Bourdieu, P. (1984). *Distinction: A Social Critique of the Judgement of Taste* (R. Nice, Trans.). London: Routledge and Kegan Paul, 2010.

Caldwell, J. (2003). Second shift media aesthetics programming, interactivity and user flows. In: A. Everett & J. Caldwell (Eds.), *New Media Theories and Practices of Digitextuality* (pp. 127–44). London: Routledge.

Elliott, A. & Lemert, C. (2006). *The New Individualism: The Emotional Costs of Globalization*. London: Routledge.

Elliott, A. & Urry, J. (2010). *Mobile Lives*. London: Routledge.

Elliott, P. (1974). Uses and gratifications research: A critique and a sociological alternative. In: J. G. Blumer & E. Katz (Eds.), *The Uses of Mass Communications* (pp. 249–268). London: Sage.

Ellis, J. (1989). *Visible Fictions*. London: Routledge.

Evans, J. (2000). *Psychoanalysis and Psychosocial Relations: Identity in Question: D853*. [Study Guide, Block 2.] Milton Keynes, UK: Open University Press.

Frosh, S. (2010). *Psychoanalysis Outside the Clinic*. Basingstoke, UK: Palgrave Macmillan.

Grolnick, S. (1990). *The Work and Play of Winnicott*. Northvale, NJ: Jason Aronson.

Hollway, W. & Jefferson, T. (2012). *Doing Qualitative Research Differently: a Psychosocial Approach*. London: Sage.

Katz, E., Blumer, J. G., & Gurevitch, M. (1974). Utilization of mass communication by the individual. In: J. G. Blumer & E. Katz (Eds.), *The Uses of Mass Communications* (pp. 19–32). London: Sage.

Klinger, B. (2006). *Beyond the Multiplex, Cinema, New Technologies and the Home*. Berkeley, CA: University of California Press.

Lacey, J. (1997). *Seeing Through Happiness: Class, Gender and Popular Film: Liverpool Women Remember the 50s Film Musical*. [Unpublished PhD thesis, Goldsmiths College, University of London.]

Lapsley, R. & Westlake, M. (1988). *Film Theory*. Manchester, UK: Manchester University Press.

Layton, L. (2003). That place gives me the heebie jeebies. *Critical Psychology*, 10: 36–49.

Lopate, C. (1977). Daytime television: you'll never want to leave home. *Radical America*, 11(1): 33–51.

Mann, G. (2002). Transformational, conservative and terminal objects: the application of Bollas's concepts to practice. In: J. Scalia (Ed.), *The Vitality of Objects* (pp. 58–78). Middletown, CT: Wesleyan University Press.

McQuail, D. (1987). *Mass Communication Theory*. London: Sage.

Modleski, T. (1982). *Loving with a Vengeance: Mass Produced Fantasies for Women*. Hamden, CT: Shoestring Press.

Morley, D. (1992). *Television Audiences and Cultural Studies*. London: Routledge.

Ogden, T. (1989). *The Primitive Edge of Reason*. Northvale, NJ: Jason Aronson.

Ogden, T. (2004). On holding and containing, being and dreaming. *International Journal of Psychoanalysis*, 85: 1349–1364.

Parker-Pope, T. (2008). A one-eyed invader in the bedroom. www.nytimes.com/2008/03/04/health/04well.html (accessed 17 June, 2012).

Silverstone, R. (1994). *Television and Everyday Life*. London: Routledge.

Spigel, L. (1992). *Make Room for TV: Television and Family in Postwar America*. Chicago, IL: University of Chicago Press.

Walkerdine, V. (1986). Video replay: families, films and fantasy. In: V. Burgin, J. Donald, & C. Kaplan (Eds.), *Formations of Fantasy* (pp. 167–199). London: Routledge.

Walsh, F. (2011). Can watching TV make you die younger? *http://www.bbc.co.uk/news/health-14534025* (accessed 16 August, 2012).

Whitehead, S. M. (2002). *Men and Masculinities: Key Themes and Directions*. London: Polity.

Whitehouse-Hart, J. (2010). Subjectivity, experience and method in film and television viewing: a psycho-social approach. [Unpublished doctoral dissertation, Open University, Milton Keynes, UK.]

Whitehouse-Hart, J. (2012). Surrendering to the dream: an account of the unconscious dynamics of a research relationship. *Journal of Research Practice, Special Edition, Psychodynamic Research*, 8(2). *http://jrp.icaap.org*

Williams, R. (1974). *Television: Technology and Cultural Form*. London: Routledge.

Winnicott, D. W. (1965a). Ego distortion in terms of true and false self. In: *The Maturational Processes and the Facilitating Environment* (pp. 140–153). London: Karnac, 1990.

Winnicott, D. W. (1965b). The theory of the parent-infant relationship. In: *The Maturational Processes and the Facilitating Environment* (pp. 37–55). London: Karnac, 1990.

Winnicott, D. W. (1971). *Playing and Reality*. London: Routledge.

Wood, H. (2009). *Talking with Television: Women, Talk Shows and Modern Self-Reflexivity*. Urbana, IL: University of Illinois Press.

List of television programmes cited

Doctor Who (1963–present). BBC1, UK.

Frasier (1993–2004). Creators and producers, David Angell, Peter Casey, & David Lee, NBC, US.

Simon Birch (1998). Director, Mark Johnson, US.

Twin Peaks (1990). Director, David Lynch, ABC, US.

PART III

TELEVISION EXPERIENCES

Television as "docutherapy": an interview with Richard McKerrow and Jonathan Phang

Siobhan Lennon-Patience and Marit Røkeberg

This chapter contains the transcript of interviews with Love Productions' Creative Director, Richard McKerrow, and television presenter and fashion manager, Jonathan Phang; these two interviews were conducted in connection with the documentary McKerrow and Phang made in 2009 about the 1989 *Marchioness* disaster: *The Marchioness: A Survivor's Story* (2009). The documentary, produced by Love Productions, tells the story of the sinking of the pleasure boat, *Marchioness*, on the Thames: a horrible accident that took the lives of fifty-one people, including some of Phang's best friends. The focus in the documentary is on Phang's journey, in which he comes to terms with what happened, as he returns to emotionally evocative locations, seeking out other survivors and relatives of people who died. Throughout the documentary process, Phang's recollections and thoughts about the disaster and his life before and after are recorded, as well as his emotional experience of encountering memories and old friends and acquaintances.

McKerrow and Phang had already built up a professional and personal rapport through their collaboration on a number of projects when they decided to make the twenty-year anniversary documentary about the *Marchioness* disaster. For McKerrow, the aim of Love Productions is to devise programmes focusing on topics that are emotionally engaging for both audiences and contributors. He suggests that participating in this type of documentary has the potential to be therapeutic for contributors, with the scope for them to go on an emotional journey. In 2010, McKerrow and Phang participated in the Media and the Inner World (MIW)/Freud Museum conference "Remote Control: Psychoanalysis and Television", held at the Anna Freud Centre in London. At the event, they talked about how the process of making reality television is experienced by both producers and contributors, drawing on their own experiences.

The "Remote Control" conference created a space for dialogue between media practitioners, psychotherapists, and academics; it was a space to explore the possibilities of interdisciplinary ways of thinking, practising, and researching. A particularly lively discussion arose following the contributions made by McKerrow and Phang, with some arguing that there *could be* such a thing as honourable filming, indeed suggesting that television had the capacity to provide a kind of cathartic experience for the participant. In contrast, for other contributors to the discussion, there was a view that reality television appeals only to our baser instincts with participant as exhibitionist and viewer as voyeur. Perhaps what is revealed in these exchanges, are the tensions of contemporary society that Silverstone (1994) says can be both articulated through and ameliorated by television. For Silverstone, television is both a "disturber and comforter" (p. 3), as on the one hand, it provides an arguably vital platform for self-expression, yet on the other, it represents a powerful international cultural-industrial complex, underpinned by the machinations of the market.

The value of such an exchange of perspectives is that it allows for the exploration of views, whether positive, negative, or ambivalent. It is in the consideration of these attitudes towards the reality television genre that we can think about what is at stake for subjects in a mediatised environment. Does reality television provide a space for the subject to tell his or her own story as part of a recovery process, or does this form of television represent a step too far in the blurring of the boundaries between the public and the private sphere? The following in-depth interviews arose from the MIW/Freud Museum conference and seek to explore in more detail some of the key themes emerging from McKerrow and Phang's talk.

* * *

Richard McKerrow is the Creative Director of Love Productions, a UK based independent production company that he set up in 2004. He began his career in print journalism, writing for *The Nation* magazine in New York. Subsequently he moved into television production, joining Yorkshire Television, making internationally focused documentaries for ITV's *First Tuesday* (1983–1993), and working on the weekly live international news show for Channel Four, *The World This Week* (1989). Later he joined Channel Four as a commissioning editor in education before setting up Love Productions in 2004 with the aim of making "thought-provoking, entertaining television". He has been the executive producer for shows such as *The Baby Borrowers* (2007), *Make Bradford British* (2012), and *The Great British Bake Off* (2010–present), among many series and documentaries. We began by asking McKerrow to tell us more about what he thought the potential therapeutic possibilities of television might be.

Interview with Richard McKerrow, 5 April, 2012

RM: "Docutherapy"—that's what I call it, I suddenly realised that's what we were really doing—making, practitioning docutherapy. Documentary made in the right way, is a form of docutherapy; for the producer, as long as you are open to being changed by what you are doing, and brave enough to go forward, and ask questions that are psychologically exploratory. It is definitely therapeutic for the contributor, because the presence of a camera can act as a form of catharsis, as a cathartic tool. If you can pull off those two things, then the viewer will go on a journey. It is a therapeutic journey, because the viewer sitting alone at home, thinks all their problems are all their own, then suddenly they see someone brave enough to explore something emotional from their past, their history; and it connects and then suddenly they realise that they are not alone. Television can be, I think, an incredibly powerful tool.

MIW: You say the camera is a particularly useful tool, why do you think that would make a difference?

RM: If I bring a camera in here now it changes the situation: it heightens it, it carries a form of electricity. Everyone is suddenly very aware that it's there. I think handled in the right way it can act a bit like a priest in a confessional, except it is even more powerful because it is not private and confidential. It is incredibly public and it is incredible because you know what you say then could be seen by millions of people.

MIW: That is quite a departure from how people may usually perceive a therapeutic dialogue, which would usually take place in private.

RM: Yes, I think that it is not for everybody. I think that human beings, particularly in Britain, we are a very closed culture, and we are not very pro-therapy. I mean, I do therapy, and I try to force myself to admit that to people, because I think that that is important, because most people are embarrassed about it, and keep it all private. I do actually think that it can be good for everyone to open up and talk and communicate. Because what is wrong with communicating to people?

MIW: So your contributor to one of your documentaries, who is it that they are talking to?

RM: Obviously, I accept that whatever I think, it might not be for everyone; privacy is a personal choice. I can say what I think, but as long as I ask the question of someone, "Would you like to talk about it?" and they say, "I don't want to talk about it", but it is better to have asked the question than to have never asked it at all. I think that Jonathan is a very good example; it will be interesting to talk to him later to see if he is in the same space. Because Jonathan is quite a public facing person, he's an extrovert, he is an organiser, he brings people together; that has been the story of his life. I think for him, the act of making the programme made him, he wanted to do it publicly. That, for him, was therapeutic, opening up and doing it publicly. Even though within the programme he does do a therapy session, he actually said that he had never done therapy. It will be interesting to talk to him today to see whether that helped. For him, the public sort of thing was more useful than the private sort of thing.

MIW: Have you found that experience with other contributors? That they found it useful to communicate knowing that it was public?

RM: Definitely. I would love someone to do some proper research into the effects of television on contributors. I think that there is a kind of blanket lazy, oh, television screws people up, it exposes them. Actually, I think the right sort of television made by proper professionals, and actually most people have really a qualitative emotionally enhancing, emotionally healthy experience, which helps them and takes them forward. I would like to see that body of work shown to the government so that the government and broadcasters actually put money into looking after people and continuing that work after people have been in television programmes. For me, that is the thing that I feel most concerned about, in the sense that, we are making a television programme that involves a group of people, taking them on a journey, or an experience that hopefully will be beneficial. We can do that by talking to them in the first place about what the programme is about, and whether it is going to be good for them. We can then look after them, be honest with them about how hard it is going to be, the good things, the bad things, the difficult things are. We can then do that through the process of filming, questioning them, making sure that the experience remains positive. When the filming is finished, we always show them the cuts of the films before they are ever transmitted. That is just a particular philosophy and policy that we have at Love Productions.

MIW: Do your responsibilities go beyond the programme after it has been aired?

RM: Yes, but the problem is that those responsibilities are not funded. Yes, they go beyond filming, they go beyond edit, they go beyond press and publicity, but all we can do is offer a phone line. We have in the past funded therapy sessions if that is required or needed and we have sometimes persuaded broadcasters to give us money so that we can support people around the time of the transmission of the programme. But, I have to be honest, soon after that—bang—it all fades away because there is no budget, there is no money, there is no funding. Maybe, in most cases that is fine, people are happy, they have been through the experience and they can return to their normal lives. But that's where I can't absolutely put my hand on my heart and say that there isn't a bit of a kind of cliff fall.

MIW: Do you think there is a long-term benefit in the way that you are working?

RM: Definitely, I think so. We have to move forward and carry on making programmes. I haven't done scientific research on it. I wouldn't ever present this argument without couching it very carefully by saying it is just my impression. It is certainly the kind of verbal evidence, verbal feedback we get.

MIW: So would you argue that you take your responsibilities seriously?

RM: Very seriously. The point is that, aside from the fact that the regulation of television is extremely strict, I think that there is a level of professionalism within television. Certainly we have protocols and guidelines that we devise for all the programmes. We have done constructive documentaries involving children, where we have worked closely with the psychologists and psychiatrists. We take even more responsibility than even OFCOM (the regulator) does, in terms of being careful and making sure that it is going to be a beneficial experience. That doesn't mean it's not going to be a tough experience, but that is where there is a close relationship between therapy and television, because when you go and see a psychotherapist, they don't say it is going to be easy, they say this is going to be hard, but I'm going to look after you. The way that we approach television producing, in the right way it is quite similar, it's a bit like the therapist, it's a bit like you are the parent. And any TV producer who isn't honest about that to the contributor is lying, because when we get to the cutting room with the footage we are the parent, we are the author, we are the person that will frame the story.

MIW: You have used the term, therapeutic journey, I wondered to what extent you think that that journey is a shared experience.

RM: Totally. That is something I fundamentally believe: that you cannot make brilliant factual television without it being a shared journey. I would like to look at the whole canon of our work at Love Productions, back to the first year. We did a film called *Having a Baby Ruined My Life* (2005), that was the year that my partner and I had our first baby: now that didn't ruin our life, but it was a funny film about talking about things that people don't talk about when they are having a baby. We did a series called *Kidnapped by the Kids* (2009), which is about workaholic parents because I was worried about work/life balance. When I became a father of a son, I did *I Want My Dad Back* (2008). We have done a lot of films about the treatment of old people in Britain. When I have done those films they have changed the way I have thought about my own parents and about what I might be prepared or not be prepared to do later in life.

MIW: So you are hoping to elicit personal change?

RM: If you are making a factual programme you change in the making of that programme.

MIW: Is that what you are hoping for your audience as well?

RM: Absolutely. If I am making a programme about you, hopefully you change me, I change you and the audience start at the beginning of watching it in some place, and in the end they change and that is the really important thing.

MIW: You are using quite a few terms that we may usually expect to hear in therapy. I am wondering, to what extent somebody who works in television, in production, is qualified, so to speak, to be so comfortable using those terms quite as freely as you do?

RM: Well, I'll be honest, one of my beefs with television, and this just goes to prove that I am a hypocrite, and contradict myself because I think that it is a justifiable thing to say, that you are using terms but you are not professionally qualified to use them. And I would say I'm not professionally qualified to make television programmes, other than the track record of making them, which brings me on to my beef, which is the fact that television is an incredibly important, responsible thing to be doing. I mean, we are broadcasting programmes that change children, they watch it and they are influenced by it. And we are looking after people who appear in them and yet we haven't passed any exams, we haven't passed any certificates. You don't let a surgeon operate on somebody unless they are qualified, you don't let a lawyer go into a courtroom unless they are qualified. I would like to see a professionalisation of television, I would never seek to argue against that—but that is not the current situation.

MIW: Do you think that television producers in general are aware of their power, how they can influence?

RM: I couldn't absolutely say that all of them are. I hope they are and I like to think that I am. But one's always got to stay open and listen and self-criticise and self-doubt.

MIW: Is that something you set out to do as a team, to explore and criticise?

RM: Yes. I think it is really important. When you do a single documentary, you've got a small team, and when you do a big constructive documentary series, like *Baby Borrowers* and *Young Mums' Mansion* (2008), we've got very big teams. We try to create teams that talk to each other, that are not worried about raising concerns, and doubts, and morals and ethical questions. You constantly have to be re-evaluating. In that sense, I suppose again, it's a bit like therapists, to be a therapist, you have to be in therapy right? So I would like to think that the way we work collaboratively, although someone has to be the boss and ultimately make the decisions, we listen to each other and seek to executively produce each other.

MIW: Do you seek input from therapists?

RM: Totally, in fact, obviously, when we started doing, I'm trying to think on which series, but certainly *The Baby Borrowers*, which was a very challenging piece of work, I spoke privately to psychotherapists. We then hired a psychologist to work with us. There was a steering committee and the psychologist worked with us to screen the contributors that were involved, and to make sure that we do reports. Interestingly, the best psychologist I have ever worked with was an American who does a lot of reality shows in America. I worked with him there on *The Baby Borrowers* and I brought him to Britain and he did *Young Mums' Mansion* and *Boys and Girls Alone* (2009). He understood really clearly that we were morally and ethically principled, concerned, television producers, but we were also making a programme. Yet he believed it could be good for the contributors in the programme. We worked very closely together. He kept us in check, but supported us, supported the contributors, and it was a really fantastic process. In that sense he showed a capacity to be open to television production. One of the reasons I am doing this interview is because I think that historically, psychologists and psychotherapists have been at war with television.

MIW: Do you think that part of the concern is the breaking down of the boundaries between the private and the public? Or is it that they may be worried because the responsibilities towards the contributors are not taken seriously?

RM: Well, it is definitely not the latter, because they wouldn't be there in the conversation if we weren't taking it seriously.

MIW: I am just wondering where you think that the hostility comes from?

RM: One of the biggest challenges we have all got is obviously, that psychotherapists are concerned about the vulnerability of a contributor and whether or not this can be a beneficial experience for that contributor. You know, if you like to take the hard line view—this person's vulnerable, they can't be in a television programme—there would not be any television programmes about anything remotely serious, remotely important.

MIW: Ultimately then, who are you making the programme for? Your contributor or your audience?

RM: Both. Being really honest, it's for myself, for the contributor, and for the audience. And that is the careful balance you have to get. One of the reasons we are called Love Productions is because we like to—quote "love" unquote—our contributors and take care of them. But that doesn't mean you don't ask them the hard questions, because you also have a duty to the audience—who are going: "Why am I watching this? Who is this person that gets to stand up on television?"—to ask them the tough questions. And you have a responsibility to yourself, to reach into yourself, to think what the tough question is. It wouldn't be fair to Jonathan [Phang] to do the *Marchioness* film with him, and not ask him the tough questions. A good friend tells you what you don't want to hear, they ask the question that you may not want to answer.

MIW: It seems to me, when I am watching that documentary, that Jonathan is very much the driving force. How much of it was just him going on his journey, and how much was he guided through?

RM: Well, it's a combination really and again that's the kind of careful balancing act—as the producer of a television programme you have to plan it. Logistically, you have got to tell people what time the cameraman comes. You have got to have a notion of what you are going to do. You want to be thinking about the beginning, the middle and the end, where do you want to go. There's the simple start, which is, we want to take Jonathan to a better place, we want him to feel better about himself for it to be a therapeutic journey. And then there is the practical side, let's see if we can meet these people on the way. Is that the best thing to do, and what order can it be done in, and how should it be done? So lay your plans, a bit like a scripted drama, however, this is where factual television making is absolutely 100 per cent different from drama. I think the kind of good factual television programmes and programme making, and why I find it exciting to do, it's not scripted, therefore you have a plan, but you had better be prepared to rip the plan up.

MIW: But, to a certain extent, you have clearly got in mind what makes for good television.

RM: What makes good television is keeping it real. You might ask someone to do something that is a challenge. The cameras are there so the big challenge is to get someone to be themselves. My job is to make you forget the camera is there. And when people go "Oh, what do you want me to do now?" I go, well what are you thinking? Now, as we were making this series, and you start to interrogate why they are in it, because you are asking deeper therapeutic questions about why they are really doing it. We made a documentary about British Asian contestants entering a competition to become a Bollywood star. A lot of the participants were doing it because they were trying to figure out their relationships with their parents. Which is why I think that actually, all factual television making is about loving your parents.

MIW: Tell me more about what you mean by that.

RM: It means making peace with your childhood, with what happened and asking what were your parents like as people. For example, one of the main contributors, when we questioned her, ultimately one of the reasons that she was really doing this was because it was her mother, who had been a bank clerk who had always dreamed of being a Bollywood star and had never been able to do it. You produce factual television by both producing it and knowing when not to produce it. What I learned through years of doing interviews with cameras, I used to have my list of questions, they would never forget that the camera was there, I never got any really good material. And now, if I do an interview, if I can't forget that the camera is there, then how are *you* going to forget that the camera is there? Sometimes I do an interview and you are talking to people right in the moment, in the zone.

MIW: I am interested to know how you enable that space, for the contributor to feel that the camera is not there.

RM: Depends, different things on different documentaries, from the kind of single documentary to the big constructive documentary where you have got lots of characters. If you are doing an intimate interview then quite often it will be just, you know, a cameraman or woman. A lot of our programmes are done with individual, what we call individual DV directors, who have a relationship with the contributors. They spend quite a lot of time and they've got solo cameras, maybe someone helping. But they will have conversations with the camera there and in those moments something will happen, or a conversation might lead to an interview that goes down a personal direction.

MIW: You are talking about moments here that are often emotionally charged, particularly when someone is revealing something very personal about themselves. We have talked about the responsibility you have for the contributor, but what about the production team who have to potentially carry that experience with them?

RM: Well, in an ideal world, on the shoot, where we have numbers of people working, like *Young Mums' Mansion,* we had [a psychologist] who was there for the entire shoot, for the contributors, for me, for the production team. Because of the tension between the psychotherapeutic community and television, we haven't worked as closely as we ought to be working, and as we need to be working. That is part of the reason I am doing this interview, to say that we are pointed in the same direction. Factual television, done properly, has the ability to improve the emotional health of this nation and the people of this nation. Which is exactly what psychotherapists, as I understand it, and psychiatrists, want to do. And, it is what governments should want us to do. So that is why I want us to come together and work together and figure out how to do that.

MIW: So essentially, you are taking part in this interview as a call to the therapeutic community to say that you would like to be engaged in a dialogue.

RM: Totally, because I mean here is the problem. We have been historically attacked by, and in a lot of the attacks on our programmes there have been psychologists involved and yet I have always been prepared to meet and talk with them. What I encounter is first of all they judge the programme before they have even watched it. They've made judgements that appear in the media, before they have even asked us about all the work that we have done previously.

MIW: You have been very prepared to fight your corner and were vindicated.

RM: Absolutely, we have been vindicated every time. For example, I think that when it comes to children, there are the kind of people who claim to be protecting children who don't want children on television crying, and it is a form of censorship. It's okay they are crying in the playground because that is where they do it, but don't let it happen on the television, because there, children should be seen and not heard. When we did a series called *Boys and Girls Alone*, there wasn't a child under eighteen who complained about that series. When the parents and the children saw it and went through the whole process, they all put their hands up afterwards and they asked two questions. One, can they be credited for it, and I had to explain that actually it is a documentary and you can only credit drama. And in the years since, I have thought, you know what, they are smarter than us, they sort of know that they are acting. And the second thing the kids said is, "When can we do it again?" And if you saw the levels of attacks that came on that series, and here's the point, the irony of all this is that the impression that television producers are irresponsible and everything else is actually not true. We are totally regulated, and we regulate ourselves; it is created by the press and the media who are unregulated—which we have now seen quite openly. Clearly, these are the people who come along and cause psychological distress, the people who are running the newspapers. Because, for some reason, in this country, the government does not see fit to put them under the same regulation.[1]

MIW: One of the things that you say you want to get out of this is to engage in a debate, particularly with psychotherapists about how to perhaps move forward and to achieve something more positive, but do you have concerns that there are some elements of television media that are perhaps irresponsible on how they film contributors, particularly on emotive subjects? Is that a worry for you, do you think that the regulations are strong enough?

RM: There is always a worry, but I do think that the regulations are strong enough. We must never stop worrying. We must never stop questioning ourselves every time we do a programme. Because there is one thing that I always say to contributors, is that we will be here to talk and we will be here to help you and we won't transmit anything which we believe could hurt someone when it goes out. But I don't control the reactions, we don't control real life and so I can't give you guarantees about how you are going to be perceived. But interestingly, the people, and this is a kind of general rule of thumb, the people who appear on television programmes but then don't open up and trust and be themselves, tend to be the people who then get grief from the public. It's very interesting that that's what I often say to people: if you are yourself you may feel like you are exposing yourself, and I am telling you that will go down heroically, people will come up to you afterwards and go, "You were amazing, you spoke about something". For example, you know, "Oh, I lost my mother too and that helped me get through that".

MIW: So when you are in the editing process, you have a goal of portraying people authentically, the way that they are?

RM: Absolutely, I mean one of the reasons that we show contributors the cut before they are absolutely finished, editorial control must reside with the producer and the broadcaster, we are always very clear about that up front, we are not going to be able to change things that happened. But in order to have a conversation, in order for them to say "That is not how I remember it", we sometimes have to have difficult conversations, and we have sometimes had to make changes because the contributor made a point, and we have thought that is fine, because in the end you film lots of rushes yet you only show a tiny minority. This is the funny thing, what is broadcast is true and yet also not true because it is only a bit of the truth isn't it. These are the kind of moral and ethical decisions we have to make.

MIW: So you make clear boundaries with your contributor?

RM: So the steadfast thing, is that, if you behave in a way and start screaming and shouting, and we filmed it and you said you did not want it to be shown, sorry, we are going to show that because that is how you behaved—if it is not going to hurt anyone to show that particular footage.

MIW: When I was watching Jonathan, he doesn't really show a lot of emotion, but I became quite emotional watching it, maybe because of that. But then you have talked about crying as sort of, the money shot, crying as a cathartic thing.

RM: Well, crying on camera, it's an interesting thing. How do you feel when you cry? How do you feel after you cry? Do you feel better? Forget television, forget everything else.

MIW: Depends on the circumstances.

RM: Do you think that therapists when they reduce their patients to tears at the end of a session, they think that was a good session?

MIW: I would be very worried if they did think that. That's quite a powerful position to be in, to feel that you can "reduce" someone to tears.

RM: I think that we all cry as an act of healing don't we? I mean, I don't know, that's a whole PhD that would be interesting in itself.

MIW: It serves a function.

RM: I mean, why do people cry at the movies?

MIW: So would you feel disappointed if your contributor did not experience that during the filming?

RM: I mean, it's not crying for the sake of crying. So, I wouldn't necessarily feel disappointment. It's about, well, it could be laughing, crying, laughing, releasing. Being honest and being open, moments of realisation that take you forward.

MIW: It's about lending a sort of authenticity to their journey?

RM: Can I give you an example? When we did this show called *Kidnapped by the Kids* (2009), and we were working with a guy who was a workaholic and never spent any time with his kids, and he ran, ironically, guess what, a child's play centre that he had set up when his father had died. His father had raised him and then he is in a situation where he is spending more time there than at home with his own children. He believes that he is in a documentary about work/life balance, we've told him the truth, but we haven't told him the whole truth. Then one day we set up with our crews, he thinks he is off filming and we line up his kids, we line up the mother, and his work group. The kids have written letters, and he comes in through the door going, "What's going on, what's going on?" His son steps forward and says, "Dad, you never spend any time with us". And he starts to cry, I start to cry, the cameraman starts to cry, we all go. Did we go to a better place? Did it affect the way I am with my kids? Yeah, it did. It took me to a better place. Do I now spend more time with my children as a result of doing that programme? Yes. Does he? Yes. Is that good?

MIW: It sounds to me like it had a very positive impact, and a good result. But my worry, just hearing about it, is, a slight feeling of ambush. And I wonder how you would have dealt with that if it hadn't had that sort of cathartic impact that you describe. How would you have been able to provide a degree of protection for contributors if, for example, he had just walked away, not wanting to face it.

RM: We would have worked with it. Obviously we couldn't have predicted it. If he had wanted to pull out we would have talked to him, we would have asked him what sort of help he needed. If he had felt so appalled and violated that he had pulled out, then that programme would never have been transmitted and we would have done all the things that we could do to repair that. The thing is that living life and making television is a risky process. All you can do is make the best possible, any more than a psychotherapist asks a question, and the patient goes, "How dare you ask that?" and storms out. What does the therapist do then? They look at the fact that, "Should I have gone that far? Was that the right button to press?" As someone who has been in and out of therapy, my big problem in recommending therapy is that it took me about nine or ten therapists over a period of fifteen years, to find someone any good. Now I have found that person's good, I've been with them for ten years and I can't imagine being with anyone else. So, just in the same way, that is what I always say to people, it's interesting, people say, "Should I be in a television programme?" And there are two things I would say. One is what is the programme about? I hope that Jonathan would say the same thing, if it doesn't matter to you, what they want to talk about. Is it something that is really important? And secondly, who is making the programme, research that person, speak to people who have been in their programmes, meet and assess them. If you trust them and believe in what it is about, then I would say, do it, because I think that it can be a really brilliant experience.

MIW: What would you recommend then, television or therapy?

RM: Television or therapy?—Both, and that is where we can work together. Interestingly, with my therapist, I talk about my programmes, she interrogates them. She makes me think about them in a certain way. I think that a lot of our output has been incredibly affected by my personal engagement with psychotherapy. The conversations I have had with people in psychology, about our programmes, they really influenced it. I am proud of the programmes we've made, and what I have learned is that they have been very influenced by my engagement with psychotherapy, which is why I want to see a closer professional relationship between documentary producers and psychotherapists.

MIW: A place for both to work together. I think that is a good place to end.

* * *

When Jonathan Phang, manager in the fashion industry, decided to participate in the making of a documentary about his experience surviving the 1989 *Marchioness* disaster, he was already highly experienced within the medium of television through various reality shows, notably *Britain's Next Top Model* (2005–2007) and *Britain's Missing Top Model* (2008). However, *The Marchioness: A Survivor's Story* (2009) sees him taking two positions—one as a presenter and one as a contributor with a highly traumatic personal story. Phang therefore brings a unique perspective to the emotional processes of documentary film-making.

Interview with Jonathan Phang, 5 April, 2012

MIW: You have said elsewhere that your journey in television led you to the point where you felt able to make this documentary.

JP: Looking at it, it's quite an unusual arena to air one's washing. At the same time, it's quite abstract to real life as well, so I found that more comfortable. I found that having a team of people who I understood and trusted a little bit, who had no preconceptions of who I was or no judgements of how I behaved, just impartial and a bit neutral, was really quite refreshing. I think for me when there's a goal, when there's a common pursuit that everyone's working towards, I feel more obliged to actually see it through. Whereas say, for example, therapy for me—I know I would find every excuse under the sun not to go. I would create obstacles, and probably not use it correctly. Whereas, because I was so exposed in this environment, and knew at the end of it there was something that potentially lots of people would see—I didn't expect to want to explore myself and my feelings towards the disaster in that place, but I'm actually really glad I did and I think it was the best place for me to do that.

MIW: From what you're describing, it sounds like you felt very contained—it felt like for you there was a beginning and an end and a direction.

JP: Well, I was ready to deal with my demons, and I don't think you always know what they're going to be at the time that something happens to you. So, I found that when therapy was offered to me, it was probably too early. I didn't have time to reflect at all, or to see the consequences of it, and I wasn't mature enough, or there were other things that I found more of a priority that sort of prevented me from getting there. And then I think I got to that age, early forties, or whatever, when we started making it. Everything else that was going to happen, the natural things— when your parents die and things like that—had happened and I just thought, I don't care what people think of me any more, so I'm ready to just be open. And it's for me, not for anybody else. So I had a vague notion of what I wanted to discover about myself. I'm sure the result is pretty good, and I hope people liked it. But it didn't matter to me, because the process delivered what I wanted it to deliver for me.

MIW: Did you feel as if you were talking to somebody or was this very much a personal journey for yourself?

JP: Thankfully I was experienced enough to know what to expect, and I think for someone less experienced in television it might have been different. Because I knew that a production company has to have an agenda, there has to be a framework. And as the subject of that programme, you're not privy to it. If I was more paranoid about it, I would think, well, okay they're making assumptions and making decisions behind my back and I might have felt used by that. And all of those kinds of things that contributors normally have a complaint about. But because I'd done several shows before, and with Love, I didn't have an expectation of it, and I knew, that's their business and I have to do what I have to do. I do feel sorry for people who suddenly find themselves in the midst of a documentary who don't understand that process, because they really have no clue. I just was really open to the process and really honest and able to use it to my own advantage, and to hopefully Love's, everyone's advantage, really. So, I think, hopefully, that's why maybe our film is—not better, but a bit more useful than others.

MIW: The way it comes across is that you appear to be quite in control.

JP: I felt I absolutely was. Because, I was so determined. I thought, "I'm in my forties, I don't care, I have to do this now, this is the only way that I'm going to actually condense it and pressurise myself and make myself confront my issues and explore what's gone on". I still knew I wasn't going to go and sit in some high street room with somebody that I may or may not like or respect. I respected Richard, so I knew I was as safe as I could possibly be, having done three shows with him prior to that one, and I also knew the responsibility was on me to make it interesting. Because again, knowing a bit about television, I know if I'm being boring they're going to have to concoct something from elsewhere; 'cause they have their own reputation to think of as well, so, I think we came from an area of mutual respect anyway.

MIW: Richard has talked about the type of documentary making that he does as a sort of therapeutic journey. Is that something you recognise in what you do?

JP: I think it definitely was a therapeutic journey for me. I didn't know what to expect from it, I just had this urge to do something, and to have a voice within it. I was going into the unknown, I suppose, and I think it was my version of therapy. It was the most appropriate way for me to do it, and the most productive way. I had left the experience putting to rest all the issues that I needed to resolve, and not feeling like I need any more help. So, it's about what provokes you to deal with certain situations and what comes up along the way, and we communicated every step of the way. And I knew if there was ever a problem that Richard would understand the sensitivity of the topic, so if I was out of my depth, or feeling a bit vulnerable about it, which I never did, in fairness to me—but I never had to call Richard.

MIW: But you needed that rapport to get it to work.

JP: Yes you do, because it's so intense, and even if you know they're playing with tricks, in a way, you have to forgive them for it and understand them for it.

MIW: To what extent do you feel that you were very much the author of that journey?

JP: I had to just turn a blind eye to maybe what they expected and wanted. When I'm interviewing somebody, I know that there's a manipulation gear that kicks in to get what you want. I think they, on certain occasions, were assuming certain things were going to come out, and they just weren't. And that is disappointing if you have a framework in place.

MIW: So you felt that they had an agenda?

JP: Yeah. But I don't mean that in any negative way. I think, luckily enough, that I was vulnerable enough and compelling enough to keep it going when we had disappointing contributors or their stories just didn't make sense with mine. It's a very harsh thing to do, because every story is very valid and very personal to them, and then when it doesn't end up in the film everyone wants to know why. Everyone has various opinions about what's strong and what isn't. But, I didn't question too much about it, because I just thought that would actually prevent me from working on myself through it. If I'd gone home and analysed everything that had gone on that day, and worried about how they edited it, I would have driven myself crazy, and I don't think that I would have got what I needed out of it. So that's that point of having done a lot of TV before, that I was able to do that.

MIW: You were familiar with the inner workings of it, but how about the other contributors you worked with?

JP: They were supported, but you see, the difficulty with a documentary is that you can't put words into someone's mouth. So, although I felt instinctively that they had what we needed them to say inside them, for whatever reason the circumstances dictated something other, so it wasn't the right moment, or the right situation, or just not the right day. It's a very intricate thing. I just think it's a really massive skill to give something a beginning and a middle and an end. For example, with hindsight, everyone said "Oh, yes, at the end, isn't that psychiatrist marvellous?" He was a perfectly nice guy. For me it was slightly deflating that that is something everybody takes away from that film, somebody that literally spoke the obvious in one sentence. Well, I did kind of know that. It would have been nice if it had been another survivor to tell me that, not a psychiatrist. You don't have to be a rocket scientist to have dreamt that one up. It gave us a nice end, but part of me wishes that wasn't even in there, because I think there's so much that is more thought provoking, and that is a very convenient end for a viewer, actually, to just let them encapsulate it into one sentence, something that was such a massive journey.

MIW: So was the programme for you, or was it for the audience, ultimately?

JP: Ultimately it was for me, it's why I haven't really watched it. I watched the rough cuts of it, because I had to, but it wasn't a comfortable watch at all. I wanted it to be for the audience. I initially wanted it to be something that anybody could watch who was experiencing grief, any kind of grief, and would find it really useful. I hope that is the case. I think it's really nice for people to look at it to see different points of view. There was a general attitude that nobody really cared too much about it. And I understand why. Unless you know someone personally involved, why should you care, really? Life's hard enough as it is, so I get it. But because we were quite young, and sensitive, and rightly so, it did very much feel that out of all the disasters that had happened around that time, which there were many, it really was kind of forgotten about and no one really cared about it. And it was that "Thatcher's ark" sort of thing, and it was all a bunch of yuppies, who could more or less afford to … die, if you like. And that was quite difficult to deal with on top of everything else. I really wanted somebody who had that attitude to have their eyes opened a little bit. When I looked at that film, what really struck me was the physical change in me. I always felt that I was in control of my mental state and attitude, but there was clearly what you'd call body-shock, if you like, practically putting on five stone overnight, sort of within a month, and I've never lost it. But I've always had a gregarious personality and quite a forceful one, so I've always been able to pull the wool over the eyes of everybody I've ever met. And I suppose that's what's given me the profession I'm in, but also, when I had counselling sessions, a lot of the people that I was offered were probably too young for me, and I didn't respect them at all. The only time that I did respond favourably to a psychiatrist was on the recommendation of the *Bowbelle* owners' solicitors, who sent me to a charming psychiatrist who was about sixty-five. At school there are certain teachers that you are just really respectful of, and you don't really know why—and this felt the same. Whereas, with the other lot I had that attitude of, "They're seventeen and got a psych A-level, and I hate them". It wasn't good. It's opened my eyes to myself as well and made me realise how much effort had gone into covering everything up. And how unfortunate it was that I wasn't able to just say, "Yes, it's bad", or ask for help in any way.

MIW: And yet, it's been something that you've not felt that you particularly wanted to see. To sit down and view from beginning to end.

JP: No, because it doesn't matter to me. When you do a lot of television, you realise by the time it's done, it's in the past because it's three months down the line. And you have to let things go and you have to let people do the edit and not ask to see it and stuff like that. And then also, this one was so exposing, it's uncomfortable. It's like, "Oh God, am I totally embarrassing myself and was this the right thing to do?" I feel that it was a brave thing to do. There have been even bigger fall-outs with the survivors from it, who were very judgemental of it. And I now feel very solitary, but relieved that I don't feel responsible to other survivors. I think I suffered from feeling judged by them all the way along. I'm sad that they can't just think, "Well, good for him that he did something for himself. It's maybe not the way I wanted to do it, but if it's helped him, fine". Right? The result has been sad on that level. On a personal level, I feel that I've helped myself. But it's created enormous division with the few survivors that I was in contact with, and I've more or less now made the decision not to be in contact with any of them. But that is actually something that I needed to do, to feel strong enough to say that, because with my post-traumatic distress syndrome, survivor's guilt, call it what you want, I always felt that I had to please the fellow survivors. And I never had to. And I never demanded that in return from them. And I could tell by comments and the sort of critiques that people were writing me about it, and this is like, you've so missed the point.

MIW: Did you expect to sort of experience a journey where you found out so much about yourself?

JP: I was just hell-bent on making a good bit of television. That's how it started as well. I did want to work on myself, but that probably shifted somewhat. Because, after having done three seasons of *Britain's Next Top Model*, then a great show with this lot, called *Britain's Missing Top Model* with disabled girls, and then *Naked* (2009), I just thought, I really want people, also people in the business, to see that I have a bit of substance, instead of just talking this absolute rubbish that I was, that I've spoken a million times before. I also knew that I wouldn't work after that as well, for a long time.

MIW: So you were prepared to take a break?

JP: Yes, I was. How do you do these fluffy shows where people perceive you in a certain way, then do something that's quite hard-hitting which people are quite embarrassed to talk to you about, 'cause they don't really know what to say, other than, "Wasn't the psychiatrist marvellous at the end? I hope that made you feel better?" Well, actually, no. And I did know that would happen, but that's why I've felt that the whole reason I'd done the TV in the first place was leading to that moment. I needed a place to have my voice in, and that genuinely was it. And I'm very proud of it, I'm proud that I've done it, and I was happy to go into the unknown at the end of it. I didn't know how the survivors would feel about it, but that was a paranoia that I had to really get over, because I realised that this was exactly what had been causing me the problem for the previous twenty years.

MIW: A therapeutic environment is something that's actually quite private. And yet you felt comfortable enough to talk about something very private in a very public space. Has that changed the way people feel they can talk to you? Are people more willing to talk about it?

JP: I think people still are frightened to talk about it, because they don't know. I suppose if they've watched that, they realise how deep an effect it had on me. And so they're probably even more worried about discussing it with me. I think that it's probably made me shy to watch it because it's such a weird thing to do, in a way, to be so open in such a public environment. But, I don't really know how to rationalise that, other than, when somebody has that commitment to you, you are obliged to give it back. Because once you start it you can't turn back. For Harry and Richard to get it commissioned by BBC1 is a big thing. For the commissioners at BBC1 to fund it—you cannot turn back. And I suppose that's why I chose it, because I knew I'd have to see it through.

MIW: You said that you had to not be boring. Were you also thinking about the audience at all when you were filming?

JP: That is true with hindsight. I suppose because of my experience in TV, I knew if a contributor was being boring. And I would maybe, on occasion, try and make them to be less boring, and I would kind of instinctively know at the end of it why someone made the cut and why they didn't. When you do have a disappointing day, in documentary, you really cannot be too manipulative about it; you can only push that to a certain point. You cannot feed the line to the person. But, I understood it, because people are very freaked out by a camera, suddenly they can't say a word. I felt part of that process of making it, being the key contributor. To me that obligation was as great as theirs. And so, I saw it from both perspectives, I suppose. But I wasn't changing myself in order to make myself interesting.

MIW: To what extent were you able to have input into the editorial control?

JP: Not at all, I didn't ask and I didn't expect, and I didn't mention it. That's why I was an easy key person for them to work with too, because I knew better than to do that. But, as I said before, I'll say a million times again, it was all about what it was doing to me, not the end of it. Nothing's perfect. Nothing's ever what you want it to be. And you've got four or five people that want something out of it too. I wanted it to be good, but I didn't expect it to be everything that I've wanted. I wasn't paying for it, I wasn't producing it, I wasn't editing it.

MIW: Richard sees his type of work as something that could be widely beneficial.

JP: Yes, I agree.

MIW: That marrying of therapy with good TV. You had the advantage, I would say, because you knew how it worked. But is this something you would recommend?

JP: For a certain type of person, and I think they need to go into it with their eyes open, and I think there needs to be consideration for care during and after, whether one decides to use that or not. I think they should be reassured to know that facility is available to them, as an option. Because you are opening Pandora's Box. I didn't expect, as a result of it, to feel so cleansed, but also, to not want to see anybody else ever again. And those are two big things, right? But at that I lucked out. That may not have been the case. It could have set me way back. And I could have then decided, "Well, what I really do need is another year of therapy" or something. I didn't.

MIW: It was a risk.

JP: It was a major risk. So, you can't be sure what the outcome's going to be. I think that I'm quite rare, but it was almost an end for me. Also, I don't think there's going to be that many opportunities for people to do that style of work, to mark a twentieth anniversary, you're going to want it a lot before. When it's a lot more raw. Had I done it ten years or five years before, it would have been a completely different experience with different results.

MIW: Knowing how it turned out, if you could go back in time, would you have done it again?

JP: Absolutely. Yes. I did it at exactly the right time. I was emotionally and experience-wise at the right time in my life, and I think, had my parents been alive and all of that, I would have still cared too much about offending somebody.

MIW: Richard talks about the idea that the contributor gets into a space where the camera's not there any more. Is that how you experienced it?

JP: See, I'm different, though, because I start thinking "How's my hair?" or "Is my collar sticking out?" I think what did annoy them, occasionally, was I kept editing myself. So I would sort of say, "It's warm outside, isn't it? It's a lovely day". Sometimes I'd say something and I'd suddenly think, "My syntax was terrible" or "I sounded like a right idiot". So, how I would normally do it if I was being paid to do it. When you're presenting, if you like, that's a godsend, so the producer doesn't have to stop and start when you just know instinctively that you can say it better. You just do it and deliver it, but that does take the spontaneity out of it. So occasionally I had to stop myself doing that. And then when I was with a contributor, I think I was quite good at letting them talk and giving them enough space to do it. Because, when you are up against it on time, just being really brutally honest here, you do want to start putting words in their mouth if you're ever going to get to the point. Because we're now an hour late for the next one, or something, or "Time's money" and all of that. So I did have to retrain myself a little bit, but in the really intense moments I completely forgot the camera was there. I don't feel at all self-conscious in front of the camera anyway, I suppose.

MIW: We talked, again with Richard, about some of the extreme emotions that we get to see on camera, like crying.

JP: I was trying to avoid it. I really was. Because I'm always blubbing all the time, and I thought, "No, I cannot do this all the way through it". although I wanted to. But when we did that scene on the boat, I just became totally hysterical. I did not expect it at all. We went on this small boat to go on the Thames, and I've never been on the Thames before. I don't know if they did this on purpose or not, but they just left me outside on it whilst they were doing stuff inside. And this boat went by which was the spitting image of the Marchioness. And I was hysterical. That's the tears they get out of me, but it was completely spontaneous. It was before we'd even set off, and it was looking at that boat, because it was exactly the same as what it would have been, and it just totally came flooding back.

MIW: Richard described that experience, for people he felt it was cathartic, to be able to cry. Is that how you felt?

JP: I think it is. In life it was awful, because it knocked me for six. We'd had a laugh when I got on the boat because I didn't know how to get off the jetty. There was like a "Hello Dolly" moment, and sort of "You might want to do that again". So we're all laughing about it and they went inside, I went to this side of the boat, looked up, and I just went. And I don't think they noticed it for a while, but it was only because I had the microphone on that I think they heard me snivelling. And it wasn't a trickle of tears, it was complete hysteria, and it was like this pent-up— I mean, you don't even really notice in the film, you don't rea- lise how intense it was, actually. I don't even know what I was crying for. It was like twenty years of this, that, and the other, and then crying for my youth and friends and the situation, and, like, "Oh my God, what has happened for twenty years". It was like a memory of getting on the boat as a carefree person and then getting on it again middle-aged and overweight. The last time I did this, in 1989, having a great time, the best time of my life. Overnight, then—for twenty years I've held on to all these issues. So it was crying for all sorts of reasons. Parents, family, thwarted career, of feeling like an idiot for having all this stuff that had prevented me from doing the stuff I wanted to do in my life. And my life hasn't even been that bad.

MIW: You were asked to return to a very poignant part of your life.

JP: There was no stopping it. What they wanted to happen, not that anyone's told me this, but I know this, is—they took me to the place where Antonio was found, at St Saviour, that's where they wanted the breakdown. But by that point I'd cried it out. So it's edited to like a couple of sentences. Because they could only have one big moment like that, I suppose. It took me by sur- prise. I'm glad it happened that way because it was completely natural and spontaneous. But it was quite shocking to be me at that moment, is the only way I can put it. It's not so much about the vanity thing, which does exist, but I did need somebody there whom I knew was one hundred per cent on my side, and someone who wasn't a friend or a family member, just some- body who was looking out for me in a very impartial way. So I was very pleased that someone was there. It was a really big, big moment for me, and it was just totally stripped down. There was no concern for who was watching it or what we were doing or anything like that.

MIW: I think the experience as a viewer is the need to feel that that person is then okay in some way. And supported.

JP: Yes, that's true.

MIW: You don't always get to see that. Obviously because of the way it's edited.

JP: "Oh great, he's blubbing. Let's get more". I think there's probably an element of that. I don't think anyone intentionally made me feel that, but being the cynical world we're in, it is the moment you're waiting for as a producer, I would say. Because you have to have it in the programme, it has to have an emotional arc to keep the viewer there. Because the viewer wants it, I suppose. I don't think, unless you are a therapist or have studied psychotherapy or been through any kind of trauma—they're not going to understand how those things feel. And you don't want people to. You want to save people feeling grief, don't you, as long as possible. I do, anyway. Because it takes an innocence away from somebody. Let's face it, you'd rather learn lessons later in life. So when I'm having my breakdown on the boat it's like, did I really have to learn all of these things at twenty-three? Did I have to have lost both parents by thirty-three? All of those things I think came out in that one moment. I think when you get older and you have all those things happen to you, you are almost affectionate to people that don't have it. And I think that's what I wanted. I wanted that empathy from the viewer actually watching that. I think everyone takes comfort from knowing that we all get screwed up by various things and grief. Life's so fragile—you can just go off a rail that changes the course of your life, and that can be taking one drug too many, one drink too many, or just being in the wrong place at the wrong time. And I think it's a very important lesson. I work in a shallow world, and it was important to me to explain; the catharsis was about not caring about what people really think but at the same time caring so much that you want them to know what substance you're made up of. It's like, "This is who I am". By saying that, that's me coming to terms with who I am as well, but if someone can learn something from it, great. It's very easy to see my life as something really quite flippant, because that's how I've always shielded myself from anything that's too painful to talk about.

MIW: The scenes I find most moving were when you were holding back your emotions. For example when you visit the flat.

JP: What I didn't want to be criticised of is—the whole film being so self-serving, if you like, and self-indulgent—"Oh well, he's really milking it". There wasn't a day that I didn't cry at some point. It might have been on my own when the cameras weren't on, or it might be when I got home and thought about what went on. But I think it really diminishes it. I didn't want to come across like that. I wanted to appear to be stronger, and I wanted to be strong, because if you start breaking down all the time, then everybody starts offering you the tissue and the moment goes, doesn't it.

MIW: There's something quite interesting about this television genre, where they are behind a camera, not able to get involved, that actually allows some sort of freedom to work through whatever it is.

JP: Yeah, and to be thoughtful about it. For me, the scene that upsets me, when I saw it in the rough, and I looked at myself in a different way, was in the cathedral. There's something about that man shaking my hand at the end of it, which really upset me. I felt a real fraud being in the middle of a service, being filmed, actually. It was a very weird situation, because I didn't know where the camera was. I didn't question it, but when it dawned on me it was slightly uncomfortable. I look at that and I was certainly holding back my emotions then. I genuinely felt quite exasperated and knackered by that point, and I knew that was it. That was the last day of it. Which is a scary moment, actually. Because it's all a bit of a flurry and you're working towards something that's all very busy and all of that. It's like a loved one's funeral, when you're on autopilot, and then suddenly the funeral's over. Then what? And the phone stops ringing. So I was very aware of that and sort of feeling that mixture of emotion. But I felt really lonely with it. I have been, actually, and I've been fooling myself into thinking that I haven't been. That people's reactions to me were good or honourable or whatever, and they haven't been. And it spoke volumes to me.

MIW: I find that interesting, that you've described that it's been lonely. Because actually, the shot of you at the end of that element in the programme, you are seated alone. And the camera pulls away. And I have to say, that is how it felt as a viewer.

JP: I just think it speaks volumes about me, and I think it was a real eye-opener to me because there's that moment and then there's the sort of false smile that goes on my face when I shake the man's hand, which is exactly how I've lived for twenty years. And I can turn it on just like that. And it sort of slapped me right in the face. And then, when we're walking out of the cathedral and it's all the smiles and the hugging and all of that, that sums up everything. That one last minute of it, of all the good and bad that I'd experienced in the last twenty years, I think is there. So that scene gets to me, and I suppose that's why I probably haven't watched it.

MIW: You saw some rough cuts. Did you feel like that was you—that you recognised yourself?

JP: I find it really hard to watch, because there's so much that goes on in your head. And there was one thing that I wasn't happy with, and I thought, "It's not my business to say". And it was quite minor, and then Richard took it out. And I thought that was really terrific, because he understood me. I think he was sensitive enough to see it and to realise that it could be construed in a negative way. And that's what I'm talking about by having somebody behind you whom you know and trust, which I was in the luxurious position to be.

Note

1. In the UK, the Leveson report on press ethics and questions of regulation was published as the manuscript for this volume was going to press. The recommendations made by the report were under scrutiny and subject to debate in the House of Commons and it was not yet clear whether the proposed new regulatory body for the press would be underpinned by statute or fully independent.

References

Media and the Inner World conference (2010). Remote control: psychoanalysis and television. 30 October. Anna Freud Centre, London.
Silverstone, R. (1994). *Television and Everyday Life*. London: Routledge.

List of television programmes and films cited

Boys and Girls Alone (2009). Channel 4, UK.
Britain's Missing Top Model (2008). BBC3, UK.
Britain's Next Top Model (2005-2007). LivingTV, UK.
First Tuesday (1983-1993). Yorkshire Television (ITV), UK.

Having a Baby Ruined My Life (2005). FIVE, UK.
I Want My Dad Back (2008). Channel 4, UK.
Kidnapped by the Kids (2009). Channel 4, UK.
Make Bradford British (2012). Channel 4, UK.
Naked (2009). BBC3, UK.
The Baby Borrowers (2007). BBC3, UK.
The Great British Bake Off (2010–present). BBC2, UK.
The Marchioness: A Survivor's Story (2009). BBC1, UK.
The World This Week (1989). Channel 4, UK.
Young Mums' Mansion (2008). BBC3, UK.

CHAPTER EIGHT

TV times at the Freud Museum

Ivan Ward

The Freud Museum has had a long engagement with television in one form or another—production companies wishing to film at the museum, TV screens and video installations used in contemporary art exhibitions, and, in 2010, the museum itself becoming the subject of a BBC documentary *Behind the Scenes at the Museum* (2010).

There were even occasions when I had the temerity to approach TV myself. I once wrote to Lewis Bronze who had recently taken over from the legendary Biddy Baxter as producer of the BBC's flagship children's television programme, *Blue Peter* (1958–present), proposing a biography of Sigmund Freud. Intelligent biographies of famous historical characters were a regular feature on the programme, and it seemed to me that Freud was a suitable choice. What sort of story would it be? Obviously a story of "growing up"; being clever at school, falling in love, making a great discovery, being driven from his home, and dying here in England. The biography would be a tale of courage and achievement, hard work and triumph over adversity, from childhood poverty to international fame. There were the years of "splendid isolation" and rejection, the tragedy of his sisters' deaths in concentration camps, the final triumph of his legacy helping thousands of people suffering from "mental problems". My intention was to present an inspiring story of Freud's life while trying to educate in a child-friendly way about some of Freud's ideas. Needless to say, the pitch was not successful, but the rejection letter did not give a reason. The production team were off on their summer break but I could rest assured that, if a suitable opportunity arose, they would get back in touch. You can probably guess that I am still waiting for the phone call. I like to think that the reason for the rejection was more obvious. You can't get round the "sex" thing, or as Freud put it in his BBC recording of 1938, his "unsavoury ideas". Most people did not believe that Freud was a proper subject for children's TV.

Another proposal that hit the buffers was about the children's toy, *My Little Pony*, which I pitched to an independent production company with an associate producer and a BBC editor. Parents of a certain age will know that *My Little Pony* is big business. Within months of its launch in 1983, it was ranked the number one girl's toy in America. Mass produced in dozens of countries and distributed across the globe, they are destined for a little place in cultural history, and our programme was hoping to explore some of the mysteries of this luridly appealing cultural object. Adults, children, innocents, and experts would tell us what it meant to them, and what they imagine it could mean to others, all taking place in a world of sparkly colours, smooth horsey limbs, and flowing streams of plastic hair. Always, however, the programme would return to the particularity of the object itself. By taking seriously this ostensibly absurd creature, we wanted to remind ourselves how objects like this have been important for our children, and through them, for us. Superficially adorable and cute, but hideous to adults, it may be one of the means whereby children learn to negotiate their deepest fears. The model, of course, is Freud's observation of his grandson's game with a cotton reel, which was the subject of a video installation in the museum by American artist, Renate Ferro, in 2012. With his astonishing insight into the *fort-da* game, Freud opened up children's play (and adult behaviour derived from it) to analytic investigation:

> The child had a wooden reel with a piece of string tied round it. It never occurred to him to pull it along the floor behind him, for instance, and play at its being a carriage. What he did was to hold the reel by the string and very skilfully throw it over the edge of his curtained cot, so that it disappeared into it, at the same time uttering his expressive "o-o-o-o" [German "*fort*"—"gone"]. He

then pulled the reel out of the cot again by the string and hailed its reappearance with a joyful "*da*" ["there"] …

The interpretation of the game then became obvious. It was related to the child's great cultural achievement—the instinctual renunciation which he had made in allowing his mother to go away without protesting. He compensated himself for this, as it were, by himself staging the disappearance and return of the objects within his reach. (1920g, p. 15)

Through the *fort-da* game, the child achieved symbolic mastery of the inner world and the outer; of the recalcitrant object (his disappearing mother) and the traumatic separation anxiety. As Winnicott was later to generalise:

Whereas it is easy to see that children play for pleasure, it is much more difficult for people to see that children play to master anxiety, or to master ideas and impulses that lead to anxiety if they are not in control. (1964, p. 144)

Freud called this game a "great cultural achievement" not only because of the factor of "instinctual renunciation", but also because the child is entering a world of symbolic language and symbolic objects. Dependence and powerlessness is being transformed through the symbolic ritual into illusory "mastery". The toy in the game might be called the first symbolic object, and its use may be a prototype for how other objects such as television are used to regulate emotions in later life—"symbolic" objects rather than "transitional" ones.

My Little Pony was more complex than a cotton reel, and our proposal emphasised the fact. Through the contributions of adults and children we wanted to show that the importance of an object subsists in the phantasies and feelings that are mobilised around it, and that behind the conscious use we make of our objects, an unconscious logic is also at work. Each of the characteristics that are positively valued by the child—the shiny colours, bubblegum smell, long flowing hair, the ability to fly, and so on—can be shown to have something of the opposite valuation working within it. That is, behind the enchantment with this little toy animal, we find the common anxieties and phobias of childhood.

Despite our enthusiasm for the concept, the proposal met with the same fate as the Freud biography. The ideas were not strong enough and I was not committed or ambitious enough to carry them through. But there may be another factor as well. Perhaps there is something incompatible about "television" and "psychoanalysis". Could it be to do with Freud's unsavoury ideas about sexuality, or could it be, conversely, that we are confronted by an unconscious dimension of sexuality with the advent of TV?

It is difficult to know how we might examine such a contention. Jo Whitehouse-Hart's reminder that television is referred to as "the box" and sits innocuously in the corner of the room and the bosom of family life, only reminded me that the word "box" in Freud's work is usually a euphemism for the female genital. The same symbolic equation can be found today. In an episode of *The Big Bang Theory* (2007–present), "Penny" is initially surprised that "Leonard" will not play with the Star Trek Transporter toy she bought him, until he explains that "Once you open the box, it loses its value". "Yeah, yeah", she interrupts impatiently, "My mom gave me the same lecture". An installation at the Freud Museum by the Austrian feminist artist, Valie Export, evoked this strange sexual dimension in a direct way. Displayed on six monitors set in a semi-circle in Freud's dining room, *The Power of Speech* (2004) showed the male epiglottis in action as it is speaking the words, "The power of language is measured after the trace left even after silence". On one level, the piece was kind of a joke: here is the place where words come from—but of course that's absurd! We shall see later that television does indeed emphasise "the power of speech", but as *Time Out* reviewer, Sarah Kent, observed, the mesmeric power of the piece lay not in the words, but in the quasi-sexual image. Isolated in a pool of darkness, the larynx uncannily resembled the female sexual organ, which made its emphatic openings and closures distinctly alarming. "Any anxieties you may have about female sexuality—in particular the existence and threatening potential of the *vagina dentata*—will be confirmed", she asserted, "especially given that you're standing in the home of the man who specialised in repressed desires and fears" (Kent, 2004, p. 40).

If an artist can put the voice box on the box to create something uncanny—an enigmatic signifier—it is because the term itself is twisted by inherent ambiguity. We say "on the box" rather than "in the box" (as people want to be "on the telly" rather than "in television"); space collapsing into surface, surface covering void. This raises the disquieting possibility that everything that appears on the box, the television programmes themselves, are first and foremost a means of covering "the box". The symbolic object used by Freud's grandson to mitigate separation anxiety may be transformed in later life into the fetish object that circumvents the threat of castration. For the fetishist, that is to say all of us to a certain extent, the fetish object becomes a necessary condition for a sexual relationship, which can have a compulsive hold over the subject. Since it is intimately connected to the visual field and processes of looking, or looking-but-not-seeing in Freud's account, the idea was soon taken up in film theory to describe the voyeuristic activity of film spectatorship. In her comprehensive review of the literature about psychoanalysis and film, Flitterman-Lewis (1992) acknowledges the importance of fetishistic voyeurism in the experience of film spectatorship but discounts its role in television viewing:

> Whereas the aura of cinema spectatorship produces hypnotic fascination, the atmosphere of television viewing enables just the opposite—because the lights are more likely to be on, one can get up and return, do several things at once, watch casually, talk to other people, or even decide to turn the television off. (p. 217)

We are not fascinated by television in the same way, it does not hold our gaze, the image does not have the same compelling lustre as its cinematic equivalent. Theories of the "distracted gaze" of the television viewer have a common sense appeal in an era of multiple channels and competing digital media, but millions of people, young and old, still find themselves glued to the box for many hours a day. Such is the ubiquity of fetishism in human affairs that it is difficult to imagine how fetishism could not be a component of the televisual experience as it is of the cinematic one. The screen, after all, is a *screen*. The "window on the world" as television is often called, hides something from us, and if it functions as a (Freudian) "fetish", we must assume that it hides acknowledgement of a lack. Students left alone in the Freud Museum with "nothing to do" sometimes allay their boredom and agitation by sitting in front of the blank TV screen in the video room, waiting expectantly for something to happen. In doing so, they remove themselves from the real situation in which they find themselves—in the home of the man with "weird" ideas, who was "a bit of a pervert" (as they say), who may be able to read your mind and whose ghost may be haunting the place right now.

Much vaunted for its unrivalled ability to capture reality, and "reality TV" in all its guises replacing soap opera as the television form *par excellence*, perhaps reality is precisely what it obscures. As John Ellis puts it: "There is too much missing, both in sensory evidence (no smell, no tactile sense) and, more importantly, in social involvement. ... This is the conundrum of 'realism' ... The feeling of witness that comes with the audio-visual media is one of separation and powerlessness ..." (2000, p. 11). Or, as I remember the great Brian Clough once saying while commentating on a particularly exciting international football match: "This is live football! This is what you're missing!"

Before I turn to "reality", let me recapitulate. The argument has been put forward in this book that television is a particular kind of "object", most often a "transitional object", which has been linked to the phenomena of play and creativity. I have pointed out that other objects may also be candidates for offering a key to understand television, such as the fetish object or the "first symbolic object" used in the *fort-da* game. We might, at the very least, consider the binary function of the on/off switch in relation to the "good" and "bad" objects that have been discovered in infantile experience, reflecting emotions of satisfaction and frustration, love and hostility. In all cases, we look to the structure and function of the infantile object to offer a psychological precursor to the structure and function of television in the adult. It may seem that the "fetish" and the "transitional object" belong to quite different realms of experience, but there is an extensive literature looking at the relationship between them, and both are concerned with the experience of "illusion". Introducing sexuality and sexual anxiety into the equation as a basic dimension of television experience may seem eccentric. But for Winnicott himself, the arena of play was not divorced from sexuality or, indeed, the Oedipus complex and emotional ambivalence. Play links inner and outer reality for the child, as Winnicott says, but we less often hear his view that children's play is enriched by sexual ideas and sexual symbolism, or that play "links ideas to bodily functions" (1964, p. 145). Bodily functions are underpinned by the drives in one direction, subject to parental approval and disapproval in another direction, and incorporated into our phantasy lives in a third direction. If we want to use psychoanalysis to understand the activity of "watching television", then it is at the level of unconscious wishes and often bizarre phantasies that we will be able to find the link, and these are by definition hard to reveal. The fact that all commentators stress the role of television within the domestic sphere (Flitterman-Lewis, 1992, p. 217 quotes Barthes with approval: "Television condemns us to the Family, whose household utensil it has become") might alert us to the fact that this is the same family that Freud identified as the site of the eroticised psycho-drama that foreshadows the rest of our lives.

A recent conversation in the Freud Museum may give a flavour of what I mean. It was with a fifteen-year-old Muslim girl from east London, studying GCSE psychology. She was on her own in Freud's study, gazing at his collection of ancient objects, when she started to smile.

"That Freud, he's got a one-track mind".

"What do you mean?" I asked, feigning surprise.

"All these objects, they're, you know …" and she made a gesture with her hands, drawing them apart, "either up and down or …"—another gesture cupping her hands together—"opening out, like … you know".

"Do you mean they are either male or female symbols?" I asked.

"Yeah—he's got a one-track mind".

"Well, Freud didn't make the objects, so he can't be the only one".

"Mmm …"

She did not sound very convinced, so I tried another tack. "You know, you have spotted something that most people miss—most people only see the 'phallic' objects and miss all the bowls and containers that you have noticed. You're like an anthropologist who has gone into a different culture and seen that all the objects of that culture can be classified as either 'male' or 'female'. Then the anthropologist might realise that one of the organising principles of that society is the difference between 'male' and 'female'—except you've put it all in Freud's head!"

"Do you think it is one of the organising principles of society, then?'" she asked.

"What do you think?"

So what *do* we think? If we say that TV is a "transitional object", then following the logic of the transitional object—the first "not me" object between the inner world and the outer world, in the intermediate space between child and mother, and retaining tactile and olfactory qualities associated with the maternal function—it is basically the mother we are relating to when we watch TV, and the "good enough" mother at that. I am suggesting that this is inherently unlikely, given the complexity of our ordinary relationship to objects. Anna Freud, for instance, traces the subsequent development of the transitional object and the increasingly convoluted emotions with which they are cathected:

> Clinging to one specific transitional object develops further into a more indiscriminate liking for soft toys of various kinds which, as symbolic objects, are cuddled and maltreated alternately (cathected with libido and aggression). That they are inanimate objects, and therefore do not retaliate, enables the toddler to express the full range of his ambivalence toward them. (1963, p. 258)

It is not difficult to list a whole range of possible ways in which objects can be used, which might suggest parallels in the domestic viewing of television:

> Egoistic use of objects—objects used in an instrumental sense, to achieve certain ego-syntonic aims and ambitions, such as recognition by others.

> Narcissistic use of objects—objects used to promote an inflated sense of self-esteem and a fantasy of omnipotent self-sufficiency (so a narcissistic use of an object often involves disparaging the object).

> Hysterical use of objects—objects used as a means of expression or display (often sexual) of the "personality".

> Obsessional use of objects—objects used to achieve control over self and others (especially over death), and to keep the world intact—collecting may be an example, whether of things or "facts".

> Phobic use of objects—objects used for the purpose of avoidance, of condensing inner fears and displacing them to the outside world.

> Counter-phobic use of objects—objects used to evacuate and "transcend" fears—often through play activity.

> Fetishistic use of objects—objects used to circumvent castration anxiety, or as a necessary condition for sexual

gratification. "A certain degree of fetishism is habitually present in normal love". (Freud, 1905d, p. 154)

Paranoid use of objects—objects used as vehicles of projection. For Freud, "The purpose of paranoia is to ward off an idea that is incompatible to the ego, by projecting its substance into the external world" (1895, p. 109). The "paranoid" use of objects involves the evacuation of unwanted parts of the self into the object.

Sadistic use of objects—objects used to vent aggression or hatred (that perhaps cannot be directed elsewhere).

And yes, there are objects used for artistic sublimation, thinking, reverie, or reverence, or "being taken out of ourselves" (Stokes, 1966) which should also be included in this list. No doubt different types of "personality" have different styles of relating to objects, and use and are transformed by them in different ways, project different idioms and different ways of "being a character" (Bollas, 1992), but in all cases we expect a complex array of possibilities because people are three-dimensional and multi-layered.

In his paper "Some unconscious factors in reading" (1930), James Strachey looks at another domestic activity—reading—which he relates to unconscious coprophagic phantasies. Traces of pregenital forms of gratification, sadistic and destructive impulses, unconscious threats, and unstable sublimations are found in the often fraught activity of reading. Like my GCSE student in Freud's consulting room, Strachey wants to know what it all means. "What, we may ask, are these books, these words, these printed pages, from the point of view of the unconscious? What do they symbolize?" (p. 327), and following the lead of Melanie Klein and Ernest Jones, he makes the bold suggestion that words = faeces = the father or his penis. Thus "reading" involves a large number of unconscious attitudes in relation to the father: "… on the one hand feelings of rivalry, contempt, hostility and destructiveness toward him … and, on the other hand, feelings of guilt and a need for self-punishment arising out of these" (ibid., p. 330). By adding "babies" to the equation, as Freud does in his famous paper on anal erotism (Freud, 1917c), the presence of feminine wishes towards the father are also incorporated, as well as the desire to devour all the baby-rivals deposited in the mother. Does that sound completely ridiculous? How do we picture "the unconscious"? As a domestic front room with the TV in the corner in which our fondest desire is to "relate" to other people and engage in healthy "creativity" in a "transitional space"? Or as something that contains elements of the polymorphous perverse, inchoate urges, unacceptable ideas and basic anxieties? The opening credits of *The Simpsons* (1989–present) shows the eponymous family coming together from the various locations of their separate lives—school, factory, supermarket—in order to watch TV. Just as they are about to sit down on the sofa, something weird happens and the cartoon world is suddenly transformed in an unexpected and bizarre way—a sequence which has come to be known appropriately as "the couch gag". The characters may suddenly become paper cut outs, crumble into dust or be swallowed by the sofa as it turns into a giant octopus. Perhaps the "weirdness" may be an index of the unconscious elements mobilised in the act of watching TV itself.

Our relationship to reality is a precarious one, governed by the libidinal and affective relations we establish with the outside world. We do not perceive reality directly, but on the basis of a mental "representation" of that world, which becomes elaborated into what Sandler and Rosenblatt called the "Representational World" (1962). Ferenczi first investigated the libidinal relations to reality in his paper, "Stages in the development of the sense of reality" (1913). Forty years later, in the same year and published in the same journal as Winnicott's "Transitional Objects" paper, Lacan put it like this:

> [W]hile reality precedes thought, it takes different forms according to the way the subject deals with it. Analytic experience gives this truth a special force for us and shows it as being free from all trace of idealism, for we can specify concretely the oral, anal, and genital relationships which the subject establishes with the outer world at the libidinal level. (1953, p. 11)

Despite the misleading idea of "reality testing", the ego is first and foremost a "protective shield" (Freud, 1940a, p. 145). We deal with the outside world in small doses in order for the ego to make a judgement about the dangers that lurk there (dangers to its own integrity and sense of safety) and thus what it wants to, or is obliged to, recognise as "reality". Hence Freud's assertion in his last book that "The equation 'perception = reality (external world)' does not hold" (ibid., p. 162). It could be said that the main tenor of Freud's work on the ego, with its "dependent relations" to the id, superego, and external world is that the ego sets itself against the "outside" in general, that is to say, the drives on the one hand and "reality" on the other (1923b).

If "reality" is partially determined by perceptual modalities and sensory systems that underpin the "libidinal subject", it is also determined by language. Addressing the problem from the side of the signifying act, psychoanalyst and semiotician, Julia Kristeva, asserts: "[P]sychoanalysis reinforces the formal description of a signifying act by the unconscious psychosexual conditions of its possibility" (2000, p. 771). The psychosexual is caught up in the activity of speech, the impulse to communicate, and the desire to be understood. Language comes from the outside (from the words of parents, from a locus of authority) and imposes reality upon us. In the process of learning the rules of language, we construct a picture of the world; the categories of "reality" that we may later rebel against in the telling of tendentious jokes or the pleasure in nonsense (Freud, 1905c, pp. 125–126). It is a commonplace to say that the function of negation lies at the core of the symbolic, since the symbol takes the place of the "real thing", but it may be that negation is at the heart of ego-function itself:

> We have learned to be quite sure that when someone says "It is not so" it is because it is so; that when he says "I do not mean" he does mean; we know how to recognize the underlying hostility in most 'altruistic' statements, the undercurrent of homosexual feeling in jealousy, the tension of desire hidden in the professed horror of incest; we have noted that manifest indifference may mask intense latent interest. … [O]ur view is that the essential function of the ego is very nearly that systematic refusal to acknowledge reality which French analysts refer to in talking about the psychoses. (Lacan, 1953, pp. 11–12)

Where does this essential refusal to recognise reality, which may lie at the heart of our relationship to the world, place us in relation to the dominant genre of TV—"reality" in all its forms? The astonishing variety of forms almost defies classification. Researching the subject sociologically, Annette Hill argues that "Viewers do not experience factual genres in isolation but as part of a chaotic mix of factuality" (2007, p. 2) and coins the term "genre work" to describe the way audiences make sense of the multiplicity of forms. "Genre work involves immersive and reflective modes of engagement with factual genres, allowing viewers to personally respond to programmes and themselves in conscious and unconscious ways, and often in contradictory ways" (ibid., p. 2).

Despite the acknowledged debt to Freud, the concept of "genre work" is not comparable to the unconscious logic of Freud's "dream work" or "joke work"; however, the term invites us to consider how viewers and programme makers both contribute to the construction of the sense of reality: "These viewing strategies highlight how audiences engage with and reflect on various representations of reality" (ibid., p. 2). Viewers have all kinds of knowledge and experience about the world and different representations of that world—TV, radio, newspapers, websites, chatting with friends and family—and this prior knowledge mixes with the experience of watching a particular programme and transforms it. "Factual genres are often called 'leaky genres' because they are porous, absorbing other generic conventions, mixing with other kinds of media content, running off in various creative directions" (ibid., p. 84). "Viewers are alchemists, transforming factual genres from audio-visual documentation into cultural and social experiences" (ibid., p. 84). In this state of flux, "Hybridity is now the distinctive feature of factuality" she argues, and continues: "The boundaries between fact and fiction have been pushed to the limits in various popular factual formats that mix non-fiction and fiction genres" (ibid., p. 2).

The staff at the Freud Museum are well placed to confirm the truth of this statement after the museum was made the subject of a BBC documentary, broadcast in 2010 as one in a series of three hour-long films called *Behind the Scenes at the Museum*.

Being the raw material for a reality TV programme is a sobering experience. The filming was done three or four days a week over a period of five months. The question of "what's missing?" becomes reduced to its simplest formulation—it is the hundreds of hours of footage left on the cutting room floor. Despite the illusory experience that you are involved in a collaborative process—if the producer is any good at his job he will rely on your conscious and unconscious narcissism to draw you in—you know at the same time that you are being manipulated and enlisted in the service of another agenda. You do not "get used to it", except in the most superficial sense. The camera is always there, not so much "fly on the wall" as "elephant in the room", and you know that collusion with the ideology is a form of disavowal. If the technological development of TV somehow embodies an infantile wish to see "everything" and be "everywhere", like the magic Tarnhelm that Wagner's idiotic hero, "Siegfried", rescues from the ferocious dragon, then it is also the dream of being naked and exposed in public. You worry about looking "bad" or looking "stupid", unleashing expectant anxiety of impending shame. In the family of unpleasant emotions, shame is both self-referential and inter-personal, linked to our sense of exposure and scrutiny by others. For some psychoanalysts, humiliation and the fear of humiliation are some of the most devastating experiences of childhood (Nathanson, 1987; Sandler & Sandler, 1986; Yorke, 2008) and, as adults, we spend a great deal of our psychic energy trying to avoid their repetition. We do not want to look stupid. We do not want to be caught with our pants down. We do not want to be spotted *making a scene*. After the first broadcast of the programme, strangers came up to my colleagues and me to say "I saw you on the telly", and walked away. They just wanted to let us know. We can watch people being stupid and humiliated on TV or, which amounts to the same thing, being threatened with potential shame and managing to avoid it—so that we do not have to feel it ourselves. It is as if the person who has "been on the telly" has accomplished a difficult feat, and they have done it for the rest of us. The sense of immediacy that characterises TV, one of its defining features according to Flitterman-Lewis (1992, p. 219), may be little more than a sense of immediate psychical danger. Readers might like to ponder some of their own childhood experiences of embarrassment, shame, and humiliation to see what traces of these experiences can be rediscovered in the formats of reality TV.

Similar considerations apply to comedy. We laugh but we do not know why, and we fail to appreciate the anxiety and libidinal agitations bubbling under the surface that may be determining our laughter. Billy Wilder's masterpiece *Some Like it Hot* (1959)—about death, cross-dressing, and thwarted love—often considered to be the funniest film ever made, reaches its climax with an extended dialogue skirting around the problem of castration. Unable to extract himself from the demands of his impetuous suitor, "Osgood", "Daphne" takes off his wig and finally reveals the truth ("You don't understand, Osgood … Oh, I'm a man!")—only to be countered by the triumphant transcendence of the threat that ends the film: "Well … nobody's perfect".

While participants are trying not to look "bad", the programme makers are trying to make a "good" programme. Nobody's perfect. The publication of Robert Thirkell's *C.O.N.F.L.I.C.T.* (2010) gives us an "insider's guide" into the process. Brutally honest and based on a series of seminars to media professionals, the book is a road map for producing reality TV by a BAFTA-winning former producer and commissioning editor. As the process unfolds, revealing one Machiavellian subterfuge after another, the reader (perhaps I should say the "normal reader") is shocked and excited in equal measure. This is how TV conducts itself. It is shameless and it is brilliant. At a 2012 conference on media ethics, the producer, Dan Chambers, recounted the story of a professional decision of which he was most ashamed. All was not well on *The Farm* (2004–2005), ratings were poor, and viewing figures were falling off alarmingly. Something had to be done to bring the programme to the public imagination and crisis talks were held about the Channel 5 show. The radical decision was made to persuade one of the female contestants to masturbate a pig on screen, and the person chosen for the task was Rebecca Loos, recently transformed into a celebrity by association with the footballer, David Beckham. The story became front page news; outraged viewers were quoted by the press ("It was just vile. It was probably the worst thing I have seen on TV. I just couldn't believe it was on television"; "I was absolutely speechless"); the programme makers received a "stinging rebuke" from the then culture secretary, Chris Smith, and the ratings improved (Plunkett, 2004). Hearing this tale of shameful regret, I could only sit in the audience and think "How brilliant!" Perhaps, like Lacan, we might imagine that when someone says "This is the thing of which I am most ashamed", we may have to read "This is the thing of which I am most proud". And is it not possible to detect a reciprocal gratification in the viewers' excited outrage?

Thirkell's book contains similar examples of creative thinking on the job, peppered as it is with illustrative tales and advice from media insiders. The director of *Behind the Scenes at the Museum* was clearly a follower of the Thirkell approach, and parallels could be seen at every stage of the process. Thirkell shows that "persuading people to take part" is a kind of seduction. You may have to change tack many times in order to reel someone in. "The negotiation for access and performance is a tender dance—in essence a courtship ritual ..." he says (2010, p. 40), and quotes Michele Kurland, executive producer of *The Apprentice* (2005–present): "You have to give them a reason for doing it—they're never going to do it because your programme is going to be better. It could be anything: sharing a problem, a passion, something that matters to them" (ibid., p. 41). When the staff of the Freud Museum were being courted, a similar variety of options was given. After the initial approach was rebuffed—"We are making a series of programmes about small museums under threat and how they are fighting back against the odds" ... "But we're not under threat, we're doing very well thank you"—a number of different reasons were given: it's a chance to promote "Freud" and psychoanalysis; it's good publicity for the museum; it will show the important work of a small museum, and so on. Just as with real courtships, "A careful and gradual approach, not scaring contributors off, can be very important ..." but you also have to be realistic: "When the courtship is properly underway, and they are hooked, you can afford to take more risks. Tell them that there will be bits that make them look bad, and point out more downsides", he advises. "The fact that you have thought it through, and are willing to mention the downsides, should make them feel more secure, not less! Remember, it is all about trust" (ibid., p. 41). You can imagine that some museum staff felt a little betrayed when, after being promised to show the work of the museum during a five month period of our most intense activity, the promises were ignored. I naively asked the director to consider a small change to the end credits of the programme: "Why not list the events and exhibitions and conferences that actually went on during the time you were filming so that people can see that the programme they have watched is a particular 'take' but it can never be the whole story—you can be a bit post-modern and self-referential!" Sad to say, my powers of persuasion were not enough to overcome a golden rule of TV documentary film making: "Never cede editorial control to a contributor" (Jan Tomalin quoted in Thirkell, 2010, p. 42).

From "persuading people to take part", through choosing "characters" and making them "stronger", to "finding an arena" and "thinking out of the box", Thirkell's book is a revelation about the mindset of the reality TV producer and how the process works. But there is one thing above all that drives the programme making and is its ultimate goal. The clue is in the subtitle of Thirkell's book: "An insider's guide to storytelling in factual/reality TV and film".

The debate about whether the heterogeneity of television forms, the "leaky genres", and the variety of perspectives, results in a medium of fragmented looks that eschews the telling of stories (Flitterman-Lewis, 1992, p. 220), should be finally decided by Thirkell's account. It's the story, stupid. Big stories organised into little stories, each with a beginning, a middle, and an end; with an authorial voice from which they originate. Flitterman-Lewis's contention that "Such a concept of authorship is literally nonexistent in television ..." (ibid., p. 220) is flatly contradicted by the TV insiders: "The best programmes absolutely don't come from committees, they come from authored voices … [Y]ou need a singular vision" (Alan Hayling, former head of BBC Documentaries, quoted in Thirkell, 2010, p. 23). This certainly accords with our experience "behind the scenes". The director had a story to tell and he was going to tell it, adapting to the demands of the "unpredictable" footage he acquired but definitely with a singular vision in mind.

If we look at his story from the standpoint of psychoanalysis—"I want to tell a story about small (quirky) museums under threat"—then we have to accept the possibility that the director may not have known where this story came from, or even what it meant. On one level, it is close to an industry standard, a set of basic forms that "work", that appeal to the viewer and help organise the mass of material that the documentary maker collects. Thirkell is adamant that the stories must resonate with cultural forms, they must have a mythic dimension:

> I specialise in telling one main classic story—the hero with a quest—again and again. (2010, p. 30)

> In each film we follow the hero through successive hurdles, as he (or she) fights other characters and obstacles. Things look tougher and tougher until he wins through, in the process revealing his true character under pressure, leading to transformations and ideally redemption. (ibid., p. 31)

So for *Jamie's School Dinners* (2005) the story became:

> An evil giant—big bad food—was rampaging round the land, leading to illness in children and even eventually to their early death. The government didn't seem to know what to do about it. So the big fairy-tale question became: could plucky Jamie slay the monster of big bad food, and show the wicked king—i.e. the government— that it could be done better, across a whole London borough? (ibid., p. 100)

The idea of a narrative arc is a familiar and basic one. In this regard, Thirkell and Kristeva are in complete accord. Thirkell says: "Telling our own stories is a defining characteristic of humans. Onto the mass of chaotic material that makes up our lives we try to superimpose cause, effect and narrative" (ibid., p. 94) What is important, he says, is finding the right question, the *quest*, a view that is echoed by

Kristeva: "Every tale follows the ascending/descending, questions/answers logic of an ordeal", she asserts, comprising "… initiation of the ordeal … development of the action—*dénouement*" (2000, p. 772) For Kristeva, the narrative form resonates with the basic structure of human language.

> This curve of logic forms part of a larger and more universal structure … which is none other than the logic of the sentence—a subject, a verb and an object. The hero is the grammatical subject, the action is the verb, the *dénouement* of the plot is the object. The story thus becomes an extension of the logic of the sentence. …
> (ibid., p. 772)

When the mad Daniel Paul Schreber wrote of the "not-finishing-a-sentence-miracle" in his brilliant *Memoirs*, he enabled us to glimpse the hidden sensuous activity of the sentence form itself. Created by God to torment him, the "miracle" allowed only fragmentary thoughts and incomplete sentences to enter his head, in order to deny him the feeling of bodily "voluptuousness" that accompanies *the completion of a sentence* (Schreber, 1903, pp. 172–173). We find a narrative logic in the circuit of tension and satiation that exists in the early feeding relation, and Daniel Stern (1993) has spoken of a "pre-narrative envelope" that precedes and governs even these early experiences. But we also want to hear *other people's stories*. As Thirkell says: "As humans we have a deep need to read, hear or view stories that help us create our own tales and meaning—the archetypal stories that enable us to make sense of our own lives" (2010, p. 94).

For Freud, the cultural forms existing in the signifying landscape outside the self—the myths, and archetypal stories of culture—are an essential part of the inner world. The creative writer disguises the content of his conscious phantasies, which are themselves revised versions of unconscious phantasies (Freud, 1908e). That is the "art" of the writer. "The tale, in its pure form, is compromised", agrees Kristeva. "As a result, the narrative plot is often difficult, if not impossible, to spot" (2000, p. 772). The use of sensorial metaphors, subordinate clauses, digressions, and ellipses are some of the ways that the narrative is disguised, and each of these forms of enunciation has its counterpart in television production. The beautiful, colour-saturated, soft focus establishing shots of the museum that open *Behind the Scenes* is a case in point, inviting the viewer to suspend disbelief and enter a dream-like world. As Thirkell puts it: "A key part of the job is to disguise your endlessly repeated story as innovative television!" (2010, p. 31).

But in essence, the story means something. Early psychoanalysts funnelled it down into the Oedipus complex, and Freud and his followers discovered an endless variety of forms in which those emotional relationships could be played out. Father-figures and mother-figures can be split into their good and bad aspects, siblings can perform multiple roles as helpers or hinderers to the hero's quest, and Oedipal resolutions can include being reconciled to a loving father as much as overcoming him and "winning the girl".

Behind the Scenes at the Museum was no exception to this logic. The director came with a story he wanted to tell—an organisation under threat—and in offering to bear witness to the trials and tribulations and struggles against adversity, he placed himself in the position of saviour, of saving the humiliated and weak and battered institution. His previous series was about family-run department stores "under threat". Given the compelling nature of this story for the director, how did he cope with the cheery news that we were not under threat and did not fit his agenda? He told the same story! But instead of the "institution" being the humiliated and ridiculed father-to-be-rescued, it became one of the protagonists in the film itself, the long-serving caretaker, Alex. The requirements of the story meant that while Alex was pictured as slaving away "downstairs", ignored and unappreciated, staff "upstairs" were shown contemplating their navels or, like the gods of Mount Olympus, frittering away their time with silly pranks. Hence the refusal to acknowledge what actually went on during the period of filming. Alex himself was suspicious of the filming process from the start, but, like other members of staff, he was unaware of the editorial decisions that would create his "character" and make it "stronger" for the demands of the story. Such was the strength of this narrative arc, reinforced by the dominance of the voice-over in documentary forms, that even in scenes in which the putative hero was shown remonstrating with other members of staff, or arguing his point at staff meetings, he was represented as silenced and humiliated.

In the desire to see "behind the scenes", we activate fears associated with the parental couple. The good and bad breast of early infancy becomes the seducing and betraying mother-figure of Oedipal dramas;

the loved, feared, and admired father becomes the subject of ridicule and derision. Ambivalence is the order of the day, and we construct our stories in order to allow both sides of the ambivalence to be expressed. The director of *Behind the Scenes* managed to ride the horns of this Oedipal dilemma by vindicating and humiliating the father at the same time. The quest is completed, the father redeemed. Effaced from the film itself in an act of self-conscious erasure, the film-maker is the true hero of the story, who rescues the father, completes his quest, and *satisfies the mother's desire*. Indeed it was the film-maker who set up a scene in which precious "lost" Freudian objects were discovered by Alex and offered to the dominant female character of the programme— objects which, far from being lost, had many times been on display in the museum or had exhibitions built around them. The dramatic force is intensified by the fact that the mother-figure had previously been represented as self-absorbed and impossible to satisfy, shown in an earlier scene expressing doubt that her desires (for the museum) will be fulfilled before she dies. In finding these precious objects, which could function as both cause and satisfaction of desire, the humiliated father was both vindicated and redeemed.

It took Wagner fifty years before he came up with a formula to kill the father and save him at the same time, in the *dénouement* of his last opera, *Parsifal*. Reality television does it as a matter of course. Lacan's weighty aphorism, "There is no Other of the Other" (1960, p. 311) clearly shows that he never watched *Ramsay's Kitchen Nightmares*, in which the plain-speaking chef introduces the economic and Oedipal "facts of life" into the narcissistic bubble of a domineering father-figure, humiliates him in public, and saves his ailing restaurant. As viewers we identify with both sides of the dramatic conflict. The impulse to rescue the father is a powerful one, as is the impulse to undermine and criticise him. Just as with dreams, jokes, and fictional stories, reality television offers a huge variety of ways in which such Oedipal narratives are played out and troubling emotions contained. There are multiple forms and television formats which enable us to link ideas to bodily function, inner reality to external reality, and to master anxiety; or, as Winnicott also insisted, to *master ideas and impulses that lead to anxiety if they are not in control*. The process of "watching television" becomes a complex version of the *fort-da* game, leading not to emotional change but, if we are lucky, a little reassurance and distraction.

References

Behind the Scenes at the Museum (2010). The Freud Museum. BBC4, 20 May, and repeated nine times in the following two years. Director, Richard Macer. Manchester: Platform Productions.

Big Bang Theory, The (2007). Warner Brothers Television. Episode shown Channel 4, 20 January, 2013.

Bollas, C. (1992). *Being a Character*. New York: Hill & Wang.

Ellis, J. (2000). *Seeing Things: Television in the Age of Uncertainty*. London: IB Taurus.

Ferenczi, S. (1913). Stages in the development of the sense of reality. In: *Contributions to Psycho-analysis*. London: Hogarth.

Flitterman-Lewis, S. (1992). Psychoanalysis, film and television. In: R. C. Allen (Ed.), *Channels of Discourse, Reassembled: Television and Contemporary Criticism (second edition)* (pp. 204–246). London: Routledge.

Freud, A. (1963). The concept of developmental lines. *Psychoanalytic Study of the Child*, *18*: 245–265.

Freud, S. (1895). Draft H.: Paranoia. In: J. Masson (Ed.), *The Complete Letters of Sigmund Freud to Wilhelm Fliess, 1887–1904* (pp. 107–112). Cambridge, MA: Belknap Press.

Freud, S. (1905c). Jokes and their relation to the unconscious. *S. E., 8*. London: Hogarth.

Freud, S. (1905d). Three essays on the theory of sexuality. *S. E., 7*. London: Hogarth.

Freud, S. (1908e). Creative writers and day-dreaming. *S. E., 9*. London: Hogarth.

Freud, S. (1917c). On transformations of instinct as exemplified in anal erotism. *S. E., 17*. London: Hogarth.

Freud, S. (1920g). *Beyond the Pleasure Principle. S. E., 18*. London: Hogarth.

Freud, S (1923b). *The Ego and the Id. S. E., 19*. London: Hogarth.

Freud, S. (1940a). An outline of psycho-analysis. *S. E., 23*. London: Hogarth.

Hill, A. (2007). *Restyling Factual TV: Audiences and News, Documentary and Reality Genres*. London: Routledge.

Kent, S. (2004). Export opinion. *Time Out*, 29 September, p. 40.

Kristeva, J. (2000). From symbols to flesh: The polymorphous destiny of narration. *International Journal of Psychoanalysis*, *81*: 771–787.

Lacan, J. (1953). Some reflections on the ego. *International Journal of Psychoanalysis*, *34*: 11–17.

Lacan, J. (1960). The subversion of the subject and the dialectic of desire in the Freudian unconscious. In: A. Sheridan (Trans.), *Ecrits: A Selection*. London: Tavistock, 1977.

Nathanson, D. (1987). A timetable for shame. In: D. Nathanson (Ed.), *The Many Faces of Shame*. New York: The Guilford Press.

Plunkett, J. (2004). Farmyard furore as Five lets Rebecca Loos on porker. *MediaGuardian*, 6 October.

Ramsay's Kitchen Nightmares (2004). Channel 4. An American adaptation of this show, titled *Kitchen Nightmares*, debuted 19 September, 2007, on Fox.

Sandler, J. & Rosenblatt, B. (1962). The concept of the representational world. *Psychoanalytic Study of the Child*, 17: 128–145.

Sandler, J. & Sandler, A. -M. (1986). The gyroscopic function of unconscious phantasy. In: D. Feinsilver (Ed.), *Towards a Comprehensive Model for Schizophrenic Disorders* (pp. 109–124). Hillsdale, NJ: Analytic Press.

Schreber, D. P. (1903). *Memoirs of My Nervous Illness*. I. MacAlpine & R. Hunter (Trans. & Eds.). London: Dawson and Sons, 1955.

Stern, D. (1993). The "pre-narrative envelope": An alternative view of "unconscious phantasy" in infancy. *Bulletin of the Anna Freud Centre*, 15: 291–318.

Stokes, A. (1966). On being taken out of oneself. *International Journal of Psychoanalysis*, 47: 523–530.

Strachey, J. (1930). Some unconscious factors in reading. *International Journal of Psychoanalysis*, 11: 322–331.

Thirkell, R. (2010). *C.O.N.F.L.I.C.T.: An Insiders Guide to Storytelling in Factual/Reality TV and Film*. London: Methuen Drama.

Winnicott, D. W. (1964). *The Child, the Family and the Outside World*. London: Pelican [reprinted London: Penguin, 1991].

Yorke, C. B. (2008). A psychoanalytic approach to the understanding of shame. In: C. Pajaczkowska & I. Ward (Eds.), *Shame and Sexuality: Psychoanalysis and Visual Culture*. London: Routledge.

List of television programmes and films cited

Behind the Scenes at the Museum (2010). BBC4, UK.

Blue Peter (1958–present). BBC1, UK.

Jamie's School Dinners (2005). Channel 4, UK.

Some Like It Hot (1959). Director, Billy Wilder, US.

The Apprentice (2005–present). BBC1, UK.

The Big Bang Theory (2007–present). First broadcast on US cable channel, CBS.

The Farm (2004–2005). Channel 5, UK.

The Simpsons (1989–present), First broadcast on US cable channel, Fox.

INDEX

Fictional characters are entered in double inverted commas, listed by first name, with the series in which they feature being entered in brackets after their names.